Away From Home
A Life in Football

Nicholas Harling

First published in 2023 in the UK
3P Publishing
C E C, London Road
Corby
NN17 5EU

A catalogue number for this book is available from the British Library

ISBN 978-1-913740-60-3

Cover design: Ian Willsmer

For my children, on the understanding that they will not be offended by the contents, and my grandkids on the condition that they, too, will be similarly broadminded.

Contents:

Foreword	1
Author's Note	3
Part One: Away From Home	5
The birth of an obsession	7
Supporting dilemma	11
1966 and all that	13
Getting plastered	16
Mexico mayhem	20
Sliding doors	25
Boxing clever	31
Favour from Fergie	35
Friendly causes friction	40
Disguised for Wembley	42
Second team syndrome	45
A Swedish sojourn	48
Time to go	50
A Romanian rhapsody	52
A Copa half full	58
Familiar territory	61
Monkeying about	64
In France without tickets	68
Copa capers	76
Who needs boots?	80
A bridge too near	82
He just wasn't my type	87
The magic carpet	92
Train takes the strain	94
Asian odyssey	98
The scrapbook survives	104
Sights to behold	108
Three disappointing gorges	113
Going Dutch	116
Ticket palaver	121
Suzie one frock	128
Getting my dong out	133
The enormous shadow	138
A controversial sleeping remedy	142
Parrot lost for words	147
Tracks in the sand	155
A boat ride like no other	158
A bumpy ride	162

No justice for Hodd   167
Hitching a lift   171
Tension at the turnstiles   173
Fifa's nasty little scheme   177
Where eagles dare to dive   181
Wedding flashes   184
Friends rally round   187
English cowards in Marseilles   193
Beckhaaam gets lucky   198
The woes of relegation   201
Respite in Poland   204
A relentless rhythm   207
Sliding door opens for De Boer   211
Maltese melancholy   214
Russian resistance   220
Runway to the Rock   226
Ode to Patrick   230
Getting in with a squeeze   233
Storks have the best view   237
Foiled by Damo   242
A relic from the past   247
Refs wave play on   253
Part Two: Up For The Cups   259
Who needs a goalkeeper?   261
Revie to the rescue   265
A low blow in Maastricht   268
A bunch of fives   275
Laugh time in Lisbon   279
Hooping along   282
From the depths to Palace's zenith   285
Deep pockets   290
And finally   294
Acknowledgements   298

Foreword

If you were to ask me how many football matches, I have seen with Nick Harling, I'd have to reply 'about half of them'. The enigmatic response is because so often I have been entering a restaurant to meet one of his lady friends and he will whisper 'by the way, you were with me in Barcelona a fortnight ago.' Of course I wasn't in Barcelona, but a woman from the subs bench certainly was!

This book is based on adventures around football and the fairer sex, because Nick's life, indeed his sole purpose, is based around football and the fairer sex. One of his goals is goals, the other – well you can imagine. I have tried to stick to the pitchside part of his passion but one evening does stick in my mind.

We were on the Isle of Man for the Inter-Island Games (of course we were) and Nick was accompanied by a Mexican lady (of course he was). At dinner he mentioned a trip to a match in Italy with Susan. Immediately the Mexican lady's demeanour changed. 'But you told me you had gone with Roger,' she spluttered. 'Oh, did I,' said Nick, in a manner reminiscent of Sergeant Wilson of Warmington-on-Sea (Dad's Army). The lady said nothing for the rest of the meal as clearly a Latina volcano was heating up. With tension in the air, we retired to the hotel, where their room was next to mine. I went to clean my teeth and on finishing the task could not help but hear the noises of enthusiastic intimacy through the wall. How Nick was able to turn that situation around, I cannot fathom to this day.

Nick summed up his adventures in the 'Up For The Cups' chapters at the end of this book, when he said of another acquaintance: 'He knew me well enough by now to realise that my perfect trips were a combination of football, train rides and boat trips in delightful female company.'

While Nick may not yet be ready for acceptance into any monastic order, even the most chaste of his critics must tip their hat to his life-long love of football in general and Crystal Palace in particular. Now in his mid-70s, he embraces life and will travel by any means possible, chat to anyone or sniff out a story anywhere. For a man from his background to gain the utmost pleasure in riding a suspension-free bus for several hours to see a Third Division game in Peru is simply extraordinary and a story that deserves to finally be told.

I have come to realise that it is probably best to witness Nick in action from a balcony seat, rather than actually being on stage with him. Nevertheless, I have often been close to the action and can verify that the stories in this book that may seem just too ridiculous, actually did happen. Some will make you laugh hysterically, others will make you cringe, no doubt some will make me check old diaries to see if I really was on that trip ...

Neil Morris
2/9/21

Author's Note

The idea of writing my memoirs, so to speak, first surfaced when I was regaling someone or other with a story from my travels. And he or she said: 'You really should write a book.' Then years later the same conversation happened again. And then yet again the same scenario was repeated. So the idea gained some substance to the extent that I told my parents about it.

The biggest influence was my father Robert Harling, who found the time to be a prolific novelist when he was not editing *House and Garden* magazine. He often asked how my book was coming along. He had written several novels, most of them thrillers revolving around the newspaper industry in which he worked, mostly as a creative art director with *The Sunday Times*. But his last work was a biography on his great pal, Ian Fleming with whom he had worked at *The Sunday Times* and in naval intelligence during the Second World War. As it was often suspected that my Dad was James Bond in Fleming's eyes, I signed copies of the book: A Personal Memoir at the book launch – after my father's death – 'Son of Bond.'

As my father never relented in his questions about my book which had yet to be started, I resorted to changing the subject or twisting the truth about the progress I had made. It was the only way to keep him quiet. And then 12 years after his death we had lockdown. The days hung heavy. There were fewer football matches to attend and more time to occupy. There was nothing else for it but to embark on the blessed book. As soon as I started on it, I wondered what had kept me away from the computer for so long. It got to the point where I felt I lived not only for the next football match, but also for my writing. I could not fathom why a friend, also long since retired from Fleet Street, told me he suffered no withdrawal symptoms after penning his last article.

Football has subjected many of us to its inexorable grip. So far as I was concerned, it was all the better if the journeys to games and tournaments were taken in delectable female company on trains or boats through mountain ranges or on scenic rivers. There were scrapes galore and adventures along the way which I have attempted to describe in addition to the more spectacular places I visited and the most interesting people I encountered, all in pursuit of watching football around the globe. I have tried to steer well away from writing a kick-by-kick summary. Or to go too deeply into tactics. There are enough of those books already on the market.

Circumstances have determined that I have reported on less than half the football matches I have seen but if I could not keep a cutting as a record of my attendance then invariably I collated the match programmes, thousands of them, dating back to the late 1950s, which have gathered dust on the shelves of my flat. The excuse for keeping them was that I could eventually use them for research if I ever got round to writing the book. As it happened, I never had the need to refer to a single one of those piles of progs which will eventually be sold on Ebay. Google and Wikipedia came to my rescue whenever I needed to check a fact or a date. For which I thank them sincerely. As well as Mark Burton for his painstaking editing. Not for nothing did he gain the nickname on The Independent and other papers who employed him of David Fairclough or Supersub.

Part One
Away From Home

Chapter 1:
The birth of an obsession

As I spread the sports pages of that day's Times on my parents' marble hall floor, I hardly sensed to what extent would be my future involvement with that newspaper, The Thunderer - as it was nicknamed - or, indeed, my obsession with the great game.

My father had promised to take me to the following day's home international and I could hardly contain my excitement. It wasn't a bad first ever football match for a young boy of not quite ten years old. England v Scotland at the old Wembley. Beat that. The Times had previewed the game and had detailed a list of the likely starting line-ups and I daresay I memorised each player by heart. Among them were Tom Finney, Stanley Matthews, the captain Billy Wright and, of course, Duncan Edwards who played for my then favourite club, Manchester United. (I was to see the light a few years later) .

In the blue of Scotland was their giant centre half George Young. God knows how my Dad had got us tickets, but I was eternally grateful that he had managed to do so.

The next 24 hours passed at a snail's pace and then the big day dawned. It was a sunny one and off we went but not alas with hours to spare, in my mother's car. She drove us to Oxted station from where we caught a train to Victoria and then an underground to Marylebone and then another overland train to Wembley. Soon after we had disembarked from the train I fell over and bloodied my knee. But no matter, after a swift patching up session aided by my father's handkerchief, we hurried on towards the stadium and up the stairs. Hardly had we taken our designated seats than there was an ear-splitting roar and Scotland had indeed scored. "Are they still warming up?" I asked my father who airily dismissed my question with the reply that Scotland had gone ahead through Tommy Ring in the opening minute.

England duly equalised through Derek Kevan - who was later to star for my beloved Crystal Palace - and a wonderful game ensued until with about eight minutes left, my father announced that we should leave so as to avoid the crush of the crowds on the way out. I begged him to let us stay until the end, but he assured me that there would be no more goals and that we should depart. And so, we did but as we descended the stairs, there was another howl from within the stadium and Duncan Edwards had evidently scored the winner with a fulminating long shot. To this day,

7

I have never seen a replay of the goal so I never knew just how good it was, but my father suspected - perhaps correctly - to his dying day that I had never completely forgiven him for his sad lapse of foresight.

But the intense disappointment of missing that goal did nothing to cloud my love of football. I was at prep school and enjoyed playing despite some awful thrashings. I remember that we lost one game 13-0 and regarded it as something of a triumph to lose the return match on our own pitch only 2-0. Although predominantly right footed I was used as a left winger, helped in no small way by the long practice sessions I had with my Dad who insisted that I should use my left foot more. It was probably the only way I could get into the team. To this day, I often wonder why managers and coaches don't insist on their players spending long hours kicking the ball with their weaker foot. Just think how good Messi would be if he used his right foot with just a fraction of the success he employs with his cultured left foot. Or take Eden Hazard. He would be even more mesmerising if he could do with his left foot what he does with his right.

Anyway, I digress. My interest in football was fast becoming much more than a mere interest. If I was not thinking of girls the way any boy does in his formative years, then football dominated my waking hours. Playing and watching. Playing and watching and practising. I was forever grateful to my parents, especially my father - who invariably had the last word in such matters - that they wanted me to go to Westminster School rather than the then solely rugby-playing school, Whitgift which would have been so much more convenient as it was far nearer our Godstone home. But Westminster is a famous football playing private school where possibly the game of football originated 500 years ago in the cloisters leading up to the Abbey. So I took the special entrance exam for Westminster and thankfully passed and was soon representing the school's under 14 and Colts teams. As I liked flinging myself about to the extent that I was employed as a slip fielder in cricket teams, it was not long before I was used in goal. But it was a frustrating experience that ended soon after a Colts game at Ardingly which we lost 10-0. "Westminster needs good goalkeepers," our master in charge Stewart Murray told my father who had chosen the wrong game to come and watch.

And so, shortly afterwards I relieved myself of the goalkeeper's jersey - or perhaps was relieved of it - and returned to a more constant active role. Not that it was a roaring success at first. At half-time during another Colts match at Charterhouse where we were enroute to a 5-1 thrashing, Mr Murray singled me out and said: "Harling you're doing fook all." Right up until the end of my school days I had to endure school pals

8

imitating Murray's broad Yorkshire accent and teasing me in no uncertain terms with "Harling you're doing fook all." Schoolboys can be very cruel, I was soon to learn.

Outside Little Deans Yard which was the focal point for Westminster School with its classrooms, main assembly hall and various "houses" adjoining it, and through the stone arch lay an acre or two of grass, known as "Green." With homework very much of secondary consideration, it was there in every spare minute after school that I rustled up enough pals to make up two decent teams. The goals, as ever, were coats or jackets and the games were intense, just what some of us required as the foundation for selection to the various school teams who lined up for games against other schools on the playing fields of Vincent Square, half a mile away.

The in-word among pupils more academically inclined was 'keen'. If anyone showed undue enthusiasm for sport or any other kind of activity that required exercise, he was labelled as keen. Bearing in mind my success as a middle-distance runner, I was forever being criticised for being "too keen or "Harling you're so keen." It was typical of Westminster's dilettante attitude towards sport and those who excelled at it.

However, one thing I did not excel at was the compulsory CCF afternoon which was part of the school curriculum in those days. We had to dress up in military uniform which I detested as the khaki army gear itched horribly especially on a hot day. My classmates would take up to four hours a week cleaning their uniforms and woe betide them if the masters in charge could not see a reflection of their faces in the boys' sharply polished boots. I hardly ever spent more than a quarter of an hour a week cleaning my kit with the result that I was invariably forced to do extra parade. After a while I reasoned that two hours extra parade was far better than at least four hours cleaning the damn stuff so I appeared on these weekly afternoons of hell, looking shambolic and a complete mess. My respect for the various drills also left much to be desired. A photograph taken at the annual march-past in front of parents at Vincent Square showed that I was 100 per cent out of step. While everyone else had their right foot forward, I led with my left foot. To this day, that photo remains my pride and joy.

My house master, who was the extremely approachable Dennis Brock, a maths teacher was not only involved in this Friday parade on the naval front but luckily for me, he also doubled up as a part-time athletics coach. He eventually tired of my token efforts to look smart in khaki and told me that I'd be of far more use to the school if I spent my Friday afternoons training on the school's 'long distance race' course of 3.3 miles along the towpath from Barnes to Putney. This was manna from heaven for me and I'd like to think that the school did actually benefit as I went onto break the school record - running 17min 31sec - and win 880 yards and mile races in athletic matches against other schools. It must also have sharpened up my fitness for football.

After my baptism in the younger age group teams, I made the first X1 with a year to spare. By now Stewart Murray had been promoted to take charge of the school's senior team which was not, I first thought, a promising turn of events so far as I was concerned. But he was a fair man, however critical he had been of my efforts a couple of years earlier and in the classroom where he taught geography. With my career as a goalkeeper now in the distant past, he gave me a place on the left wing where I rewarded him with a few goals, none better than the left foot belter I managed from outside the penalty area in a 4-0 win over Forest. My euphoria at scoring such a spectacular goal was tinged with disappointment when I learned that my father who accompanied my mother to most of the school's home games after his stint at the Sunday Times had finished, arrived at Vincent Square too late to see my goal.

The highlight of my second year in the team was the centenary match against Charterhouse for which we wore a smart new pink and black kit. So it was that we were somewhat dismayed on arriving at Godalming to find that our hosts had not treated the occasion with the same significance. For them, judging by their scruffy appearance in stark comparison to the smartly turned out visitors, it was just another game. But The Times were present and on the Monday morning there in the sports pages was a sizeable report of our 1-0 defeat, complete with action photograph, which did not alas feature my good self.

With England v Scotland now a largely defunct fixture, Westminster v Charterhouse is the oldest surviving annual game in the football calendar, and I was happy to attend the black-tie dinner that acknowledged the 150th anniversary in 2015. David Miller, an old Carthusian better known for his sports writing in The Times and Daily Telegraph, and Alan Smith, who made various amusing anecdotes that included mentions of me to my acute embarrassment, were among the speakers.

Chapter 2:
Supporting dilemma

I had got to know Smith when he went from being assistant manager to Steve Coppell at Crystal Palace to manager. Even though Palace were the nearest club geographically to Godstone, they had not really come onto my radar until one Friday in September 1960 when George the builder, asked me if I would like to accompany him to the next day's fourth division game against Carlisle. It's funny how one remembers such useless facts from such a bygone age, but I know it was Carlisle that Palace played that day and that the result was 1-1. Anyway, George had been helping to put up or take down a wall at my parents' home - my father was forever changing his mind - and he did, I believe possess a season ticket for the terraces which is where I joined him after seeking my parents' permission to go. It was my first experience of standing up to watch a game as my father had always treated Simon, my brother, and I to seats in the stand for our infrequent visits to Chelsea, Arsenal, Fulham and to the next England v Scotland international.

That draw against Carlisle was no classic but Arthur Rowe's push and run footballers featuring Johnny (Budgie) Byrne must have made some impression on me for soon after arriving at Westminster School and gaining the friendship of one Peter Dudgeon, an avid Chelsea fan, I was persuading him to join me for another Palace game, against Oldham. Feeling like an intrepid explorer, I led him to Victoria from where we caught a bus to Crystal Palace, little knowing that Selhurst Park was a further two miles away. By the time we had caught another bus to the ground, the score was 1-1. Palace went on to win 4-2 and the dye was cast. Manchester United were still very much my team but Palace had won a place in my heart. Usually on Saturdays when I was not playing for one of the school teams I would either go to Palace if they were at home, join Peter on the terraces at Stamford Bridge or do likewise at Upton Park along with another pal, Mark Van de Weyer, a keen West Ham fan who went on to become a journalist, editing the Luton News, aged 20.

Palace had begun to chip away seriously at my affections. When my parents were away one night, I abused the trust of the babysitter Doris to skip my homework and see a home game against Watford. And then on another evening, I was devastated when my parents insisted that I should do my homework rather than watch the club's prestige friendly against Real Madrid, Alfredo de Stefano et al. So it was that a major conflict developed in my stupid head; which team should I support? Like a lover torn between the favours offered by two girlfriends, I was in a state of torment. Where my anguish should have concerned the fact that I was slipping ever further behind in the classroom, it regrettably centred on a dilemma revolving around the world of professional football.

I had got into a habit of watching United whenever they came to London, besides making the odd trip to Old Trafford, once to see them clinch the old first division title in a 3-1 win over Arsenal. On such occasions Palace hardly posed a worthwhile challenge to my mental state until matters came to a head one afternoon when I went down to a sold-out Dell to see United play Southampton. I had to climb a tree behind the ground in order to see the action, skinning up too high to be drenched by the water from the hoses which the local cops had borrowed from the fire brigade to soak us renegade spectators.

United won 2-1 with one of the goals coming from Bobby Charlton but my satisfaction would only be complete if the news from Selhurst Park was positive. I found someone on the platform at Southampton Central with a transistor radio glued to his ear. "How did Crystal Palace get on?" I asked. "Beat Norwich 2-0" came the reply. Even though United had won, I felt so guilty at missing Palace's game that I knew from that day on that Palace were the team for me.

United have retained a place in my affections and I must remain one of the few people alive to have seen all five of their European Cup or Champions League finals but with Mourinho succeeding Van Gaal at the helm to produce less than captivating football, the love affair faded so fast that I now make scathing remarks to those diehards who trek long distances from their homes in the south to support the Mancunians instead of their local team. And, if my despair was anything to go by following Palace's two unsuccessful cup finals - both against United - my relationship with them is now nothing much more than an occasional friendship.

Chapter 3:
1966 and all that

On leaving Westminster and with considerable help from my father who had been in advertising before dividing his working hours between House and Garden magazine - where he was editor for 40 years- and the Sunday Times, I embarked on an apprenticeship with the Everetts advertising agency. My passion for football was fuelled by my friendships with some of the guys who worked there especially Ralph Finn, a copy writer who had been a sportswriter for The People. He was devoted to Spurs and a conscientious workhorse, never more so than when he was writing about his favourite subject. When he discovered that I had applied for tickets for the 1966 World Cup, he asked me if I would like to help him write a book on the tournament.

Who was I to refuse? Of course, I was flattered, and he seconded another chap from the agency to contribute to the tale of the England football team's greatest triumph. I only had tickets for the ten games in London for which I had paid the princely sum of 22 guineas, so I was forced - if that's the word - to sit by my parents' television and report on the various other matches I watched as they unfolded around the country. I was spellbound.

I had gone to England's opening game against Uruguay with Ray, a fellow worker from Everetts. Uruguay tried every time-wasting gambit in the book to cling onto their 0-0 draw and Ray was aghast at one particular ploy. "Look," he said, "their goalkeeper has just thrown the ball back at the ball boy. " It was a welcome to the cynical world of professionalism for me, but it could not tarnish my passion.

My father had often remarked that he had nurtured a monster in assisting what was fast becoming an obsession. So there I was, off to all England's subsequent games and indeed all the games at Wembley as well as the one between France and Uruguay which took place at White City because the greyhounds could not be shifted from their regular Friday night slot at Wembley. It could only happen in England.

Then there was consternation among many of us ticket holders after England had beaten Argentina in that stormy quarter-final because no one seemed to have the least idea whether our semi against Portugal would be at Goodison Park or Wembley. There was a "help" counter at Victoria Station where we were assured that it would be at Goodison so I was on the point of buying a train ticket to Liverpool and trying to swop my Wembley ticket for one in Everton's stadium when we were told "no, it would definitely be at Wembley," thereby giving England the massive advantage of playing all their games in the stadium with which they were most familiar. My main memory of that game against Portugal apart from Bobby Charlton's two goals was of how difficult it was to focus on the action against the glare of the early evening sunlight which half blinded me whenever I glimpsed the action at the far end.

The abiding recollection of the subsequent game against West Germany was of my subconscious telling me of how badly I wanted the game to go to extra time for which I felt incredibly guilty. Until the 90-minute mark, the game had not been a classic and, for me, it had lacked drama despite Wolfgang Weber's last-gasp equaliser for the Germans. So, I wasn't too disappointed at the prospect of extra time which, of course, contained all the drama missing earlier.

I was stationed high up above the goal where Geoff Hurst scored his disputed second goal so, of course, for decades afterwards I told everyone who cared to listen that the ball had definitely crossed the line. I revelled in the joy of England's victory, but the rest of the day was an acute anti-climax as I went from Wembley to a party where no one seemed to know or care that England had just won the World Cup. That wouldn't happen these days. Venture into the kitchen during any social gathering and one can be sure of picking up the dregs of some anal conversation about the round ball game and contributing one's threepenny worth. There was always some buffoon sounding off that Wenger must go. Or whatever.

The media duly saluted the achievement of Sir Alf (then just plain Alf) Ramsey and his merry boys, but I feel the sheer magnitude of their feat was not properly acknowledged until many more years had elapsed. And then with every subsequent England failing in the big tournaments, the 1966 triumph was magnified, the players honoured and lauded, Sir Alf and Bobby Moore immortalised. Did we really manage that, people must now wonder, regardless of the fact that we had home advantage? I was merely grateful that I had been born at the right time to witness it.

I was determined after that to go to future World Cups and European Championships wherever they were. With my oldest friend Patrick Hamilton who sadly died recently, we set off for the final stages of the 1968 European finals in Italy. Armed with a tiny tent and maps, it was with a combination of hitch hiking and train travel - when we decided that we could afford it - that we went via Hanover, the scene of what would be West Germany's revenge match against England, albeit in a friendly. They managed it with a late scrambled goal from Franz Beckenbauer in a 1-0 win.

It was a hot summer and we cursed the weight of our rucksacks as we dragged them across the fields alongside autobahns to the ideal hitching spots for the journey down to Rome. That was the venue for our semi-final, a 1-0 defeat by Yugoslavia who managed to provoke Alan Mullery into becoming the first England player ever to be sent off. In those days, the finals were a relatively uncluttered affair, whittled down to just four nations which meant that England's only other game would be the third-place final on a blisteringly hot day in a Stadio Olimpico so packed that I was only able to watch from a crouching half-sitting, half lying-down position. It was not the most comfortable viewpoint.

England's 2-0 victory was followed by Italy's 1-1 draw with the Slavs in an engrossing final which was followed not by a penalty shoot-out but a replay two days later. For a long time afterwards, I regretted that I could not stay for the replay. But with commitments back home, not least a job to find as I had been sacked from my first one as a cub reporter with the South London News Group, it was with heavy hearts that Patrick and I hitched out of Rome the next morning. Or tried to.

Italians have never earned a reputation for offering lifts to hitchhikers unless they are wearing short skirts, so we suffered a fruitless few hours under the sweltering sun sticking our thumbs out. Reluctantly we then decided to go it alone. Eventually, I was the first to get lucky, but I caught a glimpse of my friend hours later as he emerged from a car at a service station from which my driver was just pulling out. The only sensible way of crossing the Alps was by train so, on arriving in Milan at the grand Centrale Stazione built by Mussolini, I scoured the next train to Basle in the hope of finding Patrick. As this was long before the advent of mobile phones, I had no idea if he was on the train or not. So I boarded. He was bound in any case for Paris where he was working as a waiter.

15

Chapter 4:
Getting plastered

Thanks to my father's connections, my new job was at the Evening Echo, the Thomson paper based at Hemel Hempstead although the circulation area also included large swathes of Hertfordshire encompassing Watford, St Albans, Harpenden, Radlett, and Borehamwood. Although I started out on the news desk from where I was loaned out to sport on the Saturdays to cover Hemel Hempstead for much longer than I wished - as they were going nowhere and playing on a soulless ground - my news reporting left a lot to be desired. The highlight was misquoting a Bushey Councillor who despised the gypsies for camping on the central reservation of the A41. My shorthand let me down to the affect that he went in the paper supporting the gypsies. Not surprisingly he was onto the paper's editor first thing the next morning to complain with the result that I was told to have extra shorthand lessons. I never could get to grips with it though and offered my shorthand teacher a £20 bribe to take the exam for me. She had made no secret of the fact that she was hard up but, good for her, she rejected my offer.

Before I could do any more damage to the paper's news coverage, I got my wish and was moved to the sports desk full time and 'promoted' to cover the Isthmian League clubs St Albans and Boreham Wood. St Albans, under their astute manager Sid Prosser were a joy to watch. They must have been one of the best non-league sides ever and it was a travesty that they never graced the Amateur Cup final, falling one round short in 1970. The compensation were the few occasions I managed to persuade the sports editor Bryan Stiles to let me cover Palace for the paper's Saturday classified edition even though I can't imagine many readers in the vicinity of Watford were remotely interested in what Palace were doing. Fortunately for me, Bryan was a Welshman from Cardiff who probably had scant knowledge of the local geography.

All the extra driving which included trips to Palace's midweek games for my own enjoyment, culminated in a driving ban. I was told I would be sacked if it happened again which, inevitably, it did. Us reporters needed cars to get to jobs. I learned later that the editor had no right to threaten me with dismissal for a driving ban, but this was unbeknown to me, so I carried on driving the firm's cars. Never has a motorist driven so carefully and studiously to avoid being pulled up. My eye was constantly in the mirror. The six months were almost up when Maggie Richards, one of the paper's staunch union girls got wind of the fact that I wasn't a law-abiding citizen. She told me that she would tell the editor on the Monday morning if I didn't tell him myself.

I had a few confidantes on the paper. One of them was a pretty news reporter Judy Graham.

"Why don't you come in on Monday incapable of driving?" she said.

"What do you mean?" I asked incredulously.

"Break an arm or a leg," she replied.

By now I was beginning to see what she had in mind. My mate Mike was a student doctor at St Thomas Hospital. I rang and told him that I needed a plaster cast. On the Sunday night, he brought one over to the Pimlico flat where I was living at the time. It had been taken off an old lady who had recovered from a broken leg. We fitted it on my right leg. I got the tube up to Judy's flat off Finchley Road on the Monday morning as she was in the habit of giving me lifts when we were both on the same shift. She was most impressed. Arriving at Hemel, I limped slowly up to the sports desk, telling Bryan the grim news that I had suffered a hairline fracture of my right leg playing football the previous day.

"But you'll still be able to drive, won't you?" he asked without a trace of sympathy for my plight.

"I'm afraid it's out of the question," I said.

So, I was assigned desk duties. Maggie gritted her teeth and grudgingly accepted my ruse. Another person in the know was my good pal Rob Freeman, an avid Watford fan and a football nut. Whenever he saw me hobbling my way to the loo or wherever, he would roll up a piece of paper and lob it towards my feet, knowing that I would be tempted to kick it. Once the plaster cast almost spiralled off my leg and into the midst of the newsroom. On days when Judy couldn't give me a lift, I made my painful way towards Hemel station. The plaster cast was excruciatingly painful as it rubbed on my Achilles tendon to the extent that it did almost give me a broken leg which would have been some kind of karma. Fellow travellers who saw me stumble into the gents at Hemel station gave me some weird looks when they saw me re-appear without a care in the world. By now the blessed plaster cast was tucked into a plastic bag that I had been carrying.

I was cursing my predilection for getting into scrapes after two weeks of this fiasco when I learned that my application to join GOAL magazine had been successful. The good news coincided with the official end of my driving ban and the paper's five-year anniversary party hosted by the editor. I was cock-a-hoop with news of my new job, so the plaster cast was shed and I danced the night away to some bewildered looks from

17

colleagues. They must have wondered how someone who had suffered a fractured limb so recently could now be so active. When Bryan joined The Times sports desk years later, we became firm friends. He told me over a beer that he had suspected all along that there was something not quite right about my "broken leg" although the truth only came out months after I had left by when it was too late to take any action.

Unfortunately, Bryan died some years after we had both left The Times. As did Rob Freeman who went from The Echo to the Daily Mail, eventually retiring to concentrate on writing about winter sports for the paper. He had become one of my closest friends, often reminding me over the years not only of the plaster cast story but of the time when his Mum drove us both to Luton Airport to catch a flight to Athens for England's Euro qualifier against Greece.

"Are you sure you have got your passport Nick? she asked me a couple of times. She was on the point of nagging.

"Yes, Mrs Freeman," I replied wearily.

I duly got to passport control to be informed that my passport was out of date. I had picked up the wrong one. I contacted my brother who lived in the flat below mine. He located the right passport and met me halfway but, of course, I had no chance of making the flight which left me with two options, either miss the game altogether or take the day trip package going out the next day. I chose the latter option, but the flight was delayed several hours. There is nothing worse than sitting on a plane knowing you are going to miss kick-off. We got to the Karaiskakis Stadium in Piraeus at half-time. I met up with Rob and Kathy, our lovely tour group leader who flung her arms around me. Thankfully England had left their goal-scoring until the second half, so I saw the strikes from Hurst and Martin Chivers that gave Alf Ramsey's team a 2-0 win. As I wasn't restricted to catching the one-day trip's flight back, I spent the night celebrating with Rob. We sunk a few glasses of Retsina over our Moussaka.

Shortly after my return to the UK, I was asked to ghost write an autobiography on Charlie Cooke, the flamboyant winger, who was then playing for Chelsea. We were introduced and on almost every Friday thereafter I would make my way to Stamford Bridge after his training had finished and listen painstakingly to the story of his life. He was great company and a willing raconteur but a typical Scot in that he didn't take kindly to differences of opinion.

Once after a disagreement he said: "So, do you want to come outside and sort it out?" Sensibly I resisted the invitation as he had doubtless been in many more skirmishes than me.

I had never done this kind of thing before and was therefore extremely naive as I had signed nothing. When I had jotted down 28,000 words, Charlie said one day: "I am sorry Nick but if anyone is going to write my life story, it's going to be me. As I had wasted time and energy on the project for no financial gain, I was fairly bitter. But when Charlie signed for Palace the next season, he won me over with some dashing displays on the flanks. I forgave him but somewhat depressingly he went back to Chelsea. He has since spent most of his life in the States where, so far as I know, he has never written his book.

After 1966, the 1970 World Cup in Mexico was a must. I made plans to go with Chris Wright a rebellious Palace fan, and John Goodbody, like me an old Westminster but two years older and now ensconced in the world of sports journalism. As England were due to play their group games in Guadalajara, we were booked into a hotel next to a lovely lake just outside the country's second biggest city. Among the guests on some football promotion was Roger Hunt who joined us poolside and regaled us with tales of 1966 and life under Bill Shankly at Liverpool. As all the photographs of that epic moment four years earlier had showed Hunt turning back after Hurst's shot had rebounded down from the bar, we had to ask him whether the ball had actually crossed the line.

"Of course, it was over," said Hunt who must have been asked the same question hundreds of times. But as Mandy Rice Davies might have said, he would say that, wouldn't he?

Chapter 5:
Mexico mayhem

England fans soon got the hang of making their cheap way to the Jalisco Stadium for the various group games. We would all congregate in the bars, restaurants and coffee bars in the centre of town, wait for trucks and vans to stop at the traffic lights and then jump aboard before the lights turned green. We got it down to a fine art. My favourite watering hole post-match was a hotel and it was there that I met Cheryl who was a budding American journo. She was a looker, a brunette with lovely long hair. We hit it off immediately. On our second meeting she told me that I could move in with the family accommodating her on the condition that I wrote an article for the husband who happened to be editor of the city's English-speaking newspaper. The subject was a basic one "an Englishman's impression of Guadalajara." I duly penned about 1,000 words and my article was given a good show with the result that I was in in more ways than one. Cheryl was soon creeping along the family's corridors to spend time in my bed. It was a belated and welcome introduction for me as to how football and sport, generally, were irrevocably linked to sex thanks to surplus portions of testosterone.

My enthusiasm was obviously infectious for when the scene shifted from Guadalajara and England faced a quarter-final in Leon against West Germany, Cheryl joined me for the bus journey. Like any couple who travel together we had some petty arguments but for the most part we got on well together and I managed to get her a ticket for what would be her first ever 'socca' game.

I was surprised soon after entering the stadium to see Peter Bonetti file out with the rest of the England team. England fans had been given no inkling of his selection beforehand, but he took the lion's share of the blame for the collapse of the world champions after they had taken a two-goal lead under the boiling midday sun. From behind Bonetti's goal, we had an all too clear view of the game's dramatic transformation in the second half. The Chelsea goalkeeper had been a late replacement for Gordon Banks who had succumbed to food poisoning, but he was a bag of nerves, in utter contrast to the many composed displays I had seen him give under pressure at Stamford Bridge.

I had been sitting on some vendor's freezer containing cold drinks in an attempt to keep cool but that was impossible as Gerd Muller inspired a remarkable recovery in what really would be West Germany's revenge match. They won 3-2 and I was devastated. Cheryl was not the right girl friend to comprehend or contend with my foul mood which lasted several hours into our return journey. She tried to placate me with the usual "it's only a game," line but I was not to be consoled for a considerable while. I must have seemed boorish in the extreme to this gorgeous all-American girl but happily I livened up by the time we reached Guadalajara, which was to be the stage once again of my next match, the semi-final between Brazil and Uruguay, won 3-1 by Brazil. As the England fans - who remained in Mexico - made their way back from the stadium on their convoy of trucks and vans, we soon realised that we had been at the wrong game. The other semi-final between West Germany and Italy had gone to extra time. Every time we asked the occupants of vehicles alongside us at lights what the score was, there had been another goal. Eventually it finished 4-3 in favour of Italy who thus took their place in the final.

As I was still ostensibly, at least, staying in the hotel by Lake Chapala near Guadalajara, I was part of the tour group still afforded coach travel to the various venues. As some disenchanted England fans had gone home, I managed to persuade the organisers to let Cheryl come aboard for the journey to Mexico City for the tournament's climax. We holed up outside the neoclassical spa resort of Tequisquiapan a couple of nights before the third-place final which nobody apart from me, seemed to want to watch. So, I collected a handful of tickets from those who didn't want to go, with the intention of flogging them outside the Aztec and refunding the money. The trouble was transport or, in my case lack of it with our tour group chief insisting that there was no way they were going to lay on a special coach for me. I tried unavailingly to persuade others to come along. We were 110 miles from the capital and some distance from a station or a train that could get me there so, reluctantly, I had to accept that the West Germany v Uruguay match would have to go ahead without me.

Our hotel was next door to stables, so Cheryl was eventually able to appease me by suggesting that we go riding. She teased me that I resembled Clint Eastwood, my screen idol, on horseback as I clung onto the reins, desperately trying to avoid a nasty fall.

The next day June 21st 1970 was the day of the final and we congregated in reception in good time, or so we thought, to board the coach and reach the stadium. We were all in good heart with the final to anticipate, little knowing then that our coach driver - who must have been a Guadalajara local - didn't have the faintest knowledge of Mexico City's frantic and snarled-up roads. As the rain teemed down, he went round and round in circles, so it seemed, as kick-off dawned ever closer.

21

Satnav was, of course, 40 years distant so I was one of many in that overheated coach getting seriously anxious that we would miss the start of the big match. The pressure on the beleaguered driver increased every time he regained his seat on stopping to ask for directions. Us passengers, hurling insults towards the front of the coach, were now all in a state of steadily increasing panic and Cheryl was hardly helping my peace of mind by announcing that she was now intent on wanting to see the game, Brazil v Italy, ticket or no ticket. Yet, all I had to help, besides my genuine ticket - and there was no way she was having that - was the handful of third-place final tickets now crumpled up in my pockets. She would have to get in on one of them.

We could hear the build-up to the game on the Spanish commentary on the driver's radio. That probably didn't help either. And then it was obvious that the game had kicked-off. It was a World Cup final and here I was, still some miles from the stadium. How could that be? This is how heart attacks happen, I thought as Cheryl tried unsuccessfully to calm me down until eventually and, by now, with the match well under way, the driver negotiated a route onto the stadium's deserted concourse. He came to a stop and we bundled off the coach, taking no notice of his apologies as we sped up the ramp leading to the entrances, populated by a mass of stewards, police and various other officials. They immediately noticed that Cheryl's ticket was not legit. It was the wrong colour for a start. They told her in no uncertain terms that she could not go in. I wanted to dash ahead but a certain chivalrous gallantry, a legacy of my public school upbringing, held me back. That was to my cost, I was soon to learn. For as we pleaded and argued, there was a mighty roar from inside the stadium. Pele had apparently scored with a header to put Brazil in front and I was still outside the fucking Aztec and engaged in the mother of all rows with Cheryl. She then did the sensible thing by bursting into tears thereby evidently gaining the pity of our custodians who suddenly waved us both through. The sun was out by now so, hot and perspiring madly, we stumbled up the remaining steps and took our places on the terraces high up behind the goal in plenty of time to see Roberto Boninsega equalise for Italy.

With that goal and for the first 20 minutes of the second half, I was entertaining prospects of the game going to extra time, in which case I wouldn't have felt quite so cheated at having missed such a sizeable chunk of the early stages and Pele's goal. It was an engrossing game but there was no empathy from Brazil as first Gerson and then Jairzinho and then ultimately, and most famously - Carlos Alberto - with that fabulous goal, put the game well beyond Italy's reach. So much for my prayers for an extra half hour.

I consoled myself with constant reminders that at least I'd seen Pele at his best. Twenty-seven years later I had the chance of meeting the great man at the FA Trophy final between Woking and Dagenham & Redbridge. He was due to present the trophy and medals at Wembley. Us journalists were told they could have a personal audience with him before the game. What am I going to say to Pele which could be of novelty value to him, I asked myself. What questions could I ask which he has not been asked on countless occasions, I thought, declining the invitation. I regretted that rebuff as the years passed, never more so than after his death on December 29 2022, the same day incidentally on which my all-time favourite Crystal Palace goalkeeper, John Jackson passed away. When Pele died, I thought back to 1970 and how I had missed seeing his goal in the Aztec and how he might have been amused had I regaled him with that story. Not doing so ranked as among the most stupid things I have ever done. Or not done.

Cheryl and I said our goodbyes the following day as I boarded a plane to London and she took a coach back to her adopted family in Guadalajara. But time is a great healer, so we kept in touch and made plans to meet 12 months later even though I had by then met Susan, a dishy 17-year-old, seven years my junior. I had plucked up courage to tell Susan of Cheryl's imminent arrival and she reluctantly agreed to be put on hold for a month. But as Cheryl emerged into the arrivals hall at Heathrow her first words were: "you don't look so pleased to see me." It was hardly surprising. The gorgeous long-haired brunette from a year ago had morphed into a dumpy, short-haired bruiser. Apparently she had taken pills for some stomach disorder that had a traumatic effect on her figure that had ballooned outwards. And she had hardly aided her new appearance by getting her hairdresser to shear off her lovely locks.

Her instant treat on arriving in the UK for the first time was an introduction to Palace and as I could do nothing about the vagaries of the fixture list - or the manner with which they contrived to combine with flights arriving from the US - it was to Southampton for a late season re-arranged midweek game that we headed straight from the airport. We stood among the away fans at The Dell, but Cheryl could not have been impressed by the manner in which Palace succumbed to a 6-0 defeat.

The plan was for her to bed down with me at my parents for the length of her stay, but I regret to recall that things did not work out. Her new look did not help. I had given my Dad, a renowned ladies man, the big build-up regarding my American girl friend but he took some convincing that she had been the bees knees just a year earlier. Appearances aren't everything, I realise, but it does help if you enjoy looking at your partner. And so it was with tetchiness always in the background that Cheryl soon decided to do her own thing and go solo, travelling around the country. I was much relieved and Susan got a prompt call to re-enter my life. Cheryl returned for the last few days of her trip when thankfully we got on better though she was by now sleeping in my parents' spare room. She must have kept my number, for years later, on a trip to London from Tucson, she got in touch and we met for a curry in Tooting. She looked much better, but she was still not the glamour puss of old.

Chapter 6:
Sliding doors

For some reasons, England's absence probably being a determining factor, I gave the 1972 European Champion-ships in Belgium a miss and was tempted to do the same when Don Revie's team failed to qualify for the 1974 World Cup finals. By then I had met the lovely Lissi who was to become my wife and it was from her mother's home in Frankfurt that I set out by train for the near 24-hour journey to the vital qualifier in Katowice. I arrived early the next morning, unwashed and unshaved, and in no condition, so I thought, to be joined in conversation at a hotel reception desk - where I had gone to see if Rob Freeman had booked in - by a beautiful Polish girl by the name of Karin. She didn't seem in any hurry to move on so we had a coffee and then she invited me to join her and her pals for what turned out to be an extremely inebriated lunch in the nearby town of Sosnowiec. As the vodka flowed in copious quantities Karin decided that she wanted to come to the match with me even though her boyfriend was planning to go. But she had no ticket. So, we returned to the hotel where we had met, the same hotel, as it happened, where the England team were staying. We encountered Alan Ball in the lobby and he, good as gold, came up with a ticket for the game when I asked him.

Forever after that I had a soft spot for the fiery redhead and could never bring myself to write a negative word about him when I was reporting on Portsmouth while he was manager there. Anyway, Karin and I went to the game but, knowing that she could not afford to be spotted, she kept her head well down, raising it only slightly when the masterful Wlodzimierz Lubanski exploited a rare mistake by Bobby Moore to score the game's only goal. Karin and I returned to the city centre and I often wonder how much differently my life would have unfolded had I acceded to her request to stay that night. But I was booked onto the midnight train back to Frankfurt and Lissi's welcoming arms the next evening. There was to be one exchange of postcards with Karin but nothing more. Sliding doors and all that.

The return match at Wembley five months later was possibly the most dramatic international of my life. Brian Clough's contentious remarks about the Polish goalkeeper turned out to be foolish in the extreme. "Tomasieski is a clown" he went on record as saying during the lengthy build-up to the crucial qualifier but Jan Tomasieski proved to be anything but a clown as he performed heroics to keep England out either side of Norman Hunter's mistake that let Jan Domarski in to put the Poles ahead. England needed to win to qualify for the finals but had to wait until the 78th minute before Mick Channon swept in the equaliser. The bombardment on the Polish goal grew ever more intense but our cause was not helped by a statuesque Martin Chivers. As Bobby Moore - who had by now been demoted to a place on the substitutes bench - pleaded with Ramsey to get Kevin Hector on, Ramsey finally heeded the crowd and Moore to introduce the Derby player. Hector nearly scored three times in the remaining few minutes, but England were left with a 1-1 draw that was good enough for Poland but not enough for England to go to West Germany.

I was bereft. England's failure to qualify left with me with a similar despair to seeing Palace relegated which was a fate to which I was forced to become all too accustomed over the next few years. As we trudged slowly down Olympic Way, Lissi did her utmost to console me. My frustration was clearly shared by Hector who poured his heart out to me a few weeks later when I was sent to see him by GOAL Magazine who were by now my employers. Hector gave me more than enough material to easily fill a double page spread.

Slowly but surely my despair subsided and I made up my mind that I wanted to go to West Germany even though England were not among the finalists. Lissi's mother helped by offering me accommodation in Frankfurt but there was a problem. Alan Hughes, the editor of GOAL was insisting that all his staff, with the exception of its main writer - who would go to Germany - would have to be in the office for the duration of the finals to edit the various reports. More misery for me until one day there was a rumour that IPC were threatening to close the magazine because it was running at a loss.

Unlike my colleagues, I felt like celebrating. When might this happen? Before the World Cup, of course, because that would cost IPC a bomb in expenses. I saw a sliver of hope that materialised one day when we were summoned into a meeting to be told that the magazine would indeed have to close a month before the finals. Glory be.

With the help of press accreditation that I managed to scrounge through GOAL, I was off to Germany via Dover and a boat to Ostende in my battered VW that was packed to the rafters. In the need to keep costs down and to save on hotels as much as possible, we had a tight schedule, leaving pre-dawn on the day of the opening game, Brazil v Yugoslavia in Frankfurt. I had become a huge fan of Yugoslav football having seen Red Star Belgrade knock Liverpool out of the European Cup with such panache that the sporting Koppites applauded the visitors off the Anfield pitch, much to the disgust of the vanquished manager Bill Shankly who had the audacity to claim that the crowd was, in fact, jeering them off.

Among my passengers on the German trip was Hy Money, the photographer I had befriended in the Palace press room a year or two earlier. She had been taking pictures of a wedding the previous day and, true to character, had stuffed all the left-over food into a plastic bag for our sustenance. So, we gorged on sandwiches and canapes as we sped through Belgium and then Germany, but Hy's popularity began to fade as we neared Frankfurt. The match was no longer her priority but her need for a pharmacy selling tampons. Consequently, I ended up screaming at her as vivid memories of 1970 began to dominate my thoughts.

I knew I was being unreasonable but so too, seemingly, were those shop owners throughout the city who were closing early in order to get in front of a television for the big game. Every single chemist and convenience store seemed to be shut so Hy did whatever women do in such dire situations. We could see the Wankdorf Stadium floodlights through the trees of the adjoining forest and eventually parked up and raced to the game just in time for kick off. That was as much a result as the 0-0 draw was for the Slavs against the world champions in a fascinating duel.

We stayed for the group games, hurtling up and down autobahns, mostly between Frankfurt and Dusseldorf. Money was tight and I regret to report that on one occasion after six of us had piled into a ground floor hotel room meant for a mere twosome, we escaped through the window early the next morning to avoid paying the bill.

Football was not quite all encompassing for me then so, since Lissi and I were still lovey dovey after less than a year's marriage, I returned to see her for a week with the intention of going back out to Germany for the later stages. Which I did, Dortmund being my first stop this time. The initial quartet of four-team groups had been whittled down to two more groups of four with the result that the final group A game between Holland and Brazil was effectively winner-take-all. And what a game it was as Brazil lost both their heads and their world title in a 2-0 defeat, to Holland's 'total footballers' secured by goals from the two Johanns, Neeskens and Cruyff. From my press seat I had a close-up view of Cruyff's speciality, his exquisite 'Cruyff turn' which left Brazilian defenders indeed turned inside out and in serious danger of ripped stomach linings. They were classic 'see you later' moments. The Dutchman was a wonderful player and I could not help but admire him and his fellow Orangemen enormously. But it was the hosts who were to

27

gain my support four days later thanks mainly to the fact that I now possessed a gorgeous German wife.

I had made some new friends in Munich and it was after I had witnessed a drab third place game in which Poland defeated Brazil 1-0 that one of my new acquaintances ruined whatever slim chance she had of acquiring a ticket for the final. Sylvia was a striking brunette from Canada but her ravishing good looks took a hit as she rushed out of the hotel where we had been staying, forgetting all about the plate glass door separating the reception area from the terrace outside. Her momentum carried her through the door, breaking the glass and she ended up in a bloodied heap on the ground, barely conscious. She was escorted to hospital by her fellow Canadians. I never did see her again though we kept in touch for a while. It was difficult to get that horrible accident out of my mind as I headed for the same Olympic Stadium which would have been the destination for Lissi and I two years earlier but for the terrorist attack on the Israeli athletes. Luckily for me, the final was an engrossing affair which partly succeeded in distracting me from all too vivid recollections of Sylvia's distress.

It remains to this day among the three best games I have ever seen and it was controlled expertly by Jack Taylor, the English referee, a butcher from Wolverhampton. He was a big man, not to be trifled with, possessing courage allied to his air of authority and discipline. That much was obvious when after Cruyff had been brought down after barely a minute's play, Taylor pointed to the penalty spot, waving away German protests to the disgust of the fiercely partisan crowd. Neeskens duly scored as did Paul Breitner for West Germany, also with a penalty, 25 minutes later before Gerd Muller swivelled to score what transpired to be the German winner just before half-time. I willed the Germans to resist the Dutch pressure after the interval and so they did but it was such a magnificent encounter that with the final whistle came a tinge of disappointment that the game was over. And yet it was with a feeling of intense satisfaction that I completed the four-hour drive from Munich to Frankfurt under a colourful sunset. A few weeks later when I bought a German sporting publication with a picture inside of Beckenbauer lifting the Jules Rimet trophy, I scanned the faces behind him to catch a glimpse of my then dark curls in the distance. I should have framed it under the heading of "Me and Beckenbauer."

There were no major tournaments in the summer of 1975 so Lissi and I embarked on a trip to Norway revolving around West Ham's pre-season tour which I thought would be newsworthy seeing as they would be coming home to participate in the Charity Shield as FA Cup winners. The Daily Express said they would take match reports which was useful as it would help cover the costs of the excursion which was never going to be cheap as Norway was, even then, one of the continent's most expensive nations. The itinerary benefitted us though as the Hammers began at Kristiansand which meant that we could take my trusty VW on the ferry from northern Denmark straight to the game against the local club, Start who lost 2-1. I buttonholed John Lyall and Ron Greenwood after the game and introduced myself to the West Ham management duo with the result that they were happy to give me the quotes I needed to embellish my reports.

The schedule was tough as the second game was the very next day which forced us to dash up the coast road to Lillestrom, just east of Oslo, for West Ham's 4-1 victory. The gap of five days before the next game at Aalesund gave the players, ten of whom had started both games, a chance to rest tired limbs.

Lissi and I saw the non-match days as a heaven-sent opportunity to explore Norway which I had not visited since a running trip ten years earlier with South London Harriers who were in a reciprocal exchange programme with an athletics club in Bergen. The two clubs visited each other on alternative years.

After taking our fill of fjords and waterfalls, we were reunited with West Ham. Two days after their 5-1 win in Aalesund, the Hammers provided the opposition for their second division hosts, Os Idrettsplass. Os is a quaint town 180 miles north of the capital. Lyall didn't want to know when I asked him after his team's 2-1 win about the wisdom of playing the game less than 48 hours before they were due to face Derby at Wembley. I walked off the pitch alongside Trevor Brooking, so I put the same question to him. He said something along the lines of: "yes, we think it's a bit odd that we should be playing this game so soon before playing at Wembley. We thought we would have had more time to prepare for that." They weren't earth-shattering quotes, so I buried them halfway down my match report.

After filing my report, Lissi and I were invited to join the players for the post-match reception. We had made particular friends of Bobby Gould and Mervyn Day. To his credit, Gould preferred to talk to us rather than socialise with the bevy of local damsels who had rather surprisingly been bussed in to 'entertain' the players after the game. For a long time, until alcohol took effect, the two parties sat around eyeing each other up as if they were coy schoolboys and girls weighing up the prospects at an end of term dance. I wondered what the wags back home would have made of the arrangement had they not been in blissful ignorance of the event.

29

When Lissi and I got home a few days later, I managed to obtain a few back copies of the Express. I was horrified to see that my report of the last game at Os bore little resemblance to what I had written. It was an inside page lead with Brooking lambasting the management for having the temerity to expect the players to compete in a friendly in Norway two days before their engagement at Wembley. I rang the Express whose chief football writer Jim Lawton had apparently been told "to make a decent story" from my efforts. I duly received a letter from Greenwood via the Express informing me in no uncertain manner that I had abused the hospitality shown by him and Lyall to my wife and I. Greenwood's letter won't go down in the annals of letter-writing tomes as one of the great passages of literature. He said all he had to say in one unpunctuated sentence of 165 words.

As bad luck would have it, the first division fixture planners had done me no favours. For I was by now sports editor of the Hampstead and Highgate Express who covered the fortunes of Arsenal, Spurs and Hendon. We reported on Hendon because the club was known as Hampstead FC in its infancy. As Richard Gwynne, my assistant, had already stated a preference for Arsenal, my duties were to concentrate on Spurs who were given an early-season derby at West Ham which was certainly not ideal from my point of view. As soon as Lyall addressed the assembled throng of hacks after the game, he pointed at me and said: "You. I want a word with you afterwards." He took me into a side room and admonished me for the pre-Wembley report I had written.

He didn't draw breath for long enough to hear my protestations. When we emerged into the corridor, other reporters were agog to find out what the fuss was all about. I regaled them with my tale. Happily that was the end of the matter. Whenever Lyall saw me on subsequent occasions, he gave me a wry smile. He was a charming man. As, indeed was Greenwood.

Chapter 7:
Boxing clever

England's failure to qualify for the 1976 European Championship finals in Czechoslovakia was followed by the elimination of Don Revie's team from the qualifying tournament for the 1978 World Cup in Argentina. Horror of horrors for a loyal England fan. I still wanted to go though it would have meant complications with holiday arrangements at the Ham and High.

My private life was by now in tatters as I had abused Lissi's love by getting involved with Diana, who was a lovely dark-haired Hampstead girl. I had met her in Hampstead's famous Flask pub, introduced by Hy Money, who had just met Di and her brother Anthony when she stopped her car in Swiss Cottage to ask for directions. And, knowing Hy, she also gave them half her life story in those few minutes. She is a garrulous lady and told them why she wanted to find Hampstead. I had asked her to come and take some photographs of John Conteh who was approaching a world light heavyweight title contest in Copenhagen. Anthony who had boxed for the police force, asked if they could come too with the result that my marriage was threatened from that moment on. As Hy drove us to the Wellington pub in Highgate which doubled up as a gymnasium for the boxers trained by George Francis, she knew exactly what I was about when I asked Anthony for his phone number, the ridiculous notion being that maybe we could go running together. Hy had already sensed the chemistry between Anthony's sister and me, she was acutely aware of my ruse to get Di's number. And that I duly did on my return from the big fight in Copenhagen, much relieved to hear that by now Anthony could not run because his wrist had been broken by a prisoner he was taking to a cell. I didn't care much for him in any case.

"Oh sorry to hear that," I said unconvincingly, "but would you mind very much if I asked your sister out?" He handed her the phone and my life thereon was in turmoil, so much so that as the World Cup neared, I convinced myself that by not going to Argentina I could sort out my dilemma. It was such a forlorn hope that as the tournament unravelled, I grew more and more frustrated that I was not in Buenos Aires and all the other venues staging games. Little did I know that I would get to Argentina and all those grounds 33 years later but that is another story.

As Di was now very much in my life and she had moved into a Hampstead bedsit with me, we watched most of the games together on television in the living room belonging to Ewen, a Scottish news reporter on the Ham and High. As the tournament progressed, I grew ever more exasperated that I was not there. I even entertained the wild notion of flying out for the final after the semi-finals but thankfully I saw sense in time. It was an idiotic idea and could have been a costly exercise and a painful one had I not acquired a ticket. So, I watched the game between the hosts and Holland with Di at her mother´s Streatham home but my concentration was somewhat interrupted by a ringing of the doorbell downstairs and a long, quite flirty conversation that followed. I could hear Di chatting to a black man she had met in a Brixton night club a few nights earlier. With my suspicions aroused, she brought him into the living room and introduced me. He finally departed but the atmosphere between us was hardly conducive to watching a World Cup final. Again, I was glad that the game went to extra time before Argentina prevailed. That was it, I decided. Never again would I choose to voluntarily miss such a game or an event.

My torment was assuaged a trifle on a subsequent excursion to the Wellington pub when George Francis ordered me to climb into the ring with Conteh. "Then you can tell your readers what he's really like," said the trainer. As I hadn't boxed since prep school where my aspirations ended with a bloodied nose, I was terrified. But downing my notepad and biro, I did as I was told and danced around with pads on my hands to give Conteh a moving target to aim for as he sparred for his next major contest. Those three minutes gave me something to boast about for years to come. I had survived to tell the tale.

By the time the 1980 European Championships came around Di had given me a son, James, and they joined me in Italy. UPI (United Press International) for whom I now freelanced, had decided that I would be their man in Milan, so I covered all the group games there which meant that I had to miss out on England´s games in Turin. That was a wrench, but I had to show some semblance of responsibility. When the scene switched from Milan, I was able to persuade an Italian journalist to ferry Di, James and myself in his Mercedes for the 5-hour journey to Rome. Luckily James slept like a log or it would have been embarrassing. They stayed a few days and then caught a plane home while I stayed on to see Italy beat the Czechs in one of the longest penalty shoot-outs in history in the third-place match in Naples. And then it was to Rome for the final in which West Germany overcame Belgium 2-1.

Di and James also accompanied me to Spain for the later stages of the 1982 World Cup. I was, by now, employed by The Times as a sub editor, permitted occasional reporting duties. I wasn´t allowed to take a whole month off my holidays for the event but Nick Keith, the sports editor, knowing only too well my passion for the game, was most accommodating. He sanctioned two separate ten-day stays while the games were on. I was based in Santander with Chris Oakley, a psychotherapist mate and his wife, plus another friend Phil Wilson. From there we travelled into Bilbao to see England's group matches besides making the lengthy road trip to Zaragoza to take in Northern Ireland's tussle against Yugoslavia. And then, reluctantly, I flew home.

Di and James joined me for my second visit at which point hotels and apartments in Madrid were full to the brim. Not being the best organised soul, I had booked nothing in advance and we had a serious problem until Di burst into tears when we were refused a room in the same block where Chris and Haya were staying. Not for the first time in my life, I was grateful for a woman's tears. The concierge took pity upon us and found us a 'matrimonial' with the result that I was able to see all the subsequent group games in Madrid, in the Bernabéu and the Vicente Calderon stadium. And then we drove south, stopping off in Cordoba where fortune smiled upon us once again as I found an open gate leading into Cordoba's stadium where James and I enjoyed a kickabout.

Our eventual destiny however was Sevilla's Estadio Ramón Sánchez Pizjuán, the venue for the epic France v Germany semi-final, made famous or rather infamous by the manner in which Germany's goalkeeper Schumacher cleaned out Patrick Battiston. The score was 3-3 after extra time but Germany, as ever, won the ensuing penalty shoot-out. That incident and the manner in which Germany and Austria had earlier collaborated to draw 0-0, thereby eliminating Algeria from the World Cup, left such a nasty taste in the mouth that I was no longer such an avid fan of Deutsche fussball whatever the love I still felt for my estranged German wife. So it was that when I took my seat behind the goal for the final in the Bernabéu stadium, I was supporting Italy and not Germany. Fortunately, Italy obliged by scoring all their goals in their 3-1 win at that end in the second half. I had the most perfect close-up view.

Thanks to my support of Palace and my burgeoning friendship with the chairman Ron Noades and his wife, Novello, a former Miss Wales, I was able to rent their spacious apartment in Cassis, near Marseille for the duration of the 1984 European championships in France. I drove down with Di and James and we made the most of their pool between games. Cassis is a delightful coastal resort, so we spent many happy hours pottering about when Chris and I were not hitting the autoroute. We seemed to take endless return trips to games in Lyon's Stade Gerland but the highlight of the tournament was undoubtedly the France v Portugal semi-final in Marseille's Velodrome, won 3-2 by the hosts who thus progressed to the final against Spain. With tickets in the Parc

33

des Princes for behind the goal, we had an all too clear view of the horrendous mistake by the Spanish goalkeeper Luis Arconada who allowed Michel Platini's free kick to slip through his grasp for the first France goal. By chipping in the second goal in the last minute to give the hosts a 2-0 win, Bruno Bellone became the only French striker in the tournament to score.

Chapter 8:
Favour from Fergie

As I had been at The Times over five years by now, I was entitled to a sabbatical. I had always been fascinated by Australia, little knowing then that I would have strong links to the continent years later thanks to having two of my sons living there. The other reason for travelling down under via a week in Thailand, was the little matter of the World Cup qualifier between Australia, the Oceanic Group winners, and Scotland, then managed by Alex Ferguson. Scotland, who were runners-up in Uefa's group seven, had won the first leg of the play-off 2-0 and were due in Melbourne for the second leg. I was hoping to report the game for The Times but the sports editor Norman Fox was so intent on keeping in with the Sydney-based freelance Sue Mott that she was told to cover it for the paper. I was incensed so I made sure that I would get work from other papers even though I was a Times staff man. I knew that was unethical, but The Guardian and Evening Standard duly gave me their orders. However, true to form, I encountered difficulty finding the Scotland team hotel and arrived too late for Ferguson's pre-match press conference. All I had were a few quotes from the Scotland striker, West Ham's Frank McAvennie who I had met while crossing a park enroute to the hotel. The scorer of Scotland's second goal in the first leg, he had been suffering toothache and was on his way back from seeing a dentist who had given him the all-clear to play, if selected.

I eventually arrived at the hotel in a panic. All the rest of the journalists accompanying the party had vanished into the afternoon to file their previews so there was no one around to tell me what Ferguson had said. I saw the team's chief steward and explained my plight to him. The team and officials were having lunch. "I'll go and see Alex," he said. He came out and said: "Alex will give you 15 minutes after he's finished lunch." I waited patiently until the great man appeared. He was as good as gold and gave me what I wanted. I couldn't have been more grateful. Thereafter I would never hear a bad word said about Fergie without leaping to his defence. His team drew 0-0 to qualify for the 1986 finals 2-0 on aggregate.

Somehow, I managed to procure press accreditation for Mexico even though I was not covering the tournament. The press passes helped to cut costs as I was by now firmly entrenched in the insane world of ground hopping. Mexico´s 11 venues were stretched far and wide but the raison d´etre was to chalk them all off. Chris and I felt like celebrating when we took in Mexico City´s Estadio Olimpico Universitario to see France beat Italy 2-0 in a group game as that visit enabled us to complete the full set. I had a brief liaison with an American lady in the artists' colony of San Miguel de Allende during one of our many stop-offs, but that particular romance was destined for the scrapheap when she asked "where do we go from here?" one hot night. She was getting far too possessive for my liking.

My relationship with Di was now on borrowed time so I considered myself a free man, never more so than at the end of the frantic day when we sped up the motorway from England´s 3-0 win over Paraguay in the Aztec Stadium to Queretaro, some 150 miles distant, for the evening quarter-final. The game between Spain and Denmark was already under way but we hurried past stewards just in time to see Jesper Olsen put the Danes ahead. Spain´s reply was a breathtaking five-goal salvo. We found a hotel after the game and instantly clocked the short-haired blonde working at reception. Bill Pierce from the Press Association and the engaging Roger Malone from the Telegraph joined Chris and I for a post-match meal, but they were all too tired to join me for a late night drink in a bar next to the hotel. As I gazed absentmindedly at my fellow drinkers, I spotted the blonde from reception at a table opposite mine. She was alone and looking at me so I beckoned for her to accompany me. She shook her head which I thought was odd until I returned to the hotel to see her lolling against a chap, watching a football highlights show. When he wasn´t looking, I blew her a goodnight kiss which was not reciprocated. No matter. By the time I reached the first floor landing she had caught up to engage me in a bear hug. This was wonderful. "Wouldn´t it be nice," she said," if we went to bed."

"Yes," said I. "It would."

"But there is just una problema," said she as I started to think that she must have her period.

"Yo soy hombre," (I am a man) she said with which I could not remove my fingers fast enough from beneath her knicker elastic where they were just starting to explore. Her mate, encased in the most tightfitting jeans, came down the stairs on hearing the commotion. "Yo soy hombre too," she said. I woke Chris up to regale him with details of my escapade. But five days later, in the medieval city of Taxaco, which we had gone to explore on a non-match day, Chris and I emerged from a restaurant to be confronted by a group of svelte looking ladies standing outside a night club. One of them, a dizzy brunette waved at me to come over. We started chatting and then she said: "I think we have met before. In Queretaro." The short haired blonde from the hotel had turned into a long raven-haired beauty. They were a group of transvestites touring Mexico.

The fixtures transpired to give us several trips to Guadalajara where Northern Ireland were based. On one such excursion and because of my nonsensical liking for running the petrol tank low so as to satisfy an adrenalin rush, we ran out of gas. However, fortune smiled upon us as we were near enough to a drive-way to push in our otherwise trusty VW. The idea was to ask the owners if we could use their phone to plead for roadside assistance but the hirsute proprietor who resembled a bandito out of a Clint Eastwood dollars movie, did far better than that. He disengaged himself from a group of chaps, drinking, smoking and playing cards to summon his six-year old son to bring his Mercedes out from where it was parked at the rear of the complex. With the utmost aplomb, the child who could barely see above the dashboard, obeyed by driving the car into the courtyard where Dad promptly found a hosepipe, enabling him to suck petrol from out of his tank into our empty one. We could not thank them enough. They refused our offer of money, gave us a cerveza each and sent us on our way in search of a gas station.

With England based in Monterrey near the USA border, we had decided to take in just two of the three group games. We flew to the first one, a dismal 1-0 defeat by Portugal, sacrificed the goalless draw against Morocco - during which Ray Wilkins was sent off - but drove the marathon journey to the winner-take-all game against the Poles in which Gary Lineker scored a hat trick. Once we had satisfied our need to do all the grounds, Guad - as it became known - became a second home helped by my familiarity with the city from 1970. It was as I made my way out of the Jalisco after the France v Brazil quarter-final - won 4-3 by France on penalties after a 1-1 draw - that I was seduced by a captivating smile from a curly haired senorita. We started talking. Her name was Rocio and she was to play a big part in my life for years to come.

Chris and I were allowed to leave our bags in her sister´s home in the city as we were only taking minimal belongings with us on a short break to Puerto Vallarta before flying back for the France v Germany semi-final. As we disembarked the plane at the seaside resort, I grabbed my luggage - which happened to be in a bin-liner - from the overhead rack only for it to snag on a hook. I was dismayed to see all my clothes, underwear et al tumble out and scatter in front of Ron Atkinson who was in Mexico as a commentator, accompanied by his new wife-to-be. I spotted him raise his eyebrows to her as I stooped to gather up the various items. It was so acutely embarrassing that I could not help but smile some years later when Malcolm Allison - who had been Palace's manager - did me a favour of sorts by referring to Big Ron - as he was known - as Fat Ron.

37

And then there was the famous occasion when after Atkinson had briefly become Nottingham Forest´s manager, he sat in the wrong dugout - Arsenal´s - before his first game. Honours were even in the embarrassment stakes then, so I reckoned.

Anyway, after we had returned to Guad to collect our gear, I agreed to Rocio´s suggestion that she join me in Mexico City for the tournament´s climax. But there was to be no climaxing for me as I was to learn after we had enjoyed a prolonged fumble in the shower that she was still a virgin at 38. Apparently, she came from a good Catholic family. For an attractive woman she must have rebuffed countless offers to deflower her, mine being the latest. Still, we had a good time. I managed to get her a ticket for the Argentina v Germany final but her joy at getting into the Aztec - for what I thought was a disappointing game, tarnished by the South Americans' time-wasting, turned to dismay when she learned that the expensive camera, she had brought with her had vanished from the storeroom where she had been promised it would be secured. Some hope. She brushed off the loss of her camera as nothing more than an inconvenience.

Rocio's innocence and naivety were as evident again 12 months later when she travelled to England to visit me. After a lengthy wait in the arrivals hall at Gatwick, I made enquiries only to be told that she had been refused entry through passport control and into the UK as she did not possess a visa. I was escorted into a special office where, dressed all in virginal white, I saw her looking a picture of elegance. No matter, she was not allowed into the country however much we both pleaded with customs officers. So back to Mexico on the next flight, she went. I suppose I should have asked her on the telephone beforehand if she had the required paperwork, but I could only assume that she had. A year later and very much wiser, she sailed through immigration at Gatwick with no problems. She got herself a room in Victoria and dead-end job which was a shame for an intelligent woman who was an English teacher back home.

I was back reporting for UPI when the football scene switched to Germany for the 1988 European Championships. It brought quite a contrast as I went from frantically searching for accommodation in Spain to being holed up in Dusseldorf´s plush Hilton Hotel. My companion now was Athena, an Australian honey blonde, as Di had dumped me unceremoniously the previous year, a week after our return from the World Athletic championships in Rome. From our first date, Athena had made it clear that she didn´t think much of my dress sense so between games she took my arm and led me towards the city´s shops. Under her approving look, I purchased a jacket, strides and a couple of shirts and began to look the part, so she reckoned. We dined out that lunchtime in the Hilton restaurant where the steak I devoured turned out to be one of the most sumptuous meals I have ever enjoyed. UPI had booked me on a flight to Hamburg on which there was no room for Athena, so I enjoyed the delights of the Reeperbahn the night before her arrival.

Chapter 9:
Friendly causes friction

As you readers may have gathered by now, fidelity was not my most outstanding virtue. I blamed my Dad whose mantra was "one's body is one's own to do what one wants with it." And to hell with anyone who disagreed. But Athena gave as good as she got when it came to staying faithful - or not - so we ploughed on for the time-being. She stayed in the hotel that UPI had booked for me while I took in the West Germany v Holland semi-final, won by Holland who thus advanced to a semi-final against Russia in the same Munich Olympia Stadium where they had lost the 1974 World Cup final so unluckily. It was a good final, but I was never able to join the throngs who claimed that Marco van Basten's goal that secured Holland's 2-0 win was one of the great goals of our time. Okay, it was a superb cushioned volley from a tight angle but over the course of a season one would expect to see a handful of those.

Athena had by now gone home which came as something of a relief as she was one of the few women, I had ever met who gave me a major problem over my footballing obsession. I was selfish in the extreme as anyone harbouring an obsession undoubtedly is and I had, I thought, made that abundantly clear on our first date.

In 1990, maybe I should have made allowances for her pregnancy when she was three months away from giving birth to our son Ashley. We were lying in the sun outside her Wembley flat one July afternoon when I rose to my feet, saying that I would see her later. I hadn't dared raise the subject of Wycombe Wanderers' pre-season friendly against Southampton in their new stadium which, of course, I had yet to visit. "Where do you think you're going?" she asked.

"To Wycombe," I replied.

"What for?"

"Football."

"But the season hasn't begun yet."

"I know but friendlies have started.'"

"But you are not covering it."

"I know but they have got a new ground and I want to see the game."

A major row ensued, taking up more time than I had bargained for. She told me that I was being callous which brooked no argument. I finally insisted that I was going and would be back by 6.30 pm - in plenty of time to enjoy more of the hot day - but I was now on borrowed time. I made good progress along the M40 but finding the new Wycombe stadium proved a nightmare. By the time I stepped inside Adams Park, as it was then known, the game was well under way and I had missed the only goal of the afternoon, a Jimmy Case penalty for Southampton. Somehow, I got over my anger in time for us to have a pleasant evening in Wembley.

A life of hedonism continued to have its blips. Late the previous year when I joined Athena in her native Sydney, the plan had been for us to spend a week, driving up the Pacific Highway, returning via the New England Highway about 100 miles inland, in time, I had hoped to see three games in the New South Wales Premier League on the Friday, Saturday and Sunday before flying home. True to form, she wasn't very keen on the idea so, being a sensitive soul, I reluctantly agreed on a compromise of just one game, on the Sunday. We arrived at her parents' home on the Saturday evening and she immediately vanished into the kitchen with her Mum, finally emerging to say that her parents had arranged a special farewell dinner for me. So, my one game was scuppered as I had no idea how to get to Paramatta without her help. When we sat down to eat on the Sunday, it was a regular meal, nothing particularly special about it at all.

Chapter 10:
Disguised for Wembley

By now I had been at The Times ten years and had only ever taken four days off sick because of a horrendous bout of flu. Other sports subs had taken weeks off at a time especially one individual who came out with outrageous excuses for not coming in such as that he had been hit on the head by a cricket ball. And that was long after he had given up playing. So, I wasn't too conscious stricken about pulling a sickie, so to speak.

Knowing full well that I was a staunch England fan and would be desperate to be at the friendly against Brazil in March, my bête noir Keith Blackmore made sure that I would be on the desk that night. And yet I knew that I would be nowhere near the desk as I had devised a cunning plan. The Times football team had a game that lunchtime on the pitches behind Canary Wharf in Millwall Park near the river. The guy who reported on our games for the house magazine came along. As soon as the match was over, I told him that I had been concussed in a clash of heads. He was a little bemused as he had been standing on my side of the pitch where I, right back for the day, had been occupied during the second half. He had not seen me collapse. Anyway, he was a good lad and, after the game, whisked me in his car to the Royal London Hospital in Whitechapel Road.

As soon as he had gone, I donned my civvies and left the hospital's accident and emergency wing and rang the sports desk to tell them of "my plight," adding for good measure that doctors had told me to go straight home and rest. All I had to do now was avoid being spotted by anyone who might give my game away. The sooner I got to Wembley therefore, the better as there'd be less chance then of bumping into anyone on the tube who knew me. I found a cafe near Wembley Central station and killed time. I had come armed with a deer stalker hat that my Dad had given me for God knows what reason as it certainly wasn't my style. It looked incongruous in the surroundings but there was nothing else for it but to wear the damn thing. Alan Leather, the Palace secretary, had a ticket for me and had insisted on meeting at the foot of the steps underneath the twin towers, the last place I would have chosen for our rendezvous. I couldn't have looked more conspicuous if I'd tried, standing there in that ludicrous headgear.

Alan was a benign character' known as Clouseau by the Palace players for his resemblance to Peter Sellers who played the bumbling inspector.

Alan smiled quizzically as he saw me and handed over the ticket. I gave him the money and disappeared into the crowds. I saw Gary Lineker score to give England a 1-0 win and, after the game took the least direct route I could find to the Wembley Tandoori where, amid much hilarity, I regaled the lads with my story. I had recovered well enough to go to work the next day when Paul Harrison, a fellow sub, asked me how I was.

"Strange that you should get concussion on a day when England were playing Brazil at Wembley," he said rather pointedly.

By the time that Italia 90 came round, my relationship with Athena was on its last legs in spite of her pregnancy. I wondered if it was just me but when my mate Chris stated that she was the most selfish woman he had ever met, I knew that I had a case. As a psychotherapist, Chris should know what he was talking about. My feelings for her were not helped by the fact that I had by now expertly timed my excursion to the coffee dispenser at Wapping and summoned up the courage to chat up Gill, a comely secretary working for The Sunday Times. I had had my eyes on her for a long time. She proved much more amenable to being a party to my obsession and joined me halfway through the World Cup finals when I was working once again for UPI for extremely limited rewards. I started by being their man in Milan just as I had been at the Euros in 1984.

The idea was that I covered all the games in Milan and filed stories from the German training camp near Como on intervening days. The trouble was that the Germans weren't desperate to share hotel foyer space with British journos and even when I did manage to gain entry past the heavily manned security, I had no idea what anyone was saying as I had no knowledge of the language despite being married to a German. Silly me for not bothering to learn the lingo from her. And, of course, the German reporters who had deadlines to meet, were not too eager to share the thoughts of Franz Beckenbauer et al with foreign scribes.

It was a nightmare scenario, so I thought "sod this" and started offering UPI statistical pieces on the World Cup, number of penalties, sending-offs, background on scorers etc which they seemed happy with. This permitted me time to drive to Verona to see all three group games there which I was not, in fact, covering. With the autostradas taking a hammering from my VW Beetle, I even found the time to motor to Udine on the other side of Italy for the Spain v Uruguay tie which had caught my attention. With my luck holding, I finally had the audacity to fly from Milan to Cagliari for the England v Republic of Ireland game which was, like Spain v Uruguay, extremely dull and goalless. But the England game was not quite bad enough to influence my decision to drive down to Bologna for David Platt's last-gasp winner against Belgium in the round of 16 game.

43

For an obsessive like me, there could be nothing worse, I reasoned, than sitting around on match days not actually seeing matches. It was unprofessional in the extreme, I knew, but UPI weren't paying me mega bucks. I was utilising my press accreditation to the full to broaden my knowledge for their benefit, I kidded myself. And yet UPI must have been quite content with my efforts thus far for they then dispatched me to Naples just to report on games, thank God. Gill joined me there but she was naive in the extreme when she announced her arrival by permitting a pock-marked Italian from whom we had asked directions to dip his grubby paws into the passenger side pocket and steal a bundle of liras we had stacked there for supposedly safe keeping. That left us a bit short of readies, but Gill's humour and sensuality provided ample compensation. Thankfully she wasn't desperate to come to games or sourcing tickets would have been a problem.

UPI's head of delegation, the extremely affable Morley Myers assigned himself to cover the England v Cameroon quarter final in Naples, but I managed to procure a ticket for behind the goal where I had a grandstand view of the heroics of Gary Lineker and Terry Butcher in England's dramatic 4-2 win. Nothing, not even Gill was going to stop me then from seeing England's semi-final in the Stadio Delle Alpi where Morley managed to find an additional press ticket for me. I caught the lunch-time train to Turin and groaned with despair as Stuart Pearce and Chris Waddle missed their penalties in the shoot-out. The pain of that defeat by Germany was on a par with how I felt in 1973 after our exit by Poland or as witness to one of Palace's many relegations.

The night special train back to Mafia country was rammed but I eventually managed to find a seat next to a fellow Brit who was as miserable as I was. But fortunately, he was engaging company. I arrived back in Naples the next morning after little sleep, so I caught up with a few zzzzs before that evening's second semi-final between the hosts and Argentina who possessed the villain of the piece in Diego Maradona despite his massive contribution to Napoli's first ever Scudetto. He was no longer flavour of the month having netted a penalty when 90 minutes and extra time once again failed to produce a winner. And so, we had another West Germany v Argentina World Cup final which transpired to be the worst one ever. The Argies seemed to perform as if they believed the whole world was against them and not just Italy. They hurled themselves into one illegal challenge after another and had two men sent off before Andreas Brehme scored the decisive goal for the Germans from the penalty spot. No one had wanted this one to go to extra time, let alone a shoot-out - except possibly Argentina - so the rest of us were indeed thankful that 90 minutes proved sufficient for once.

Chapter 11:
Second team syndrome

David O'Leary once said preposterously that everyone's second team was Leeds. Which could not have been much further from the truth because, since the days of Don Revie, Leeds have not exactly been the most popular club in the land among the footballing universe, let alone the second most popular for those of us whose priority is some other club. But it did raise the question of second teams. How many of us have a second team that we favour? It's a childish notion perhaps but a valid one, nevertheless. For a long time, Man United were mine until I discovered Swansea. My devotion towards the Welsh club began during my early days on The Times when Nicholas Keith was sports editor. With Swansea going for promotion from the old second division in 1981, he asked me one day if I'd like to cover their midweek home game against Luton. It was a lively 2-2 draw. Nick must have been pleased with what I wrote as he then delegated me to go to the next Swansea home game which happened to be against Chelsea on the Saturday. They won 3-0. By now I was hooked and so desperate to see John Toshack's team clinch promotion that I begged Nick to let me cover their game at Preston which could lead them into the promised land for the first time.

Never the best timekeeper, I didn't allow quite enough time for my journey by train and tube from Wimbledon. As I raced down to the platform at Euston, I saw, to my horror, my train pulling out. My car was at home. The next train to Preston wasn't for another couple of hours. I thought about flying but I didn't have the flight schedule and Preston, is in any case a long way from Manchester and Liverpool airports. There was nothing else for it but to catch the next train going in a northerly direction and hitchhike. The era of four trains an hour to Manchester and Liverpool was 30 years away. So, I caught a train to Leighton Buzzard and disembarked there and thumbed a lift to the MI. My look of desperation must have appealed to an Indian gentleman who was approaching the slip road where I was standing. He stopped and I got in. He told me he was going to Birmingham. He was good company. The miles sped by. We passed the signs for Coventry but then as Birmingham came into view, he kept his foot down. We went past Walsall and then Wolverhampton. Eventually I said: "We have gone past Birmingham."

"It's alright," he said. "I have got plenty of time. I will take you to Preston."

I could hardly believe my luck. This guy was effectively going 200 miles out of his way to give a lift to a scruffy hitchhiking hack who he hadn't met until a few hours earlier. I had long since given up hope of making kick-off but at least my escort could help me see a sizeable chunk of the game and get me to Deepdale in time to listen to the quotes. In fact, he pulled up outside the main entrance just as the half-time whistle blew. I got my press pass from reception and raced up to the press box to find out from other hacks what had happened in the first half. Goals from Leighton James and Tommy Craig had apparently given the visitors a 2-0 lead. I felt like a jinx when Alex Bruce scored to give Preston a fighting chance. But then came the goal from Jeremy Charles that completed a 3-1 win for the Swans who thus pipped Blackburn for promotion on goal difference which also served to relegate the hosts. There was pandemonium on the pitch afterwards as players, fans, and journalists mingled. I battled to hear what Toshack and Bill Shankly, who was his advisor, had to say. I got what I needed, and much relieved, composed my report on the train home. No one guessed that I hadn't seen the whole game.

I kept the Indian man's number and promised that I would treat him and his wife to dinner which I duly did a few weeks later. But it was a bit of a subdued evening as, with our marriage crumbling, Lissi refused to make up a four.

"Why would I want to have dinner with two complete strangers?" she argued. I was embarrassed but I hope I managed to convey my gratitude to my guests.

The die was cast however, so far as Swansea and I were concerned. They had got under my skin. Nick permitted me to report on their opening game in the first division at home, ironically, to Leeds who were convincingly thrashed 5-1. Encouraged by their spectacular start, Swansea beat the likes of Liverpool, Man United, Arsenal, Spurs and even challenged for the title before falling away and finishing sixth. But they struggled the next season - second season syndrome and all that - and were relegated.

I got to love the Vetch and its narrow wooden fire-risk corridors as I watched the club tumble through the divisions, more often than not paying my own way to south Wales as their games were seldom thereafter singled out for coverage. But they became newsworthy again when creditors lined up in the High Court with the aim of liquidating the club. They were wound up by a court order in December 1985 and, much to the amusement of my colleagues at The Times, I wore a black tie to work. The club was saved by a local businessman Doug Sharpe but years later they needed a win from their last game, at home to Hull, to avoid falling into the Conference. I reported on their 4-2 success - which sent Exeter down instead - and intermittently during the subsequent years I was summoned to write about their games. If not, I went anyway whenever their midweek matches did not clash with Palace. Invariably I stayed in one of the cheap hotels on the promenade, a short walk from the ground. One of the hotels was appropriately called The Times Hotel. Another was owned by Mel Nurse, a former Swansea centre half who had formed a consortium that confirmed salvation. Invariably I looked forward to post-match drinks with him and his pal Mel Charles, another former Swan, the brother of the famous John Charles.

Slowly but surely Swansea climbed back to the elite and they even paid three successful visits to Wembley, old and new, a penalty shoot-out success over Huddersfield after the teams had finished level at 1-1 in the Autoglass Trophy final, a 4-2 championship play-off success over Reading to reach the Premier League for the first time and a 5-0 League Cup triumph over League One Bradford. By now the club had long since moved into the Liberty Stadium on the other side of town. But I had always envied the occupants on the huge North Bank terrace, or 'big bank' opposite the Vetch's main stand for their unobstructed view. So, I needed little persuading when my mate Martin Scott said he was coming to the penultimate league game at the Vetch against Oxford as he wanted to "tick it off before it was too late." We stood together on those steps. We had a much better sight of the action than I'd ever enjoyed in the pokey press box. But it was in that press box that I had met, among others, John Burgum, the Swansea Evening Post reporter. In 2006, on the 25th anniversary of the club's elevation to the old first division, John invited me to a celebration dinner. He asked me to write a piece for the special brochure commemorating the occasion, so I regaled my readers with a tale of my panic in getting to Preston.

With Swansea subsequently back in the top-flight alongside Palace, it was difficult to maintain my enthusiasm. Too frequently for my liking, the two clubs were involved in the same relegation battle. There were some games, I must admit, that I actually wanted Swansea to lose.

Chapter 12:
A Swedish sojourn

Gill's predilection for cocaine eventually got the better of our relationship. Her two best friends who lived in Braested near Sevenoaks where she was based, were regular snorters and I think Gill reckoned that I was a bit of a wimp for my constant excuses not to join them. But this resulted in her wild mood swings. She had regaled her girlfriends by telling them she was "going out with a groundhopper" and she could indeed be as nice as pie at the regular Saturday night parties hosted by Roy, an antiques dealer. But then, more often than not, she'd turn into a harridan as soon as we crossed her threshold.

It was some time after she had left the Sunday Times for the Sunday Express to become a reporter that our rupture was confirmed. She was sent along with other journalists from other papers to stalk Prince Charles whose courtship of Camilla from Highgrove had now taken off big time. I believe she met a journo on that trip who enjoyed the white stuff as much as she did with the result that I was toast. I returned from a basketball trip to Esjberg - where she had rung my hotel to check that I was not on a sudden plane home - to find all my clothes neatly packed and my suits hung up ready for my exit from her life. That happened soon after the 1992 European Championships in Sweden.

Bobby Robson had given way to Graham Taylor as manager, but it was obvious from the dire group games in Malmo against France and Denmark - who had replaced Yugoslavia at the last minute because of the war in the Balkans - that England would not go far. Our eventual exit came at the hands of the tournament hosts in Stockholm. I had an inkling that Taylor would do the unmentionable and take off our top scorer, Gary Lineker minutes before he actually did so.

I remember saying to Chris who had somehow scammed a press pass next to me: "you know what, he's going to bring on Alan Smith for Lineker."

Chris replied knowingly: "He would never do that."

But Smith it was who came on as Lineker made way with a rueful glance at the bench. You got the impression that Taylor was a risk-taker who did things like playing players alarmingly out of position (Gary Pallister at left back for instance) for dramatic effect simply because he wanted to make a bigger name for himself. Underneath all that he was an incredibly nice man as I found out for myself when he engaged my small group in conversation as we stood around the foyer of the Lancaster Gate Hotel before a subsequent Football Writers dinner. Among the guests on my table was the commentator Jacqui Oatley, a diehard fan of Wolves where Taylor was, of course, by then manager.

Fortunately, the agony of England's dismissal in Sweden was soothed by Christine, a lovely Welsh brunette who had come into my life a few months earlier following our meeting at the annual basketball dinner. I was there in my guise as basketball reporter for The Times and on the same table fortuitously as Christine who was the guest of Bob Hope (no relation) who was a club owner. They were no longer an item, so I was delighted when Bob asked me to "look after" her when he started circulating. She told me that she worked for the Welsh Lawn Tennis Association, so I obtained their number from Directory Enquiries on the Monday morning and rang her saying that The Times wanted me to write a piece on the state of Welsh Lawn Tennis.

"Oh yeah, pull the other one," she laughed.

So, I came clean and asked her if she would have dinner with me. Two days later I was heading down to Cardiff for our dinner date that ended happily in bed. But for all her many attributes, Christine was, after Athena and Eva, who I had yet to meet, the most difficult lady when it came to tolerating my obsession.

"Do you ever take a holiday which is unconnected with football?" she once asked me to which I replied: "Er no, I don't think so."

But I have since gone on trips where I saw no football, to New Zealand to cover the Commonwealth Games in Auckland, to Bali to spend a holiday with my Australia-based son James, to Nepal for trekking in the Himalayas and to Pakistan for my son Ben's wedding. Try as I might, I could find no football to watch in any of those countries.

Christine proved something of a martyr for she agreed to a solo drive in my hire car back from Stockholm to its depot in Copenhagen as I had to travel to Spain via Faro to cover the Olympic basketball qualifying tournament for The Times. Christine never let me forget what an angel she had been to do me that particular favour. It was a wrench to leave the Euros early, but duty called and I was able, after all, to watch the semi-finals on TV in Badajoz where my room overlooked the town's lower division football stadium. To this day I have not seen a game there despite visiting around 175 stadiums in Spain. I saw Denmark's staggering 2-0 win over Germany in the final over dinner in a roadside café on the long road from Badajoz to Faro.

Chapter 13:
Time to go

Within three months of my return from Faro, I was walking out of The Times' Wapping plant for the last time, stunned and chastened by my sacking. In all, 26 journalists from the paper were dismissed on that dark Friday. Under the new editor Peter Stothard, the News International mogul Rupert Murdoch had deemed it necessary for a brutal culling of staff. Among the victims, there had to be five from the sports desk. I stood no chance of surviving as I was hated by the third in command, Keith Blackmore who was a creep, reviled by just about everyone in the department. It had been a fairly harmonious desk until 1987 when he was brought in by his mate, David Chappell who rose to become sports editor. They were like two police officers, good cop and bad cop.

Under the previous sports editors, Nick Keith, an Old Etonian, Norman Fox, the paper's former football correspondent and briefly Tom Clarke, the former Daily Mail sports editor, I had enjoyed my time as a sub, notwithstanding the time when I used a dinner break to watch Arsenal play Huddersfield in a Milk Cup (League Cup) tie at Highbury, only a few miles from the paper's then base in Gray's Inn Road.

I would have got away with it, but Norman Fox spotted the match programme on my desk and said: "You don't use your dinner breaks to go and watch football matches."

With many games to cover at weekends, the subs were allocated matches - if they wanted - in return for generous match fees. We worked a four-day week so, as often as possible, I made sure that my days off fell on Tuesdays and Wednesdays so I would be available for further midweek reporting duties if asked. The atmosphere was full of bonhomie in those days, but it was polluted by the arrival of Blackmore who swiftly grovelled his way up the desk to a position of authority. It became his task to ask the subs if they wanted games on Saturdays, but he never asked me and if I told him I was available, he prevaricated. On one occasion, he made sure that I was within hearing distance when he ordered a report from an agency. He is a loathsome individual. Whereas he steadfastly refused to give me games, he adopted a different policy with another sub, Peter Robinson, who he also disliked. Peter commuted from Bournemouth where he lived with his girlfriend, so he wasn't best pleased to be given games at the likes of Sheffield. He probably made a handsome profit on expenses but that came at the expense of a cosy weekend with his lady.

If Blackmore had an excuse for taking umbrage against the world, it was probably because he had a disabled daughter back home in Brighton which was a misfortune that indirectly cost Glenn Hoddle his job as England manager. This came six years after my dismissal. Knowing that Hoddle had some pretty outrageous views about the afterlife, Blackmore deliberately delegated Matt Dickenson, the paper's reporter to ring Hoddle for his views. Realistically, it should have been a football piece, but Dickenson got the quotes that Blackmore wanted although he buried them midway through his article. Blackmore promptly shifted the more salacious offerings into the first few paragraphs which made for a spicy headline with the result that Hoddle was cast aside within a few hours. Which was a nonsensical decision by the Football Association. Why should a good man lose his job just because he had some weird things to say about people paying for their sins in a previous life. The FA got what they deserved with their subsequent appointments of Sven-Goran Eriksson, Fabio Capello, Steve McClaren and, dare I say it, Roy Hodgson, none of whom achieved what Hoddle could have done had he been allowed to carry on with his good work.

For eight years after I had taken a £38,000 pay-off, I carried on working on a freelance basis as the paper's basketball reporter, hard as Blackmore tried to relieve me of my duties by asking other people to do the job. Out of loyalty to me, Russell Kempson, one of the football reporters - who had a connection with basketball - rejected the idea. Finally, Blackmore gave up. He could abide no more of my by-lines in the paper. He found no one else to do the job, but, out of the blue and after penning the column for 20 years, I got a two-paragraph letter from him saying the paper could no longer "afford me" which was risible. Speculation was rife that he would eventually become the paper's editor, but he managed to crawl no further than deputy editor after which he ended up at the BBC. I was delighted to read years later that he had been referred to in Private Eye as "James Harding's lapdog who has moved with his master to the BBC."

Chapter 14:
A Romanian rhapsody

It was around this time that Chris and I realised that there were other tournaments within our compass, not just World Cups and the Euros. In the spring of 1994, he joined Christine and I in Tunisia for the Africa Cup of Nations. Alas the chemistry between the two of them was not great which slightly marred for me the enjoyment of the event which was staged in the capital's two main stadiums and in the town of Sousse 60 miles to the south. My abiding memory of a game there was of the cattle on the hillside making their way down for feeding time. However, the raison d'etre was to see games in all three stadiums which was, of course, accomplished but before pulling out I was able to conduct an interview with Ian Porterfield, the manager of Zambia who had lost 18 players and staff in an air crash only the previous year. Despite that massive handicap, Zambia reached the final in Tunis only to be beaten 2-1 by Nigeria. For a man who had become something of a hero to me for his FA Cup final winner for Sunderland against the much-despised Leeds in 1973 - I was behind the goal where he scored - I had hoped that Porterfield would prove rather more engaging company than he proved to be.

1994 was also the year, of course, for the World Cup finals in America where sadly England were not among the entrants. Taylor had paid for our failure by getting the sack but there was no way I was going to repeat my mistake of 1978 when I still bitterly regretted my decision to stay away which was partly because of England's absence. The official opening game was in Chicago but sensing the possibility of freelance work (for The Independent) I booked a flight from Heathrow to Dallas, the venue for Spain v South Korea on the same opening day. It was an entertaining 2-2 draw in the Cotton Bowl Stadium.

The size of the continent made it difficult for us hoppers to complete all nine venues especially those hoppers like me who also had work to do. I was filing reports for both the Independent and Guardian but the schedule I had embarked upon was a demanding, even an insane one. On one occasion I booked a room in Boston with Ian, a Kiwi I had befriended, with the idea of seeing two games in three days at Foxboro, 30 miles away. On the middle day I had arranged to fly to and from Detroit for the Romania versus Switzerland game which was not in Detroit at all, which was officially listed as the venue, but in Pontiac which turned out to be some 70 miles distant. My flight's arrival had been delayed but I found a willing cabbie. As I was not on expenses, I persuaded him to agree to a $70 fare whatever the clock stated. But as the miles sped past, the sun boiled down and the clock sailed way beyond the $70 mark, I sensed what was to come.

The cabbie, a perspiring black guy with a towel draped round his neck to soak up the sweat, said: "come on man gimme me a bit more." So I handed him a $100 note as he finally dropped me off outside the stadium gates some minutes after kick-off.

Mad escapades like that are life-shorteners at the best of times. It is bad enough missing kick-off any day anywhere but when team line-ups have to be filed to a newspaper before kick-off, it is ten times worse. I was in a panic as I was doing the game for the Indy and I had to find the media office and obtain my pass for the game before negotiating the stairs to the press box. I missed about ten minutes but none of the goals in Switzerland's 4-1 win which was to the delight, of course, of Roy Hodgson, their manager. As I listened to his post-match press conference, little can I have guessed that one day he would become manager of the club I supported. In the panic-stricken circumstances my report was halfway decent and I took my place on the press coach taking us scribes back to Detroit where I slept on a sofa near reception at the airport hotel as I had already spent far more on this particular excursion than I had budgeted for. I arrived back in Boston in good time the next day and met up with Ian for the Bolivia v South Korea group game, a drab goalless draw.

By comparison my trips to Orlando for a two-games-in-two days fest involving Mexico and the Republic of Ireland and then Belgium and Holland, Washington for Norway v Mexico and Holland v Saudi Arabia and New York for Republic of Ireland v Italy were models of rest, relaxation and much needed stability. The games were ticking by and I was ticking off the venues. But I had been begged to take a week off by my ex-girlfriend Dean who had wanted to see something of America in company with yours truly. She arranged for us to meet in Chicago halfway between another two-games-in-two-days bonanza. I got her a ticket for the second game, Bolivia v Spain at Soldier Field, the windy city's historic stadium which, from the outside looked more like a coliseum. She had wanted to tell her friends she had seen a World Cup game but Dean was no great footie lover as I was to find out to my cost. Tennis was more her thing. We had met at the Guildford club where both our sons played.

Anyway, the idea was to fly to Denver, collect a car there and drive down through the Rockies, taking in the Grand Canyon enroute to Los

Angeles where I was due to be reunited with Christine. Somewhat reluctantly I had agreed to Dean's wish to give football a miss for those seven days, not going to games and not even watching them on television. Some hope. I tried, how I tried not to renege on that promise but for all my good intentions I failed dismally in spite of all the majestic scenery enveloping us. Every morning when we set off, I was busy calculating how I could watch this game or that game and so, glory be (but not for her), we would mysteriously arrive at some café or restaurant just as kick off was beckoning. Or, in the worst-case scenarios, a few minutes after the game had started. Woe betide any establishment that did not possess a television for its customers. We sat down to quite a few meals in sullen silences while she sulked as I took in the action on the screen above our heads. Never again would I agree to such a preposterous idea. A World Cup is a World Cup, not to be trifled with and games are there to be seen and not missed.

Dean and I said our goodbyes in LA before I headed for the hotel where I had arranged to meet Christine. She greeted me warmly, clad only in a white bathrobe, saying: "I have decided that I want to spend the rest of my life with you." Music to my ears but little did I know that 16 months later, it would be all over between us. Anyway, she was fun to be with for those last two weeks of the World Cup.

As I had formed a huge affection for the Romanian team and had even put a pre-tournament bet on them to win the Jules Rimet trophy, I was delighted to be assigned their round of 16 game against Argentina to cover the next day in Pasadena. Most of all I loved watching the hugely coiffured Miodrag Belodedici in the heart of the Romania defence. He was almost indolent the way he went about his business, breaking up attacks and stroking the ball this way and that to teammates.

Gheoghe Hagi was, of course, a delight to watch in midfield but I also savoured the efforts, alongside him, of his less celebrated compatriot Dorinel Munteanu. When Romania were on their game as undoubtedly they were then, there was no better sight in football apart from, possibly, Maradona in full flight. But Diego had been banned - again - for taking ephedrine so the South Americans were without their talisman and Romania's task eased a trifle. Three goals in the opening 18 minutes, two of them for Romania, set the tone for an enthralling game, won ultimately 3-2 by the Europeans. It was curious that they were now in the tournament's later stages whereas Switzerland who, I had seen comprehensively overcome them so recently, were out, beaten 3-0 by Spain at the same stage.

There was no time to be lost after the game for the next port of call was San Francisco or, to be more precise Stanford, 320 miles away, for the game, the following day, which happened to be Independence Day, between the hosts - who had made astonishing progress - and Brazil. Christine and I found a place to stay enroute but, after dropping her off at the hotel we had booked in San Jose, I still faced another mad dash to make kick-off. As I pulled up onto the grass parking lot, almost mowing down other latecomers, I was amused to hear one near casualty yell at me: "typical Colorado driver." Talk about leaving clues. I still had the car, complete with tell-tale license plates that I had taken from Denver ten days earlier. Somewhat fortunately I was not covering the game so was able to enjoy the match all the more. Brazil made light of playing the entire second half with ten men after the dismissal of Leonardo and won it with a goal from Bebeto.

With subsequent games taking place on the other side of the country or in almost equally distant venues that I had already visited, Christine and I headed for Reno where I had activated a timeshare exchange to book a room for six days in a hotel there. I had no idea what we were letting ourselves in for. It was common knowledge that Nevada was the gambling capital state of America, but I had assumed that the main dice rollers were all based in Las Vegas. Big mistake. Wherever we went in Reno, there were slot machines and more slot machines. Yanks, with wobbling bellies, were pulling the levers as if in a trance. And if there were not slot machines, there were roulette tables, all being exercised by obese tourists, morning, noon and night. For the likes of us who weren't gamblers - notwithstanding my bet of peanuts on Romania - it was a fairly dismal place in which to be holed up.

Thankfully we didn't feel murderous or even suicidal, but we did have the comfort, at least, of a sweltering sun and the car that took us on day trips to Lake Tahoe, an hour's drive away. The lake's contents were the icy, melted waters that had surged down from the snow-capped peaks that we could spot in the middle distance. So that made for some exhilarating, albeit fairly brief dips when we went swimming.

One evening on our drive back to Reno, we were stopped for speeding by the local cops who took down my details. For years afterwards, the Reno Police Department sent me demands for a $125 penalty. I wrote back several times saying that if they sent me the air fare, I would be delighted to come to their precious courthouse in Reno to defend myself. Without fail, their letters never differed. It was the stock one every time, never an individual reply to my request. They wanted their $125. But they never got it. Eventually the charge notices stopped coming but I did worry for a while afterwards that I might be stopped at passport control and barred from entering the States. Worse things might happen.

55

Such were the delights of Tahoe and the restaurants that provided us with gargantuan feasts on the road back to Reno that we were reluctant to leave. But Romania called or more specifically, their quarter-final in Stanford against Sweden which I was due to cover for both the Indy and the Guardian. So we left it until the last minute before embarking on the interstate back to California. Alas though, Romania didn't quite hit the high spots of their triumph against the Argies and so, after 90 minutes and extra time, the game was tied at 2-2. The tension was unbearable as my newly adopted, yellow-shirted favourites succumbed 5-4 in the shoot-out with Belodedici, of all people, wasting the vital kick. Somehow, I had to get over my disappointment to compose two reports.

I was more than ever grateful for Christine's presence back at the hotel that evening even though she found it hard to comprehend my dejection. She might have understood if I'd just seen Palace relegated or England lose a vital qualifier but Romania, why on earth Romania, she could have been forgiven for asking. Anyway, she was a rugby girl who put up only mild resistance - thank God - when we stopped off enroute back to Pasadena to see the later stages of the first semi-final between Bulgaria and Germany on TV in a bar. We took our seats just in time to see Yordan Letchkov's spectacular goal give the Bulgars a remarkable 2-1 win.

I was in full relaxation mode now. Staff men from all the papers were taking over reporting duties so I could go to the Brazil v Sweden semi-final that evening feeling much less tense. It would be stating the obvious to say that because of previous events, I very much wanted Brazil to win which they duly did with a lone goal from Romario. I suppose I had got over some of my distaste for the Scandanavians by the time of the third-place match in which they beat Bulgaria 4-0 with all the goals coming in the first half against opponents who included a sulking Hristo Stoichkov, the tournament's joint top scorer. But I felt more sorry for Trifon Ivanov, the Bulgarian central defender who like Belodedici, had earned my admiration because of his composure under pressure and also, partly and perversely because he had the look of a conniving gypsy. I learned later that he was, in fact, from gypsy stock. I was sad to hear that he died of a heart attack in 2016, aged just 50.

With scant interest in the proceedings, Christine had booked herself on a flight home that departed just as the final kicked off the next day. No wonder she got a good price.

Inevitably, in their wisdom and so that it would not clash with the tedium of the NFL on television, Fifa had decided that the final would start at midday and so it was hardly surprising that Brazil and Italy remained goalless after toiling through 120 minutes in the heat. It was however a fascinating duel which Brazil eventually won in the shoot-out after Roberto Baggio had skied his attempt to earn his place forever more in the Azzuris' 'rogues' gallery. For all that, he made the 1994 World Cup's All-Star team.

Chapter 15:
A Copa half full

As I had yet to resurrect my enthusiasm for cricket, 1995 had the look of what became known as a fallow year with no World Cups or Euros to sustain a sporting interest over the long summer months except, once again, for the Toulon Under-20 tournament. All that did was whet my appetite for more football at the Copa America in Uruguay. And so it was to Montevideo that I flew from Heathrow to meet up with Rocio, the Mexican senorita from 1986. We had kept in touch after her UK visa had expired and, as I now sensed that Christine and I were not in it for the long haul, I didn't see too much harm in sanctioning Rocio's wish to join me in Uruguay. In fact, the fortnight there proved to be so enjoyable that my mate Chris - who followed me to the banks of the River Plate with his wife Haya - and I both wondered out loud why on earth we had not ventured to South America previously for this tournament. Why, for instance, had we not bothered with the Copa in Ecuador in 1993, another fallow year?

There were only four venues and as Uruguay sits snugly between Brazil, Argentina and the ocean and is about the same size as Wales, distances were no insurmountable challenges to the Volkswagen that I rented. Rocio was worth her weight in pesos. There was a certain shyness about her, but she was as bold as brass when it came to asking directions to stadiums, hotels or press centres and it was evidently second nature for her to jump to the front of a queue if time was short and we were in a panic which was the case more often than not. I soon discovered the meaning of "disculpe" (sorry or excuse me) on the umpteenth occasion she hurtled past a line of people who had been waiting for an eternity.

I was covering the tournament for the Daily Telegraph and managed to get her day press passes on behalf of the paper for some games. For others I bought her a ticket as she was a real football nut who didn't want to miss a single kick especially when Mexico were involved. We took in the opening game between Uruguay and Venezuela in Montevideo's ancient Estadio Centenario, won 4-1 by the hosts who included the likes of the elegant Enzo Francescoli up front, and Gus Poyet in midfield. And then we spent the next ten days or so speeding between the capital and Maldonado, the resort, which was also staging games in Group A, and the two border towns of Rivera, the host city for Brazil's group, and Paysandú, next to Argentina whose team was, of course, based there.

Maldonado was on the coast, so we holed up there for a couple of days, much to Rocio's delight, as the intention was to coincide with Mexico's 3-1 win over the group A whipping boys Venezuela. Unfortunately, the contest was watched by a meagre crowd of 700 as it clashed on TV with a Uruguay game. But no matter. Mexico had won and Rocio - and I come to that - had both enjoyed the antics of Jorge Campos, their flamboyant goalkeeper. Unfortunately, however, Maldonado left me as cold as the weather at that time of year which was their winter. Montevideo, however, possessed a primitive charm notwithstanding its potholed pavements and roads which are probably still to this day awaiting repairs. I had to be doubly cautious every time I went for a run or my ankles would have been wrecked for the duration.

With only one venue for Groups B and C, games in Rivera and Paysandú came in double headers which has never been one of my favourite formats. Obsessive that I am, I prefer to concentrate on just one match rather than hang around for an hour or more, consuming junk food and sweet drinks while waiting for a second game to commence. Rivera was a particular problem with its plunging and soaring temperatures. After going unprepared to the first double header and feeling a distinct chill between games, I ventured out the next time wearing seven layers of clothing. By the time the second match had finished on a balmy evening, I was down to a single t-shirt.

We familiarised ourselves with the roads linking the venues and Rocio and I found a favourite stop-off in the town of Tacuarembó almost midway between Rivera and Paysandú. We discovered a rundown café which served coffee to our liking. A regular visitor to the café was a gnarled old boy who was a shoe shiner by trade. Rocio tried to persuade me one day to give him some custom even though I was wearing hush puppies. The rest of the characters in there looked like they had come straight out of the Clint Eastwood movie "The Outlaw Josey Wales." A weirder bunch you never did see. Further on along the road west, we invariably wondered which teams would occupy a pitch complete with goalposts in the long grass of a field alongside grazing cattle. "Maybe it's where the cows play the sheep," said I. Rocio, bless her, laughed at my feeble joke.

The bonus with Paysandú was that the USA team was based there which meant that, at long last, I could get first-hand quotes from someone whose native tongue was not Spanish. I conducted an interview with their goalkeeper Kasey Keller which stood me in good stead over the years, bearing in mind all his connections to English clubs. I also made quite a friend of Steve Sampson, the affable American coach, never more so than after his team had provided the shock of the tournament by humiliating Argentina, Gabriel Batistuta, Javier Zanetti et al, 3-0 to top the group. Diego Simeone, later to become such a foe to us Brits, was also in the vanquished team. But the best game by far, indeed one of the best I have ever seen was the earlier pulsating 2-2 draw between Argentina and Bolivia.

One day after I had filed a report to the Telegraph, my future career was determined. Brian Oliver, the paper's sports news editor, asked me if I would like to be their non-league man for the forthcoming season, covering what was then the Nationwide Conference.

"You mean that I've gone from reporting the Copa America to the Conference?" I asked him.

"Take it or leave it," he said.

"Ok, I'll take it," I replied which was a sensible answer bearing in mind the fact that his paper was to give me an average of two Premier League or Championship games a week to cover over the next 15 years in addition to my twice weekly non-league columns.

It was to Rocio's intense disappointment that the USA team went on to beat her beloved Mexico on penalties in the quarter final. She flew home to Guadalajara after that while I stayed on in Montevideo for the semi-finals in which Uruguay and Brazil prevailed. So it was that Brazil, containing such luminaries as Roberto Carlos, Leonardo and Dunga, their World Cup winning captain, took on Uruguay in the final. But such is the machismo nature of football in South America that no extra time was deemed necessary for knockout games. So, after the teams had finished level at 1-1 after an engrossing 90 minutes, Tulio missed Brazil's third spot kick with the consequence that Uruguay were Copa champions for the 14th time, beating the world champions in the process.

Chapter 16:
Familiar territory

There was a small minority among us who did not jump for joy when England were awarded the 1996 European championships. We knew all the stadiums, after all, and would have preferred a tournament in foreign climes for the purpose of exploring new grounds. But I, for one, grew into Euro 96. The longer it lasted, the more I enjoyed it apart from the nadir of Gareth Southgate's penalty miss against Germany. But more about that later.

The tournament which had opened with England's less than satisfactory 1-1 draw with Switzerland at Wembley, took off with one entertaining game after another, never more so than when England took on the auld enemy at Wembley. Paul Gascoigne, fresh from his dentist's chair escapade in Hong Kong, scored the goal of the Euros soon after Gary McAllister's penalty had been saved by Dave Seaman. England's 2-0 win put Terry Venables' side in the driving seat for a place in the knockout stages.

In between England's games, I was racing around the country taking in other matches although they all lacked the novelty value of being played on unfamiliar venues. I went to Leeds, Newcastle, Liverpool and Old Trafford, all the time clapping myself on the back that I had managed to meet Andrea, a lovely lass from Ulverston, on the edge of the Lake District. Not only was her home astutely situated given my meanderings around the country, but she had a winsome figure, lovely soft skin, a cheery face and wicked sense of humour, which were all the qualities I needed to help me over the heartbreak of being dumped by Christine some seven months earlier. The only blight on Andrea's character was her chain smoking. I do hope that she hasn't smoked herself to death by now.

At St James' Park I was able to see two of my favourites from a bygone era, Belodedici and Ivanov line up against each other. But unfortunately, neither of their teams, Romania or Bulgaria made any progress. Indeed, Romania went out without a point to their name in their group games, scoring only a single goal. When Andrea and I were not playing at being tourists around Hadrian's Wall, I used her home as a base for my northern sojourns. I also got to sample the ales in some of Ulverston's 36 pubs, not bad for a town with a population of just 15,000.

A couple of mates with slightly different schedules to my own, joined me at various junctures and still vivid is the memory of our dash down the M6 from the Germany v Croatia quarter-final at Old Trafford to that evening's quarter-final at Villa Park featuring the Czech Republic against Portugal which was won by Karel Poborsky's remarkable goal for the Czechs. We had made such good progress in my trusty Cavalier that we reckoned we were ahead of every other maniac wanting to manage this crazy double-header. Not quite so, we discovered on being overtaken by a limousine carrying the ubiquitous Serb, Bora Milutinovic, who was in the midst of making his name for managing five different nations at World Cups. He and his entourage must have recognised us from the first game as they gave us thumbs up signals and cheery waves in the process of cutting me up on the slip road leading to Villa Park. The Czechs' victory in that game took them to a semi-final against France.

England had meanwhile progressed but if ever a game stank, it was the hosts' final group game against Holland. Venables, and his pair of two-goal scorers Alan Shearer and Teddy Sheringham shared the main plaudits for our 4-1 win which was an outcome that, coincidentally or not, had assured both nations of a place in the last eight. But for all England's brilliance that night, there was not a proper tackle in the whole 90 minutes. When did you ever see that in such a crucial game? England had rattled in four goals without reply before news came through that Scotland had gone ahead against the Swiss at Villa Park which was then - surprise, surprise - that Patrick Kluivert promptly scored to edge Holland through too on goal difference at Scotland's expense.

The tradition after games beneath the then twin towers has always been for a group of us to meet up for a curry at the Wembley Tandoori. The rest of the lads were in celebratory mood but Chris who had been in a different part of the stadium to my seat in the press overflow area, was like me, deeply suspicious. We both thought it had been a fix. We will undoubtedly never find out if we were mistaken or not. But whatever the case, England were heading towards a tumultuous quarter-final against Spain and, for once, success in the penalty shoot-out which was not, alas, to be repeated in the semi-final against the Germans after 90 minutes and extra time had once again failed to separate the teams who had finished level at 1-1.

As a Palace fan who had swopped the odd post-match comment with Gareth Southgate in the players' bar at Selhurst Park during his time with the Eagles in the 90s, I probably felt the pain of his penalty miss as much as anyone. I had, after all, been the first journalist ever to interview him which was a moment the England manager acknowledged when I bumped into him at the FWA dinner a few years ago.

As he circulated after the meal, I plucked up the courage to ask him: "Gareth, this is a claim to fame moment. Who was the first journalist ever to interview you?"

I was overjoyed when he replied: "It could well have been you, Nick."

Not only did he remember the instant when I had buttonholed him, aged 17, just before he climbed onto the Palace team bus after making his club debut at Anfield, but he remembered my name after all these years. I had been working on a freelance basis, covering Palace's midweek away games for the Croydon Advertiser who could not staff them.

It was in that same players bar at Selhurst that I had also briefly met his mother Barbara who came out with her famous quote after Southgate had side-footed England's sixth penalty all too tamely at Andreas Kopke, the German goalkeeper. "Why didn't he just hit it?" she asked which was a question on all our lips for years to come. The Czechs duly beat France in yet another penalty shoot-out to qualify to play Germany in the final which, good game that it was, still ranked as a huge anti-climax for every watching Englishman. Oliver Bierhoff's golden goal won it for the Germans.

Chapter 17:
Monkeying about

The huge temptation in 1997 was to follow Chris to Bolivia for the next edition of the Copa America but then I discovered that the FA would be sending an England team to compete in the World Under-20 championship in Malaysia which happened to clash with the Copa. Thinking positively, I knew that it would also promise pastures new (from a ground's point of view) and a better chance of making money than the Copa so long as I could find papers which were not sending staff men.

England were going to compete in Group F whose games would take place in Johor Bahru to the south of Malaysia. The most expedient route from London to JB (as everyone knew it), was not via Kuala Lumpur, the capital but through Singapore. So it was to Singapore that I flew from Heathrow, taking a cab over the Causeway, the bridge separating Singapore from the mainland's fourth largest city, I arrived there the day before the games began. With no girlfriend in tow, I could have done with decent company among my fellow scribes. I should have known better or even learned from my last experience at the Toulon Under-20 tournament where I had gone, not heeding or indeed believing a warning from my journo mate Peter Lansley who had previously covered the tournament in France as a freelance. He had endured a miserable time because of the paranoia among the staff writers there - led by the obnoxious agency man Ian Whittel - that he would scoop them with an exclusive story while they were in a bar boozing the night away. And so he was completely ostracised.

Very much the same happened to me in JB. The Telegraph's Chris Davis, Matt Dickenson of The Times, Rob Shephard of the Star and Steve Curry of the Express were all there and they all virtually blanked me. Maybe Shephard thought he had a justifiable axe to grind as I had accidentally caused him a nasty Achilles tendon injury in a Times v Star game in the Fleet Street League many years earlier, but I still thought the behaviour of all of them was pathetic in the extreme. I spent the evening of my 50th birthday alone in my hotel room on a preview that I could have left for the next day. The saving grace was my friendship with an English chap who worked in the hotel's kitchens and dining room. As a recent recruit he had yet to make friends there, so we teamed up on those of his nights off which didn't clash with games.

England won all three group games in JB's Tan Sri Hassan Yunus Stadium with Michael Owen scoring in all of them. I had only previously seen him once in action and that had been a few weeks earlier at Selhurst Park, scoring Liverpool's goal in a 2-1 defeat by Wimbledon. But now I was to marvel at Owen's burgeoning prowess once more. He was at 17, by far the youngest player in the England squad but he was completely at ease on the morning he sat down in the hotel foyer to answer questions from us hacks. I was covering the tournament for The Indy and Guardian once more, so it was nice to get a decent interview out of Owen besides, thereafter, a friendly nod on the occasions my visits to the hotel swimming pool coincided with the players' rest periods. Danny Murphy who scored a hat trick in the 5-0 win over the UAE, was also an amiable soul as was the England captain John Curtis and Matthew Upson, then still a Luton player.

I had made little contact, however, with Jamie Carragher but then on the morning after England's exit from the tournament in the round of 16, beaten 2-1 by Argentina (in which he had scored England's goal) Carra summoned me over as I packed up my gear to leave.

"Hey lad, what's in the bag?" he asked in his rich Scouse accent. Why on earth he would be interested in the contents of my plastic bag which amounted to a book, T-shirt and training shoes, I should have asked myself in that instant as he leapt to his feet to push me into the pool, bag and all. Much mirth followed from his team mates around the pool as I hauled myself out of the water, feeling like an idiot and trying to conceal my embarrassment. Over the intervening years I have often hoped to bump into Carra to ask him if he has pushed anyone else into a swimming pool lately. I wonder if he has remembered the incident or maybe he has pushed in so many unsuspecting poor sods - including perhaps Gary Neville - that, over the mists of time he has completely forgotten my unplanned dip.

While the England players headed home I took a short flight from Singapore to Kuching which is based on the western tip of Sarawak which is part of Malaysia which was why Kuching was named as a venue for these championships. It is a city hovering on the brink of the third world so that made the out-of-town, state-of-the-art 40,000-capacity stadium all the more of an eye opener. It was there that I saw England's victors, Argentina overcome Brazil 2-0 in a fabulous game in front of a near full house.

Argentina had, among their ranks, such prospects as Walter Samuel - who, for many subsequent years I considered the world's outstanding defender - Juan Ramos Riquelme and Pablo Aimar - so they were a joy to behold. With my bete noires among the English reporting contingent

65

now thankfully departed along with the team, I was in a much happier frame of mind, helped by my new friendship with Conor, an Irish journo who had been sent to cover the tournament by AP in Barcelona where he was based. He was excellent company and together, we explored Kuching's night spots.

Conor had been booked into another hotel by AP but spotting the Hilton, some 200 metres from what was to become our favourite watering hole, I took a chance and asked reception what a room might cost. I could hardly believe it when she gave me a price which was the equivalent of £39. For that I would be on the 11th floor for five nights with a magnificent view of the Sarawak River winding its way towards the South China Sea.

My room was also to become the scene for nocturnal visits by Nor (short for Eleanor), an engaging local girl I had met in the bar. She had four young kids, she told me, but her mother loved looking after them, so she was free to spend her daytimes frolicking in the pool with Conor and myself, and most nights entertaining me. On the one evening when she was giving her Mum the night off from care duties, I had a meal and drink with Conor who told me that he had arranged for a 6am alarm call in order to be present at feeding time for the local Orangutan population. As an inveterate animal lover, I was irresistibly tempted even though it meant rising at the kind of obscene hour that I detest. But the Orangutans made our visit to their jungle abode more than worthwhile. The orange-haired great apes were a glorious sight as they swooped down from the trees to grab the food that had been left for them to devour.

After that our guide escorted Conor and I around a local village before we made our way back to town. That evening we returned to the stadium to see the Argentinians again in their semi-final. This time they beat the Republic of Ireland 1-0.

Reluctantly Conor and I flew out of Kuching the next morning. My sadness stemmed mostly from having to say goodbye to the lovely Nor. We promised to stay in touch but when I received a letter from her a few weeks later, she was asking me to pay for flights to London not only for herself but for all her kids too. I wasn't overwhelmed by her suggestion so that relationship promptly bit the dust. It had been a beautiful holiday romance.

The destination for Conor and I was now Kuala Lumpur or, more specifically, the 80,000 capacity Shah Alam Stadium, 25 miles away, which was to stage the final of the competition. This time we were holed up in the same hotel which was on the periphary of the city's night life. On the second night following dinner, we took a short walk from our hotel and encountered a group of enticing strangers. They were less

66

enticing the closer we got as their Adam Apples stood out a mile. They were a group of lady boys. As I chatted to one of them, making it abundantly clear that I was not interested in what they might have to offer, I could not believe it when Conor suddenly disapperared. Somewhat sheepishly, he told me later, he had been desperate and had, therefore succumbed to a blowjob behind the bushes. The next night we saw Argentina win the latest battle of the River Plate with a 2-1 triumph over Uruguay to become world Under-20 champions.

Chapter 18:
In France without tickets

As I had failed in my attempt for accreditation to the 1998 World Cup and had come across precious few tickets to the games, I came up with the bright idea of doing a daily column for one of the papers detailing my search for billets. Who better to approach than my old buddy, Paul Newman who had gone from being chief sub-editor on The Times sports desk to Independent sports editor. It probably helped that he, too, was a massive Palace fan who had, in fact, given me permission one Boxing Day years earlier to take a long lunch hour so that I could dash from Gray's Inn Road to Selhurst Park for Palace's game against Charlton on the proviso that I completed the extra hours on my return to the desk. That was the height of generosity from Paul seeing that he was probably filled with envy and would have liked nothing better than to go to the game himself. Anyway, Paul was a great one for wacky ideas, so I rang him one day a fortnight before the tournament saying: "Why don't you have someone in France giving you a daily update on how much it cost him to get into games?"

He replied: "And have you any idea Nick who that someone might be?" to which I answered, "well how about my good self?" And so the idea was borne and the Indy were to receive my daily 100 words or so under the title of "In France without a ticket."

My Belgian contact Maryan Mahieu (more about him later) had promised to sell me a handful of tickets for a small profit but apart from those I had nothing. As we hurtled round France in my Vauxhall Cavalier, I barely had time to write my pieces. We were on a game-a-day schedule, sometimes two games a day. Fortunately, I had a ticket for the opening game and so it was from the Stade de France after Brazil's 2-1 win over Scotland that we negotiated the Periphique and stopped off for the night, halfway to Bordeaux, the venue for the next day's highly entertaining 2-2 draw between Italy and Chile (I don't think I have ever seen a bad 2-2 draw). The mad idea after that was to sprint away on the final whistle for the drive to Toulouse for the evening game there involving Cameroon and Austria. There's a good 150 miles between the two French cities but we burned rubber.

Fans in cars tend to panic on big match days so I have always maintained that the ideal parking spaces are to be found nearer the stadium rather than further away. So, it was that we drove up to where the gendarmerie were blocking off traffic. We dumped the car on a pavement - which is the French custom - and legged it to the Stade de Toulouse. None of us had tickets and the game had begun but some touts were still hanging around. Chris and I paid 10 euros each and bolted into the stand from where we had a remarkably good view of the proceedings considering the pittance we had just paid. The other bonus was the scoreline, still 0-0 after ten minutes, so we hadn't missed a goal. It was all the more surprising therefore that Dave Hutchins, the car's other occupant chose not to join us. Dave, a West Brom fan was a stickler for keeping to his principals of seeing a whole game or no game. If he gained entry after kick-off, he couldn't "count it." So, we found him in a bar near the stadium after a 1-1 draw which was an action-packed thriller that vindicated our enterprise. Furthermore, the wonderful individual goal from the Cameroon full back Pierre Njanka-Beyaka that gave the Africans the lead proved to be one of the great goals of the tournament. More fool Dave for not being inside the stadium to see it. Unfortunately for Njanka-Beyaka, his goal was not decisive as Toni Polster bagged a late equaliser for Austria.

I had done some useful research before embarking for France, deciding that it would be far better to have a base somewhere at, for instance, un hote de maison (guest of the house or bed and breakfast) in preference to stopping at a host of different places on the road. Bearing in mind the tickets I already had, the games I wanted to see and the locations of the various venues, I decided that Toulouse or a village nearby would suit me perfectly. I had gone to Foyles book shop in Charing Cross Road and thumbed through the pages of a guide on 'perfect places to stay in France' or some such and alighted upon a page giving me the contact details of Monique and Frank who owned a place, complete with swimming pool in the picturesque village of Montastruc-la-Conseillere, some 12 miles out of town. Considering that it was well past the hour when she would normally receive guests, Monique was as good as gold when we finally found the way to their charming abode. She opened the door to us but insisted straightaway that we doff our shoes which brought a subsequent complaint from Dave - when we were out of hearing range - at her house rules. "I don't think much of having to take me shoes off," he said in his rich Brummie accent that led to Chris referring to him evermore as Jasper after the comedian Jasper Carrott. We had met Dave nine years earlier on an England trip to Albania just after they had opened their borders for the first time to foreigners. As our coach left Skodra following the England Under 21 team's 2-0 win and the locals - had for some unearthly reason - warmly applauded us, Dave had piped up famously from the back of our coach: "Just think if we were in Italy now, they'd be bricking us."

After the first of many tasty breakfasts delivered by Monique, the three of us headed for Montpellier and the early afternoon game between Paraguay and Bulgaria, now captained by Trifon Ivanov, the canny gypsy at the heart of their defence. But from my position behind the goal, I was more taken by the sight of the opposing skipper, Paraguay's giant goalkeeper, Jose Luis Chilavert for his ability to make difficult saves look absurdly simple and his booming goal kicks. Once he headed upfield to send a free kick crashing against the Bulgarian bar. I was not surprised to learn later that he had been an infrequent goalscorer for the South Americans. After that goalless draw we were soon back in the car with the Velodrome in Marseilles our destiny that same evening. None of us had tickets and we feared the worst as the occasion was France's opening game in the Mundiale but astonishingly the touts had fistfuls of tickets and we all purchased one for around 20 euros each. France beat South Africa 3-0 without too many hiccups. We found a place on the road for the night as a return trip to Toulouse would have meant a huge detour since Lyon's Stade Gerland was our next port of call. Mexico were playing South Korea the next day. I was surprised and delighted to be able to sit down with Paul Newman for lunch as we had entered a local Michelin Guide restaurant to find him dining alone. So, we joined him before beginning the hunt for tickets for the match which Mexico won 3-1. I felt pleased for Rocio who would doubtless have been watching on television at her parents' home in Guadalajara.

Along with my "In France without a ticket," column which was going well, I had some extra unexpected work at this World Cup which had come through my Japanese contact Yoko Kamada. She had been asked to delegate a couple of foreign reporters to the task of doing pieces on Japan's games for a magazine back home. The idea had been conceived long after the deadline for accreditation, so Kevin and I were asked to buy tickets for the games and put them on expenses. The articles came under the bizarre headings of Japan from an English viewpoint and Japan from a Scottish viewpoint since Kevin - who wasn't even a journalist - was a Glaswegian who happened to have studied Japanese. We both had our photos taken and the articles which were sent to us after the tournament, appeared under the photos and a torrent of Japanese which, of course, I never managed to decipher. The ease of obtaining tickets for the French game two nights earlier had filled me with complacency as I set out on the road to Nantes where I had agreed to meet up with Kevin. Big mistake. Japan's opponents were Argentina, it was a Sunday and there was not a spare ticket to be had for love or affordable prices. There were some going for silly money, but Kevin reasoned that the Japanese mag would baulk at shelling out so much on our expenses, so we headed to a bar with a television to watch and report on an intriguing game that Argentina won 1-0 with a goal from Gabriel Batistuta. That was the first of a few frustrating experiences for me in France.

What with having to file my piece which meant for a translation by Kevin, and the long drive back to Montastruc, it was well into the early hours when I pitched up at Monique's with the result that I was up too late for the scheduled breakfast the next morning. But Monique gave me a snack and I set off for Marseilles once more, still believing that I had plenty of time to reach England's first game - against Tunisia - by kick off. I had reckoned without the busy traffic and worse still, the riots between the loathesome element among England supporters and the local north African immigrants that had brought the city to a near standstill. I was forced into a massive deviation with the result that I entered the ground during the half-time interval. I had missed Alan Shearer's opening goal, but Paul Scholes did the decent thing on a warm afternoon by leaving England's second goal in a 2-0 win until the 89th minute. Graham Smith, an erstwhile colleague from the Times, accompanied me, as arranged, on the drive back to Montastruc where Jackie, my new squeeze, was awaiting me along with her voluptuous mate Claire. They barely had time to recover from their flight to Toulouse before electing to sit together in the back of the car the next day for the autoroute ride back to Bordeaux where I, along with hundreds of gents in kilts, was once again locked out of a game which was Scotland's 1-1 draw with Norway. That meant we had endured a 300-mile round trip for nothing. I didn't want to make too much of a habit of this.

Getting into Italy's 3-0 win over Cameroon in Montpellier the next day gave me some sort of comfort as did the wonderful birthday cake the following day created by Monique thanks to Jackie's tip-off. Luckily the schedule was not too demanding and I could relax over my birthday feast as nearby Toulouse was the venue that evening for South Africa v Denmark, a 1-1 draw.

And so the World Cup continued to unfold with me scurrying between Toulouse and Nantes and St Etienne and both stadiums in Paris for games, sometimes by train, returning when I could to join Jackie poolside at Monique's where Claire was a huge distraction. She liked nothing better than to torment Graham and I as she stood around topless while engaging us in meaningless conversations, knowing full well that we were ogling her magnificent breasts. We seldom looked her in the eye during those discussions. I don't think Jackie was too impressed.

71

But soon I was off to Nantes again, which happened incidentally, to also be the venue for Japan's second game against Croatia. This time Kevin and I were able to purchase tickets at reasonable prices after which we composed our reports on the Asians' 1-0 defeat. Likewise, we got in cheaply at Lyon six days later when Japan went out of the tournament without a point but at least a goal to their name following a 2-1 defeat by Jamaica.

By then England's second group game against Romania in Toulouse had come and gone. We had lost 2-1 on what was a wretched night for me as I had procured a ticket for behind the goal where I stood among the moronic skinheads, the tattoos and the fat guts of the fans in replica white shirts, all singing "no surrender to the IRA." From that day until Roy Hodgson took over as manager and then, to a greater extent when "my mate" Southgate was appointed, I completely lost it as an England fan. I went to games at Wembley during the intervening years hardly caring whether we won or lost. And it was the same on overseas trips. Jingoistic I was not as I often thought that the sooner England went out, the more enjoyable the tournament would become since with England's exit, most of the hooligans would go home too, leaving the hosts to pick up the pieces, remove the broken glasses and repair the bars that had been trashed. These imbeciles should not be allowed out of the country, I reasoned, and should be ordered to spend their holidays in Blackpool, Scarborough or Clacton. They were such a national embarrassment but invariably they trotted out pathetic excuses of being goaded or provoked.

Three days after completing the full set of venues with a visit to Lens for Spain's 6-1 demolition of Bulgaria, I left Montastruc for Saint Etienne, the venue for England's round of 16 game against Argentina as Glenn Hoddle's team had recovered from the loss to Romania by beating Colombia 2-0 in Lens to qualify for the knockout stages. This time I allowed plenty of time, but time was not to be on my side once Paul Newman had rung me to say that a 1,000-word piece on the ticket situation that he had asked me to prepare for later in the week would now be required for the next day's paper. Such is the unpredictability of newspapers. So, cursing the mobile phone that Jackie had got me for my birthday, I broke my journey on encountering a restaurant where I could sit in the sun and concoct my piece which probably turned out to be the best one I have ever written. Some journalists insist that they write better under pressure and that was certainly true of my efforts on this occasion. The Indy had the best subs in the business and they found the perfect photograph to go with my article, of an attractive young woman wearing a hat with the words of "I need a ticket" emblazoned on the headband. Seeing that, I was reminded of the girl I had met before the England v

72

Romania game who had promised that she would fuck anyone who gave her a ticket. I never did discover if she found a taker.

I rang my piece through to the Indy copytakers and continued my journey through the lush green and hilly countryside of Auvergne to reach St Etienne in time to meet Chris who had bought a ticket for me thanks to his membership of the England supporters club. It was a dramatic game with both sides scoring penalties within ten minutes before Michael Owen set off on the run that culminated in that stupendous goal. England's lead lasted until the brink of half-time when Javier Zanetti equalised for the Argies. Chris and I were making our way up the steps to our "seats" after downing a beer at the interval when we were made aware of a fracas that ended with David Beckham kicking out at Diego Simeone and getting sent off, somewhat stupidly. But as one, who has always felt that the guy who retaliates to provocation is invariably unfairly punished - compared with the one who commits the initial foul or remark - I had a fair degree of sympathy for Beckham who was the subject of burnt effigies and all other kinds of nonsense for years afterwards.

Anyway, no further goals ensued over the course of the second half and extra time, so England were to suffer the ordeal of a penalty shoot-out yet again. You could identify with the pain of Paul Ince when he missed but I could not help feeling that there was a certain ambivalence about David Batty when his shot was saved. I could not get out of my mind a recent article I had read about the Leeds player in which he revealed the extent of his homesickness as he loved - and missed - his wife and kids so much. Maybe and just maybe he was influenced by all that and was the wrong man, therefore, to take a pen amidst such suspense. If Batty was a trifle indifferent to our 4-3 exit on penalties, then I certainly was too. After my night of misery in Toulouse, I was now more an interested bystander than a passionate England supporter. Gone was the pain of 1973 when Poland stopped us qualifying for the West German World Cup and gone, too, was the indignity of 1986 caused by Maradona's Hand of God goal.

I set off on the long road back to Montastruc, ruminating on my sudden change of emotions as I drove through the night towards Jackie's welcoming arms. She and Claire were due to leave the next day, so I had a couple of days of solo relaxation before venturing forth again, this time by train to Nantes for the quarter-final in which Brazil beat Denmark by the odd goal in five. Chris and I met up again for the first semi-final, Brazil v Holland, in Marseille but this game was an even hotter ticket than we had anticipated. The scrum of punters desperate to get in any which way was intense as we surveyed the throbbing market. Eventually, we were offered a pair of tickets for 250 euros, but I declined despite his entreaties, thinking it was too much. In the present day and age with values much changed, I would have snapped the guy's hand off. But not now. Chris went in, leaving me to file my "In France without a ticket" piece - very much without a ticket this time - from a bar as I watched the action, albeit with a few regrets that I was outside and not inside the Velodrome. But I reasoned that the money I had saved could be used to good effect for the morrow when France were taking on Croatia in the second semi-final which had always been the priority for me.

France were the hosts and the nation had latched on to their team's progress, putting cycling, boules and rugby to the backs of their minds, but it was still surprising the number of tickets that were available. I eventually forked out 80 euros, the most I had ever paid to get into a game. That would be the cost price of a cheap ticket for a big match these days. How times have changed. The abiding memory of the game at Saint-Denis was of Slaven Bilic's despicable histrionics when he tussled with Laurent Blanc to con the Spanish referee José Garcia-Aranda into sending off the Frenchman who was thus suspended from the final. Bilic, who had clearly not been touched, tumbled over as if hit by an uppercut from Tyson Fury. Whenever I saw Bilic in the years to come, as Croatia manager praising his players at Wembley or as West Ham, West Brom or Watford manager excusing yet another defeat, I wondered if he had a conscience. And if he had ever apologised to Blanc. I wondered too how Blanc managed to recover from the agony of missing the final to continue with a splendid playing career - as Manchester United discovered - and to become a half decent manager. However, my luscious French girlfriend Nicole had hit town, so I endeavoured to put all my anti Bilic thoughts onto the backburner.

Nicole who lived in Pimlico, was from Roanne a small town which lies between Lyon and Saint Etienne. She had a French mate who had loaned her the flat she had just purchased. But it was some way from being properly furnished or carpeted. All she had were the bare necessities including, thankfully a mattress which was good enough for Nicole and I to camp on during our short stay in the capital. I spent one afternoon at the Holland v Croatia third place game, feeling suitably grateful for Maryan's ticket when I saw hundreds of fans from both countries locked out. This tournament was unpredictable in the extreme on the ticket front. Davor Suker, who I much admired, struck the goal that gave the Balkans a 2-1 win.

Back at base, Nicole continued to show me some of the sights I had missed during my previous visits to Paris and we dined out in style as the hours to the final, France against Brazil counted down. However, I very

74

nearly missed it and all forthcoming matches too. On the morning of the big game, I accidentally touched a live electric cable while shaving and received the worst electric shock anyone has ever suffered without going into death spasms. Suitably grateful for my reprieve, I headed once more to the Stade de France where Chris and I utilised the two tickets that Maryan had sold me a while back.

We had both become overnight Francophiles so from our seats in the Gods, we rejoiced at the sight of Zinedine Zidane's two firm headers that put France in the ascendancy. It all looked ridiculously easy for the hosts, doubly so since Brazil's ace striker was looking anything but his usual self. I remarked on this to my friend. "There's something wrong with Ronaldo," I said. "He just doesn't look with it." We discovered later that Ronaldo, an insomniac, had indeed been in some sort of trance after taking the wrong pills to relieve his sleep deprivation. Brazil did nothing to help their cause by keeping him on the pitch. If ever a man should have been substituted, it was Ronaldo. Maybe he had a clause in his contract that he couldn't be taken off unless injured. All of which undoubtedly assisted France. They were well on the way to their triumph when Emmanuel Petit hammered in the third goal to embellish the victory margin. It was the first time I had cheered a goal by an Arsenal man. We had a post-match drink and I returned to Nicole who joined in the French celebrations by jumping onto the bonnets of cars. And yet she had never been to a football game. And probably hasn't since.

Chapter 19:
Copa capers

Like everything else in South America, the Copa America is of a haphazard nature. But you can't blame the sub-continent for the fact that it contains officially 13 nations which is an unwieldy number when it comes to staging an international event. Take away Guyana, Suriname and French Guiana who all compete under the banner of CONCACAF, that leaves ten nations which is still an awkward figure for a tournament.

I have always maintained that Conmebol and Concacaf ought to get together and merge and have one federation of 30 odd countries. When it comes to a competition such as the Copa, they could then keep South America's surviving ten nations, add Mexico and the USA for good measure and then have a qualifying competition among Concacaf's lesser knowns to decide four other nations. That would bring the total up to 16 which is a perfect number, as we all know, for a major tournament. It's probably one good reason why I am not a football legislator. But then, when did any football authority ever make the right decision and display a single iota of common sense? Look at FIFA and UEFA for instance.

However, Conmebol in their wisdom, tend to invite Mexico and the USA or one or the other and go ahead with 12 countries divided into three groups of four who are then whittled down to a manageable eight in the group stages. However, on the occasions when either or both of Mexico and the USA are unavailable, Conmebol make the numbers up to a round dozen by bizarrely inviting the likes of Japan. It was going to be even more risible in 2020 with both Japan and Qatar lining up among the participants in Colombia until Coronavirus intervened. Is it any surprise then that the Copa sometimes has a Mickey Mouse look about it which is why my good friend and legendary groundhopper, David Nuttall refuses to countenance it and stays away? He has many principals does David.

I have never minded too much on the years when Mexico and the USA both compete. They are, after all, part of the Americas but is it any wonder that I have reservations whenever Japan take part despite the fact that I have long since had a soft spot for Japan's football team. How would it look for example if the boys from the land of the rising sun ever tore up the form book and won the bloody thing? Japan's name would be inscribed on the trophy and they would be in the record books for ever more as Copa America Campeones and little boys the world over, who had just started geography lessons, would be asking, "Dad, I thought

Japan was in Asia but it says here they won the Copa America in 2037?" Fathers would scratch their heads and say, "Son, I'm sorry but I just don't know how that happened. It must be a mistake."

I had to put aside that particular can of worms in 1999 when Japan was invited to the Copa in Paraguay simply because it would help their promotion of the World Cup as co-hosts with South Korea in three years' time. Such was my wish to continue to explore South America and to see some football in the summer months that I was therefore bound for Asuncion via a stop-over in Sao Paulo. Extra motivation was provided by the fact that Rocio could join me for part of the tournament. Mexico would have one extra fan. Before she arrived Chris and I had the mother of all rows over the trivial matter of petrol money. If he, as a non-driver, was going to join us in a hired car, I reasoned that he should pay half the gas bill rather than a third as Rocio was, if you like, simply my appendage. If she had been any other girlfriend then I might have seen his point, but she was worth her weight in gold as a Spanish speaker who would put us on the right roads and lead us to hotels, press centres and stadiums with the minimum of fuss. Why should I have to pay extra for her in such circumstances when Chris, like me, would benefit from her presence? Good friend that he was, there was still a nasty, venal streak to Chris which I couldn't abide. Brian Clarke, a mutual friend - another relic from Albania - who was sharing a cheap hotel room with Chris, was an unwitting and embarrassed witness as Chris and I argued the toss for half an hour or more. Brian, good for him, refused to take sides. It was worse than a lover's tiff. Eventually we came to an unsatisfactory agreement that Chris should pay between a third and a half which took some calculating, believe me.

I was covering the games for the Telegraph. Paraguay who included the much vaunted 17-year-old striker Roque Santa Cruz, opened the Copa with an unimpressive goalless draw against Bolivia in their Estadio Defensores del Chaco Stadium in the heart of the capital. From the open-air press box on the stadium's steep slopes, I couldn't quite fathom all the fuss being made over Santa Cruz who was soon to join Bayern Munich.

Asuncion had its benefits, one being the Paraguay River which divided the city. With my love of rivers, Rocio and I boarded a small craft over its murky waters one day, crossing to the other side for a coffee before returning. On another occasion on a warm-up pitch, a group of us fired penalties at Nery Pumpido who had been Argentina's goalkeeper in the 1986 World Cup final. Now taking time off from his job as a television pundit, he saved my weak effort easily enough, but I was impressed by the aplomb with which Andrew, a fellow journo and a Scot - based in Brazil - and a big fan of Hibernian (or the Hibbees as he knew them) sent

77

his kick past our newly acquired celebrity pal. I bumped into Andrew again in Venezuela in 2007 when, of course, he reminded me of his successful penalty.

The Defensores Stadium provided centre stage for games in Group A but there was also a need to tick off the city's other stadium, the Estadio General Pablo Rojas, another Copa venue. In between times we were invariably on the road, always in an easterly direction as Asuncion sits on Paraguay's western frontier. Getting to Luque, another venue was no sweat as it was virtually a suburb of Asuncion, just eight miles away. It was there that we saw a remarkable game in which Martin Palermo, the Argentinian striker and all-time leading scorer for Boca Juniors, missed three penalties in his team's 3-0 defeat by Colombia. He hit the bar with the first one and blasted his second effort high over. Why Marcelo Bielsa, the Argentina manager, should then have sanctioned Palermo to go anywhere near the 12-metre mark for the third one is beyond anyone's comprehension. But take it Palermo did, only for Miguel Calero, the Colombian goalkeeper to make a smart save. With Colombia scoring from the first of the two spot kicks they were awarded, it was a game of five penalties, only one of which was successful.

Distances thereafter were vast. More often than not, we were heading back and forth to Cuidad del Este where Brazil had opened proceedings with a 7-0 thumping of poor Venezuela which we had viewed on television. I had always surmised that local authorities would get their cities cleaned up and looking spic for major events which attracted an influx of foreign visitors, all needing to be impressed. But judging from the vast swathes of road deviations and repairs on the approaches to Cuidad, their bigwigs couldn't have cared less. It was pothole city. But it possessed a football ground, the Estadio Antonio Oddone Sarubbi and it was there, much to Rocio's disgust, that we saw Mexico lose 2-1 to Brazil.

Fanatic that I am, I was loathe to do the 400-mile round trip to Asuncion every other day, so we spent one rest day on the short trip into Brazil to view the mighty Iguazu waterfalls and to make friends with coati, the inquisitive creatures and members of the raccoon family, who adorn the slippery pathways. I have been informed that the view of the falls from the Argentinian side is superior but for me, nothing could beat the sights that befell us. On returning to Cuidad and on our post dinner wander around town, I spotted floodlights all lit up a little distance away. Could this be another stadium, we wondered, accommodating perhaps a re-arranged Paraguayan second division game that night. With mounting excitement, we kept the floodlights within our view, increased our pace, turned a corner, and found ...a lorry park. Our hopes of a bonus game were inexorably dashed. And I was forever reminded of my mistake.

Compensation came in the form of the one Paraguayan stadium we had yet to visit, Monumental Rio Parapiti, up north in the town of Pedro Juan Caballero. It was there in an ordinary ground that was anything but monumental, that we witnessed a none too captivating double header featuring a 1-1 draw between Bolivia and Japan and a 1-0 win for Paraguay over Peru. While we killed time in the press room between games - expressing gratitude for the fact that Japan could not now rubbish the Copa by winning it - we were befriended by a young fair-haired, English-speaking giant of around 6ft 5ins. He turned out to be Martin Scott, an Aldershot fan who had taken time off from his work at an orphanage in Colombia. He had been on buses for four days on the arduous trek from Barranquilla. We all holed up for the night in Pedro - as we named it - with Martin keen to squeeze into the back of our Chevrolet between Chris and Brian the next day. We were making rapid progress on the 280-mile ride back to Asuncion when I spotted ahead two young untethered calves crossing the road, one of them with a rope around its neck. I hit the brakes hard and reduced speed sharply but not quite sharply enough to avoid giving one of the poor beasts a glancing blow, sending it limping into a field. Over the years and with Martin very much one of the clan by now, the story has become the stuff of folklore with him regaling anyone who cared to listen with the tale of how I had collided with a cow. And then as he told and retold the story, the cow became, in turn, a bull, a bison, a buffalo and finally a yak.

The knockout stages of the Copa were now upon us but it was with a certain amount of sympathy that we watched the hosts go out in the quarter-finals, beaten 5-3 in the penalty shootout by Uruguay who subsequently overcame Chile by exactly the same scoreline to reach the final even though they had only come third in their group. Brazil repeated their victory over Mexico in the group stages to beat them again, this time by 2-0 to reach the final in which they were overwhelmingly the better side. Uruguay were beaten 3-0, conceding two goals to Rivaldo and one to a much rehabilitated Ronaldo, now happily recovered from his ordeal in Paris. Brazil thus avenged their defeat in the 1995 final in Montevideo.

Chapter 20:
Who needs boots?

The Africa Cup of Nations was upon us again in the year 2000 although not at the originally selected venue of Zimbabwe who for various reasons could not or were not allowed to stage the event. It was typical of the chaos surrounding the tournament as was the decision to award the event to Ghana and Nigeria who do not even share the same frontier. They are separated by Togo and Benin. I was with Chris and Brian Oliver, the Telegraph sports news editor who was obsessed with African football.

With all due respect to Nigeria, it didn't seem the safest place to risk a fleeting visit, so we decided to just do games in Accra and Kumasi on our own brief stay in Ghana. We regretted our paranoia on hearing that our intrepid German friend Dirk Schultz and a few mates of his had gone to games in Nigeria and returned in one piece although they had seen little of Lagos or Kano, the two venues, as they had holed up in their hotels and taken cabs straight to the stadiums and back again. On arriving in Accra for the opening game between the co-hosts and Cameroon, we discovered that chaos was far too polite a term to describe the scenes in and outside the stadium. The press centre was for instance a seething mass of humanity, all wanting press passes or the souvenir bags or both. We eventually settled down to watch an engrossing 1-1 draw between the two nations who eventually finished top of the group which took some separating as Ivory Coast and Togo also finished on four points. Cameroon progressed to become champions, beating Nigeria 4-3 on penalties after the final in Lagos had finished 2-2 after extra time.

On our drive to Kumasi the day after the opener, we stopped off to marvel at a game on a wasteland of dried mud. Most of the players wore no footwear but the level of skill was extraordinary. If they could control a ball on those rutted surfaces with rocks and tree roots protruding, it was little wonder that so many players from the dark continent were bound for the pristine grass pitches of Europe where they could make their fortunes.

We saw two group games in two days in Kumasi, South Africa's 3-1 win over Gabon and a goalless draw featuring DR Congo and Algeria but the highlight of our visit was an introduction to Dave Booth, the former Barnsley and Grimsby defender who had coached Obuasi Ashanti Gold to the Ghanaian title some years earlier. He took us on a tour of their stadium and regaled us with fascinating tales of his life. He was en route to becoming one of football's nomads with subsequent spells coaching in Laos, Myanmar, Cambodia, and India. I was delighted to bump into him again in Thailand some months later during his spell as Myanmar's manager. Our tiny group returned to Accra where I did my utmost to recover from the mother of all stomach upsets before the flight home.

Chapter 21:
A bridge too near

Like Africa with its first-ever Cup of Nations co-hosts, the same scenario was about to unwind in the European Championships that same year with Belgium and Holland sharing the duties of staging the tournament. I was all too familiar with Belgium so didn't entertain any great anticipation for the event.

My first serious and bizarre introduction to football there had come six years earlier. I had been idly thumbing through the pages of World Soccer one day when I realised that they didn't seem to have a Belgian correspondent, a serious omission, so I thought, in this esteemed mag's coverage. So, I contacted the editor Keir Radnedge - who I knew from the circuit - and suggested that I might fill that gap. "Do me a piece on the state of Belgian football," he said which would be by way of a trial. So, I drove to Belgium to see a couple of games and chalk off a couple of grounds during a hectic midweek programme just before Christmas 1994. Alas the Tuesday night game in Liege was postponed because of a waterlogged pitch which left me to write my article, based on my thoughts of a single game which happened to be Cercle Bruges against Lierse the next evening. Helped by two goals from one of my favourite Romanians, Dorinel Munteanu, the hosts won 5-0.

I must have submitted a decent fudge piece for Keir was soon telling me that I had the job which would come in handy as it could theoretically supplement my earnings as a freelance. Not that one could get rich by writing for World Soccer who didn't pay expenses, not to me at least although I took in most of the Champions League home ties played by Anderlecht and even away games at the likes of Lyon and Valencia. Likewise, I saw Club Bruges a few times. It was a labour of love and I ended up losing much more money on travel than I earned.

As I had therefore acquainted myself with most of the grounds in the top league and indeed most of those in Holland too, I did not approach the Euros in the same state of excitement with which I had looked forward to Ghana. Even the journey there left me cold for I had already crossed the channel scores of times to Calais before the two-hour drive to Flanders or beyond. But, at least, I had the company this time of Rocio who had flown over to join me for the tournament even though Mexico would not, of course, be among the competing nations.

Our first stop was the King Baudouin Stadium, now newly renamed and renovated so that it was unrecognisable from the horrors of Heysel 15 years earlier. Belgium got the competition off to a good start with a 2-1 win over Sweden after which we based ourselves in a charming bed and breakfast run by an attractive woman living on a houseboat on the Albert Canal near the town of Geel, 60 miles away and conveniently close to the Dutch border. I had discovered this waterside gem on a previous trip to Geel which had neatly coincided with Verbroedering Geel's promotion to the Jupiler Pro League earlier that year. Our room was in the house across the road from the houseboat to which we descended each morning for some delicious breakfasts on our landlady's mahogany tables. Traffic on the road alongside the canal was scarce so it was an appropriate route for my daily runs. Life looked up.

With the help of Maryan Mahieu, my Belgian friend, and World Soccer, I was accredited and by hook or by crook - usually the latter - I got Rocio into most games, including one in Charleroi, a dazzling 3-3 draw between Slovenia and Yugoslavia in a Group C that was certainly providing the tournament's highlights with Spain's 4-3 win over the Slavs being the group's finale. We saw England squander a two-goal lead to Portugal in their opening game in Eindhoven, eventually losing 3-2. Not a great start and worse still, it meant that we had to get some kind of result against Germany in the next game to retain hopes of further progress. England, under Kevin Keegan now, were of course accompanied by the usual fascist rabble that - with considerable help from Germany's Nazi sympathisers - left Charleroi in tatters before the game.

The town's Stade du Pays de Charleroi had been the subject of some intensive speculation by our red tops in the weeks before the game because of its low capacity - only 29,000 - and hazardous gradients, a combination which some said could lead to fatal consequences which was utter nonsense. The only risk of fatalities would be in the streets and bars before and after the game. It was though a probably less than ideal venue for such a big game which so many people wanted to see. Thankfully Germany were, like us, going through a transitional phase and had no reply to Alan Shearer's headed goal for England whose hopes of qualification were dashed by Ionel Ganea's late penalty for Romania in their last group game. So, once again we had lost 3-2 to Romania.

We were criss crossing the low countries on a game-a-day schedule which was not too tricky given that the distances for once were within reason. Besides Charleroi, Arnhem's GeireDome stadium was the only one new to me, but it was there we saw Italy beat Turkey, helped by a goal from Antonio Conte. Rocio had to fly home to Houston where she was

83

now a teacher as I headed for games in Holland and a new base I had booked in the picturesque village of Broek in Waterland, just outside Amsterdam. It was not easy to find so I stopped to ask an affable Dutchman for directions. He helped me and then elaborated: "You could say it is not so much a bridge too far where you have to go, but a bridge too near." When would we ever hear an Englishman cracking such a joke in a foreign language, I wondered as I drove off after thanking him profusely?

Yugoslavia had finished Group C with only four points, but they qualified for the knockout stages at the expense of Norway who had scored six fewer goals. The Slavs must have contemplated the idiosyncrasies of such mathematics as they succumbed to a 6-1 defeat to Holland in the quarter-final in front of a packed De Kuip Stadium in Rotterdam. Patrick Kluivert got a hat trick which led his team to the Amsterdam Arena for an epic semi-final with Italy who were up against it from the 33rd minute when their wing back Gianluca Zambrotta was sent off. Under Dino Zoff's astute management, Italy's riposte was a masterclass in defensive strategy in which Paolo Maldini, Fabio Cannavaro and Alessandro Nesta all excelled. Sometimes spectacular rear-guard actions must be admired as much as passages of wondrous attacking play. They can leave spectators just as spellbound. This was such an occasion although Frank de Boer obliged with one Dutch penalty that Francesco Toldo saved and Kluivert with another that hit the post. The Azzurris' ten men thus deserved to take the game to extra time and penalties which they won 3-1. I would have had an even bigger smirk on my face when de Boer missed Holland's first kick had I known what a hash he would later make of managing Palace.

With no third-place game to occupy us obsessives before the final, I used the next few days as an excuse to visit Texel, the largest and most populated of the West Frisian Islands. Two previous basketball-reporting trips with the Kingston club had taken me to Den Helder, the nearest port so I more or less knew how to get there. But it was in a restaurant in Texel one night after sinking a couple of glasses of wine that I had a close shave. I was so pleased with an article on the tournament that I had written for the Independent that I was reading it for the umpteenth time when the restaurant owner rushed in, shouting: "mister, mister be careful." Unbeknown to me, my copy of the Indy had caught alight from the candle on the table. We put the fire out before his place went up in flames.

My newly established affection for Italy after their victory over the co-hosts did not alas manifest itself in the satisfaction of seeing them win the tournament. As their final with France at De Kuip went into extra time thanks to Sylvain Wiltord's 93rd minute equaliser for France, I had momentarily forgotten about the tournament's new format even though I had seen France win their semi against Portugal with a golden penalty from Zidane. So I was for an instant confused by the extent of the euphoria among the French contingent when David Trezeguet scored in the 107th minute. His goal was, in fact, decisive as games in the knockout stages were now all being decided by golden goals. So, France were now not only world champions but European winners too.

Driving home through the night with Alicia, my Polish girlfriend who had joined me for the last couple of days, we heard on the radio the news that a little girl had disappeared in Sussex. It turned out to be Sarah Payne who was later found murdered by Roy Whiting. After the excitement of the tournament, I sobered up.

My relationship with Alicia was on borrowed time but she contacted me a couple of months later to say that she had won a competition in which the prize was a ten-day trip for two to Thailand. "Take a girlfriend," I told her, but she insisted that I should join her. We could select the dates which was a bonus seeing that I was already scouring the fixture lists to see what tasty titbits the football calendar might throw up. I couldn't believe my luck when I saw that Thailand would, in fact, be hosting the Tiger Cup in November so off we flew, heading first of all for Chiang Mai's 700th Anniversary Stadium where the Thai manager, Peter Withe gave me all the material I needed for a decent piece the day after his team's 4-1 win over Indonesia. The one-time Villa ace marksman was excellent value and I was pleased to see his team win their semi-final against Vietnam in Bangkok's cavernous Rajamangalo Stadium. By then Alicia and I had ridden elephants in the hills near Chiang Mai and visited the none too enticing city of Songkhla for more group games.

Near the end of our tour, we enjoyed a whistle-stop stay on the island of Phuket. which was where Fergie - that's the princess not Sir Alex - was once rumoured to have decamped with a lover, thereby prompting the wonderful headline in the Sun of "where the Phuket is Fergie." Alicia and I went one night to a lady boy show, sitting in the second row where I could not take my eyes off the one individual who I was convinced was all girl. Whatever its gender, it caught my eye and blew me a discreet kiss as it exited the stage at the end of one act. But not so discreet that Alicia didn't notice. She flung my hand off her lap and said: "I can't believe you are flirting with the cast." As we made our way out of the theatre, cast members were mixing with the audience in the foyer. "There's your girl," snarled Alicia, "why don't you go and chat her up."

Alicia had calmed down by the time we followed up our post show dinner by watching more lady boys performing around the tables of the town square. There was one, mincing away, handbag and all, who we

85

each thought was mesmerising. The guys on the next table clearly thought so too. One of them handed me a camera and said, "could you please take a photo of us with that one." Alicia was aghast, ordering me to refuse the request which had seemed innocent enough. As the dancer raised his/her skirt to reveal the most exquisite fanny, I lingered to make doubly sure I was focusing properly before pressing the correct button on the camera. I handed it back to its owner only to find that Alicia had stormed off into the night. I asked the guys where she had gone and they pointed to beyond the square. I rushed off but could not find her and so headed back to our hotel room. I heard her come in a couple of hours later but feigned sleep as we were making an early start the next morning. Apparently, a wealthy Arab had seen the incident and told her, when she returned to our table, after hearing her tale of woe that she was making a mountain out of a molehill. I tried to put the incident out of my mind on the flight home as I needed to write up the Peter Withe interview which the Telegraph used two days after Thailand had won the Tiger Cup with another 4-1 win over Indonesia in the final.

Chapter 22:
He just wasn't my type

The advantage of having the lovely Janette living with my parents was that one of the perks of her job as a stewardess with British Mediterranean Airways was the entitlement to occasional flights, free of charge for her friends. On one of my visits to Godstone early in 2001, she asked where I might like to go. I had a quick look at the fixtures for the next international break and plumped for Armenia as Wales were due in Yerevan for a World Cup qualifier. We arrived at the Hotel Yerevan just in time for dinner on the eve of the game after which we adjourned to the bar. Unlike many journalists with a reputation for all-night drinking sessions, I usually like my kip too much to indulge. But this was an exception. The company was so convivial that time simply swept by. Janette was there and so was Margaret, the plane's flirtatious pilot and James, her avuncular co-pilot. I was glad they were not flying me back the next day.

Trevor Haylett, the Daily Mail reporter joined our group and the bar did a roaring trade. Before we knew it, dawn was breaking and then it was 7am and guests were coming down for breakfast. Bleary-eyed, we stumbled into the dining room with them after which bed beckoned. As I awaited the lift, I was aware of the early risers among the Welsh players, Ryan Giggs among them, emerging from it to be greeted by female members of the plane's crew amid much giggling.

Fortunately, the game was a late kick-off so there was plenty of time to recover before the 2-2 draw in which John Hartson scored both goals for Wales. With the crew needing to sober up in time for the next evening's flight home, there was no post-match inebriation. But there was time for an excursion into the foothills of Mount Ararat the next day for lunch. We sampled a typical Armenian meal in a bistro on a slope close to where Noah's Ark allegedly came to rest.

With Palace heading for nothing but mid table obscurity in the old first division under Trevor Francis that April, I reckoned that I wouldn't miss too much by taking time off to see my son Ashley in Australia. But he is not the world's greatest sports fan - let alone a football fan - so I hit upon the crazy idea of seeing a game in transit. It turned out to be an even crazier escapade than I had envisaged.

After exploring the fixtures and flight routes, connections etc, I eventually plumped for a game at Miami Fusion after which I could head for Sydney via a stop-over in Los Angeles. I arrived at Miami's International Airport with plenty of time, I reasoned, to find the stadium and see them play Chicago Fire. But I hadn't done my homework properly. With David Beckham's grand scheme for turning Miami into a Major League Soccer venue still light years away, Miami hadn't really awakened to the idea of accommodating a socca club. That much I discovered on arrival upon asking for confirmation that the Fusion played at the city's downtown Orange Bowl stadium. No one had a clue, not even taxi drivers. Baseball, basketball and American Football were more their thing, man.

I began to get increasingly desperate until I calmed down and bought a copy of that day's Miami Herald. Thankfully, the sports pages had a preview of the fixture in which the writer made it abundantly clear that the game was not in Miami at all but 25 miles up the Florida coast in Fort Lauderdale's Lockhart Stadium, their home ground. I hailed a cabbie and asked him to take me to the nearest Amtrak station. When we got there, we discovered that the last train that would get me to the ground in time had just pulled out. There was nothing else for it but to tell the driver to carry on up Interstate 95. We reached the stadium a few minutes before kick-off and flashing my Times press card - this was nine years after I had left the Times mind you - I was given accreditation. With no hotel booked, my panic hadn't exactly eased until the helpful lady in the press room came to my aid saying that she would ask around while the game was on and see if anyone could suggest a place where I could rest my jetlagged self.

The guy she introduced me to after Miami's 2-1 win was a big red-necked American who promptly drove me to a lively bar. Over our first beer he said that he could put me up for the night. I thanked him and made some comment about the merits of the ladies nearest us which was obviously not something he wished to discuss. So, I broached the subject of the game we had just watched, saying that I thought that Miami's number 7 - who happened to be Ian Bishop of previous Carlisle, Bournemouth, Man City and West Ham fame - had looked the part in midfield. Larry was equally reluctant to engage in this hot topic of conversation.

Eventually he caught me completely off guard by announcing that the reason he went to games was that he got off by looking at the players' legs. Jesus, I thought, this guy's a raving queen and I'm going home with him. Over another beer he warmed to his theme and revealed his sexual orientation, as if I hadn't already guessed. Sensing my concern, he added: "don't worry buddy, you're not my type." Thank God for small mercies, I thought, but when we got back to his condominium, he still invited me to watch some porn with him to see if I'd be sufficiently aroused to change my mind. After ten cringe-making minutes of watching guys cavorting, I made my excuses and retired for the night. I propped up the door of the guest room with a chair. But it would have been a feeble barricade had he really fancied me.

There were further revelations over the breakfast I treated him to at a local diner the next morning. He was apparently a schoolteacher in upstate New York. I wondered what kind of security checks the authorities must have conducted on his background before giving him the job. Larry must have known what I was thinking as he instantly re-assured me that he would never make a move on one of his pupils, however desirable. I wanted to believe him.

And then I went for a swim and sunbathed next to the pool which was part of the complex while he entertained his latest boyfriend. When it was safe to return, I asked him the cheapest route back to the airport. We examined a few timetables before he interrupted: "Tell you what buddy, I'll give you a lift there as I'm going for a work-out and the Latinos in the Miami gyms are much better looking than the guys who use the gyms here." So, I got my lift and promised to stay in touch as I waved him goodbye. But our paths never did cross again although he seemed a nice enough chap. But luckily he wasn't my type either.

I returned from Australia to make plans for the Copa America which beckoned once more. But six weeks before flying off to Bogota I saw a vivid colour photograph in the Guardian that chilled me to the bone. It was of the sickening aftermath of a car bomb with bodies and metal strewn around the road of some Colombian city. I decided there and then not to go. 1-0 to the cartels chiefly responsible for the 37-year-old drugs war in Colombia that had claimed the lives of 40,000 civilians. I didn't feel any need to be number 40,001.

Luckily, I had not booked any flights and neither had Rocio who had planned to accompany me. There was, after all, a decent alternative. At least, I thought the NatWest Island Games in the Isle of Man was a decent alternative. They would occupy me for some of the time that I would have spent in South America. As it happens, the Copa was cancelled. But then in true South American fashion, it was back on again although Argentina had by now dropped out and most of their rivals had said they would be sending weakened teams. Such was their diffidence now, in fact, that Peru's coach Julio Cesar Uribe even promised to call up his 19-year-old son who was a reserve with a struggling club in Uruguay.

They were all very sound reasons for me not to go so I didn't change my mind.

Rocio changed her plans and flew to London. We took the train to Lime Street, met up with my mate Neil Morris - who worked for the foreign office - and his pal Dave Meeson, a social worker. We took the boat on the 3-hour ride from Liverpool to Douglas. The Isle of Man considered itself the spiritual home of the Games as they had staged the first event in 1985 and they were brilliant hosts which they had already emphasised in the brusque manner with which they had dealt with a problem that would not have looked out of place at the Copa. The draw for the men's tournament had been made with 12 teams neatly divided into four groups of three when both the Cayman Islands and Froya and Hitra, two tiny Norwegian islands (who wanted to compete as a single entry) asked if they could be included. Quite rightly their applications were rejected. Clearly the organisers were not to be messed with.

The Games have a tight format, beginning on a Monday and ending on the Friday night of the same week. I am not sure why they can't extend them to the Saturday, at least, but some of the islanders have travelled enormous distances and since all their competitors are amateurs, the majority have to be back at work on the following Monday. All of which places major demands on the participants especially the most successful footballers who must play at least four games in five days.

The tournament had got off to a lucrative start for me as I had taken the first afternoon off to watch the epic Wimbledon final in which Goran Ivanisevic beat Pat Rafter in five sets. My son James, who was in the process of becoming a tennis coach, was in the know and had, ten days earlier, told me to put money on the Croat for both of us when he was a rank outsider, backed at odds at 33-1. I did as I was told and was overjoyed therefore by the outcome. I had put £20 on with the result that James and I were both richer by £165.

Our quartet had booked into a charming bed and breakfast on the outskirts of Douglas. They had a television set in the lounge where I watched the tennis on Magic Monday. It was from the b and b that we sped between the nine football venues in our hired VW Polo. Four of the grounds were in Douglas and others were scattered around the small towns of Castletown, Port Erin, Ramsey, Braddon and Peel, the island's second largest community. The Bowl in Douglas and the Douglas Road stadium in Peel were both proper football venues with stands and terraces but the others were no more than roped-off pitches around which curious locals and a legion of groundhoppers would watch the action. There was little need of the accreditation I had acquired as entrance to all the games was free which was a blessing for me since Rocio was in tow and expecting to be paid for.

90

The Games also included a women's tournament for the first time which helped us to complete a full set of grounds, but it was the men's event that we concentrated on as the matches unfolded and the final approached. The semi-finals featuring the winners of the four groups were on the Thursday and I could not help but feel sorry for Ynys Mon (the Welsh translation for Anglesey) and Jersey as their semi-final went into extra time. What kind of state would the exhausted bodies of the winners be in for the final against Guernsey who were not taken to the extra half hour by the Isle of Wight in their semi-final? Ynys Mon duly prevailed but with the final the next day still goalless after 90 minutes, their reward was to have to grind out another period of extra time. No wonder they eventually lost the shoot-out for their players could barely have found the strength to stagger up to the penalty spot to take their kicks. When present day footballers complain at the demands made upon them, they should be relieved that they are not faced with a schedule like that.

Watching the final, I saw a legendary hopper who goes by the nickname of Hoddie (I never did discover his real name) lounging in the sun in front of us. And I was reminded of the story, possibly apocryphal, of when he had apparently borrowed an identity card from a Fulham youth team player so as to travel around the country cheaply on a child's ticket. Arriving at Crewe station one evening and being apprehended, he snatched the card from the inspector, chewed it up and swallowed it.

Chapter 23:
The magic carpet

The football was not great, only a meagre tally of six goals in the eight group games that I saw, but for all that, my visit to Mali in 2002 was one of the most satisfying footballing missions. Chris and I took an overnight flight from Paris, arriving in the bustling, ramshackle, albeit charming capital of Bamako in good time for the opening game featuring the elegant superstar George Weah who had the distinction of scoring the opening goal - for Liberia - in what was to be his last international tournament. Mali 's 87th minute equaliser from Seydou Keita was greeted rapturously by a capacity 50,000 crowd in the Stade du 26 Mars named after the date - in 1991 - of Martyrs' Day, a national commemoration of the uprising which ended the dictatorship of Moussa Traore. Keita was in the early stages of a career which earned him 102 caps and a move to Barcelona for whom he excelled.

Our rooms were less than basic but security at the plush hotel frequented by several of the teams was not tight so, during the hot days, we had the run of the grounds which were populated by giant tortoises ambling around under a hot sun. Bamako was also staging games in its Stade Modibo Keita which was where we saw Senegal's 1-0 win over Egypt the following day and the goalless draw between Zambia and Tunisia the day after. That came after rushing from the main stadium where we had seen Nigeria's 1-0 victory over Algeria.

Having witnessed the action in both Bamako arenas, Jozef, my Belgian mate, and I hired a driver to ferry us to dusty provincial towns while Chris and Brian stayed behind for a concert. I had got to know Jozef the previous year in San Marino of all places. He had ridden his motorbike down to the Mediterranean from Antwerp to see Belgium's 4-1 win in a Euro qualifier and was brandishing a Belgian flag when he emerged from his room at the same hotel where I was staying. He was married to a Kenyan lady and, therefore familiar with pottering around Africa which was a bonus for us. Our travels in Mali took us to Segou for a goalless game between South Africa and Ghana and Sikasso where there was a similar lack of thrills during the two days of our stay. Cameroon defeated the Ivory Coast 1-0 and there was yet another goalless draw between Congo and Togo.

The stadiums were charmless, all the same model, constructed unimaginatively by the Chinese Overseas Engineering Group specifically for the tournament. By now I was reunited with the others and Józef had gone his own way. We were bound for Mopti. Whenever our driver stopped off to ask for directions, young children suddenly appeared and surrounded our vehicle, rattling empty tin cans in the hunt for coins. It was a salutary reminder that Mali is one of the poorest nations on earth. We did our best to oblige the kids. It was impossible to reject their pleas of "pleeeeese meester."

Mali is flat, landlocked and on the southern edge of the Sahara Desert. It may not appeal to everyone, but I was so mesmerised by the endless panoramic views of the bushland that I was surprised at the lack of competition for my seat in the front of the minibus alongside the driver. He was forever drumming his fingers on the wheel to the intoxicating sounds of Oumou Sangare, the legendary Mali Grammy-winning singer. I hadn't heard 'the Songbird from Wassoulou' before but I was sufficiently entranced to make sure that I was among the audience at The Barbican the following year when she was on tour. We had been less than enthralled by the football in Mali, but this was a heady cocktail to compensate and raise our spirits. The scene was surreal when we stopped off for a picnic in the long grass under some trees that provided us with shelter from the equatorial heat. We espied a man in long robes striding past us on the tarmac. "He's probably on a promise 18 miles up the road," said Chris.

We eventually made it to Mopti in good time for a pre-match meal in an open-air restaurant overlooking the confluence of the Niger and Bani rivers. We watched spellbound as a huge boat arrived from Timbuktu with a cargo of sheep. It docked near us. I was impressed by the near biblical sight of the creatures being gently lifted off the top deck by the caring crew members. Much to the amusement of the others, I spent most of the duration of the meal trying to fend off a persistent salesman who was doing his utmost to persuade me to buy a carpet. By the time I had decided I wanted one, he had disappeared. He did me a favour as God knows how I would have lugged the thing back to the UK. The game was another turgid one, a 1-0 win for Nigeria over Liberia. who thus went out. With no energy left for the 750-mile road trip to Kayes, we left Mali the next day, one short of a full set of venues. Cameroon retained their trophy defeating Senegal 3-2 on penalties at the end of a final which had, inevitably, finished goalless.

Chapter 24:
Train takes the strain

Life as a freelance was not exactly making me a rich man. I was in slight financial difficulties and fearing that I would not be able to afford to go to the 2002 World Cup in Japan and South Korea until the day my accountant rang to say: "You do realise, don't you, that you've got this policy which is just about to mature with the result that you will be £38,000 better off." Wonderful, I thought. Not only might I be able to buy an enigmatic painting that I had spotted in a Sydney art gallery the previous year depicting a group of naked ladies watching a game of football - thereby encompassing my two great loves - but now I can go to the World Cup. I rang the gallery's assistant owner - whose card I had taken - and she remembered me from my visit of 12 months earlier when I had been with my then nine-year-old son Ashley. "You were the chap with a little red-haired boy?" she asked. We haggled over the price of the painting, which was to include packaging, shipping, insurance etc and finally agreed on £9,000. And then I sat down to think about how I might get to the World Cup.

As a lover of trains almost as much as football, one of my ambitions had always been to travel on the Trans-Siberian Railway - not the Trans-Siberian Express which is a misnomer - so I thought the time and circumstances were ripe for such a ride. I arranged a Russian visa from the occupants of a little office in Bayswater who also gave me guidance as to how to obtain a train ticket from Moscow to Vladivostok with overnight stays in Moscow and Irkutsk thrown in. Everything apparently had to be done through the Russian Intourist organisation, the official state travel agency. In other words, it was an invitation to an absolute rip-off. That much, I was soon to discover as added to the £120 cost of the visa was the £650, I would have to fork out for the one-way train ticket plus £200 extra for my one-night hotel stays. I thought it was all a bit steep, but it proved steeper still when I got talking to the natives on the train who had bought their tickets in Moscow for a handful of roubles. And I was soon to discover that my fellow foreigners had paid a fraction of what I had by purchasing their tickets from their own travel agencies.

Still, I would be wiser next time, I reckoned, if there was to be a next time. Two weeks before the World Cup I flew from London and boarded the train late one night in Moscow's Yaroslavsky station to find myself sharing a six-berth cabin with a friendly enough group. Fortunately, none of them snored and most were Russians who spoke just a few words of English. My knowledge of their language was zilch so every time I went to the dining car, I was relieved to find fellow English-speaking tourists. The lady behind the counter had a smiley face too and she rustled up some delicious meals as I sat talking shit with my new companions. Among them was a group of Norwegian ladies, one of whom seemed to take a shine to me. Alas there was nowhere for us to consummate our liking for one another and as she didn't seem the type to acquiesce to a knee trembler in the loo, a snog in the corridor as the train rattled on, amounted to the frustrating, physical heights of our friendship. I did try to look Ella up on subsequent visits to Oslo in my quest to complete the grounds in the Tippeligaen (top league) but she had either moved on or changed her mind about me.

As the train chugged on, I didn't realise the significance of some of the stations where we stopped off. Some of them, the likes of Omsk, Novosibirsk and Krasnoyarsk might be mentioned in the works of Dostoievski and other great Russian novelists but others such as Nizhny-Novgorod and Ekaterinburg would have meant so much more to me had I known in advance that they would be named as venues for the 2018 World Cup in Russia. And then there was Perm whose stadium Fulham would grace enroute to the Europa League final in 2010.

All those stations were long gone by the time I was forced into a parting of the ways with Ella and my new friends. They were all bound for either Ulan Bator in Mongolia or the train's terminus which was to be Beijing. For some unearthly reason I had put great store in wanting to visit Lake Baikal which happens to be the world's largest and deepest freshwater lake. Big deal. I dumped my luggage into my room at the hotel that InTourist had booked for me and took a cab to the lake which looked much like any other lake. I boarded a boat to the next small port and hung around there for a few minutes before taking a boat back to whence I had come. I found my cabbie waiting. He returned me to the hotel in Irkutsk where I had a meal and a bit of kip before being woken by the pre-arranged alarm call. I had to be at the station for 2am for the onward trip to Vladivostok. Part of me was left wondering whether my pricey stop-off had really been worthwhile. And then the train arrived and I was shown my cabin or a two-berth spalny vagan as it's known, which thankfully I had all to myself. That was the only bright note in a fairly dismal 24 hours.

When I awoke, I entertained high hopes of finding similar camaraderie in the restaurant car to that which I had happily encountered on the first leg of my marathon trek. My hopes were soon to be dashed as the lady in control was the surliest of human beings who could not or would not offer me any of the tasty breakfasts, I had enjoyed on the first train. But soon after I had sat down on that first morning with a stale piece of bread and cheese, I was joined by a couple. The lady spoke some English while her escort seemed determined to get me drunk as quickly as possible by pouring glass after glass of vodka down my throat. Eventually she called him away. "Sacha, Sacha, no more please." I was much relieved. But since I was never able to establish if the bitter hag running the restaurant car was on Moscow time, local time or Vladivostok time, my visits invariably coincided with when she was closed, not stocked up or suffering yet another menopausal trauma. I eventually gave up going, relying instead on the offerings to be found on sale at every subsequent station. There was a list up in each carriage of the stations and durations of the train's halts which were sometimes as long as 33 minutes. So, there was never much danger of being left stranded in deepest Siberia. Gnarled old women in shawls lined up on the platforms to sell their wares which were not the equivalent of healthy nourishment but, at least, their dried fish, cheeses, meats and fruits were improvements on what was on offer in the train.

For what seemed like days, the train ran alongside the River Amur or criss-crossed it. The scenery was now much more spectacular than the endless forests and pastures I had witnessed on the initial route out of Moscow. As Vladivostok neared, I got my maps of Asia out, spreading them onto the two bunks to acquaint myself with my forthcoming wanderings through that continent. A couple of soldiers appeared and feigned a deep, rather surprising interest in my future travels. I was mildly suspicious and while my back was turned, getting another chart from my suitcase to show them, they ran off. I looked round to see what might be missing and discovered that my two cans of vitamin pills had gone. Maybe the soldiers were on drugs and thought that the contents of those containers might feed their habits. In which case they would have been sadly disappointed. The attendant or provodnitsa at the end of the carriage heard the commotion and came to investigate. I managed to convey to her the loss of my precious pills and she then vanished only to return somewhat triumphantly an hour later, holding up my two cans. On every subsequent station I would disembark to seek out the soldiers, pointing to my head and twisting my finger as if to question their sanity. They looked suitably sheepish.

It was now time to hunker down though as Vladivostok was almost on the horizon and passengers were not allowed lie-ins. We were expected to troop off within moments of arrival. The station clock showed 6.06am as I climbed down onto the platform. I had travelled

5,105 miles through six nights and seven time zones, but the train had arrived on time. On the dot.

Chapter 25:
Asian odyssey

As my taxi navigated the murky light of dawn in Vladivostok, I regretted the fact that I had not allowed myself time to explore this city as it looked all the more intriguing for the fact that it is either the embarkation point or the terminus for thousands of voyages across the continents. Some other time maybe. Or maybe some other lifetime. I had banked on my train being on time as I had a plane to catch, to Seoul where Jurgen Berger, my German friend, met me. He, true to form, had a car waiting and he took me to the Happy Happy guest house which Lissi told me sounded more like a brothel when I rang her to check on the kids. But it was full of people of all ages and creeds wanting to see the World Cup. We had a couple of days to spare before the tournament, so Jurgen and I dined out two nights running at the same pavement restaurant he had discovered. Good choice as the speciality was sumptuous slices of beef that diners would cook for themselves on raclettes. It went down a treat with the seaweed they served up as well. After the hardship of searching for decent grub the previous few days, I was in clover. We finished off the evenings in a karaoke bar, the first time in my life I had visited such a dive.

Two nights later we were in Seoul's World Cup stadium to see France get off to an inauspicious start in the defence of their crown. Just like Argentina in 1990, they were beaten by Africans or, this time to be precise, Senegal. A single goal from Pape Bouba Diop did for the champions who were without the injured Zidane. On the Korean Express train the next morning I was introduced to two guys who would become lifelong friends, Ian Seymour, a Chelsea fan and Dave Nuttall, who favoured the Latics or Oldham Athletic where he lived. Although they are both English, they support Scotland which was how they had met up. They were, like me and hundreds of others, hurtling towards Ulsan, the venue for that evening's game between Uruguay and Denmark who won 2-1 with two goals from Jon Dahl Tomasson. As I hadn't relished the idea of driving in a country where the road signs in the Hangul alphabet would take some deciphering, train travel got the vote. Ian and Dave went their separate ways for a while with the result that Dave and I were often left in tandem, hunting for lodgings in erotic-looking abodes under garish neon lights that were not, in fact, the homes of hookers but simple cheap hotels.

For a while Dave wouldn't tell me what was inside the heavy bag that he insisted on carrying around with him. Eventually he relented and showed me an exact replica of the Jules Rimet trophy. His idea, apparently, had been to make money by getting the locals to pose with the "trophy" while he took photographs that he would sell them. But Dave was a bit coy in coming forward with the result that he never took any photos and never boosted his income. Eventually he dumped his precious World Cup and looked all the better for not having to haul it around, perspiring profusely, under the hot sun. The raison d'etre for both of us was to complete a full set of South Korean grounds. Dave's work as an auditor with Oldham Council prevented him from staying more than the first two weeks but I was intent on doing all the grounds not only in South Korea but Japan too. I had given the Telegraph, Indy and Guardian copies of my schedule and they gave me work whenever games were not being staffed. So, usually with Dave alongside me, I raced around the country, to games in Daegu, Busan, Gwangju, Jeonju Incheon, Suwon and back to Seoul.

Returning to Ulsan, I had seen Brazil's 2-1 win over Turkey which was tarnished by the outrageous gamesmanship of Rivaldo after he had dallied over a late corner. Hakan Unsal booted the ball at his opponent who promptly collapsed, clutching his face although the ball had hit him in the legs. The Blackburn Rovers' defender was sent off by the incompetent Korean referee Kim Young-Joo, leaving Rivaldo to say with the utmost audacity: "It doesn't matter where the ball hit me. It was only the intent that mattered. The World Cup would be a lot better off with more referees like Mr Young-Joo." Rivaldo was fined a paltry £1,000 by Fifa.

Later, with only the island venue of Jeju to visit, I flew to Seogwipo in whose stadium I saw - and reported on - Paraguay's 3-1 win over Slovenia that took them into the last 16. By then, shock horror! France had gone out. The world champions had followed up their opening day defeat by drawing 0-0 with Uruguay. Without Thierry Henry who had been sent off in that game, they then lost 2-0 to the Danes.

Continuing my travels to Tokyo the next day, or rather Narita, the airport that was nearly two hours train ride from the capital, I waited and waited for Yoko Kamada, my Japanese contact who had given me work in 1998. The Japanese are sticklers for punctuality among other things so I more or less assumed that she would honour our rendez-vous arrangement before putting me on the right train to Niigata where England were due to meet Denmark in the round of 16. But she let me down badly as I fretted the afternoon away in the arrivals hall. By the time Yoko eventually turned up full of apologies, the match was out of reach and I had to settle for watching England's 3-0 win in a Tokyo bar where we were joined by her boyfriend. The plan had been for Yoko to provide accommodation and train tickets - for which I would reimburse her - but she had only vague notions of how to be the perfect hostess. I was shown into the bedroom of her miniscule flat which she was vacating to stay with her bloke. Before leaving, she put the alarm on for 5am which was when I had to rise in order to catch a train to Oita, which is on the western fringes of the country, 500 miles and over six hours ride away on the Shinkansen, the bullet train with which I was to become familiar over the next fortnight. With most of my heavy luggage left in Yoko's flat, I was travelling light carrying only the bare essentials.

I reported on Senegal's 2-1 win over Sweden in Oita and then stopped off, halfway back to Tokyo in a Fukuoka hotel that Yoko had booked for me. And so my travels around Japan had begun in earnest with Kobe the next stop as it was the venue for Belgium's game with Brazil. My work with World Soccer had led to a fondness for the so-called Red Devils, now managed by Robert Waseige, but they succumbed gallantly 2-0. On I went to Miyagi, a suburb of the city of Sendai whose streets were ankle deep in water, the legacy of a day-long relentless downpour which continued throughout the co-hosts' round of 16 tie with Turkey that evening. Coping admirably with the saturated surface and the bedlam of the home support, the Turks beat Japan with a 12th minute goal from Umit Davala.

The powerful combination of a burgeoning friendship with Mia, a local girl who had caught my eye in a Sendai sports bar that evening and the appeal of various tourist attractions in the surrounding countryside, which were all listed in my guidebook, persuaded me to make Sendai my base from here on in. Mia paid nightly visits to my hotel room but insisted on leaving at 6am in order to be back at home to cook breakfast for her son who, she hoped, had no inkling that she had been out copulating. The few days between the completion of the round of 16 and the beginning of the quarterfinals gave me time to take a ferry to Toshirojima, otherwise known as Cat Island for all its strays. I conquered the highest hill there and the next day was ascending again onto the steep slopes of the defunct volcano of Mount Funagata. So as to further convince myself that I possessed other interests besides football and women, I also took in the resort of Goshjikinuma, the home of five lakes of varying hues including one of cobalt blue.

I had by now acquainted myself so well with the intricacies of Japanese train travel that I considered myself as something of an expert. In the evenings I returned to Sendai and, to what had become my favourite restaurant, so good was their speciality rice and sizzling beef dish. And after that sustenance I would head to the small, members only Genji bar where Mia was the hostess, conversing, flirting gently and lighting the endless cigarettes of the businessmen who were reluctant to go straight home to their wives after work. Each one had his favourite tipple in a bottle in its especially reserved spot on the shelves. This seemed to me a rather sad Japanese custom. I wondered what the wives made of it. Or if, indeed, they cared very much. Did they even bother to serve up burnt offerings when their hubbies got home?

Meanwhile Yoko was giving me grief with alarming text messages, saying that she had split up from her boyfriend who had apparently been jealous of us which was absurd -as there was absolutely no chemistry between us - with the result that she was now contemplating suicide. I tried to put this needless drama to the back of my mind when the time came to move on again. I headed back towards Tokyo and to the nearby city of Shizuoka which was to host England's game with Brazil in an afternoon kick-off under a burning sun. Michael Owen put England ahead but then, after Rivaldo had equalised, came the Ronaldinho free kick that confused the poor pig-tailed David Seaman in much the same way that Nayim had embarrassed him in Arsenal's European Cup Winners' final defeat to Zaragoza in Paris five years earlier. Ronaldinho was later sent off but Brazil's ten men prevailed.

From Tokyo, I then headed onto Osaka, the scene of Turkey's 1-0 victory over Senegal. The Shinkansen trains were a joy as they roared across Japan at speeds approaching 200mph. I have always loved eating on fast trains so there was nothing better than to watch the countryside race by as I devoured the contents of a bento box spiced up by soya sauce and wasabi dressing.

There was certainly some novelty value to this World Cup with South Korea, Senegal and Turkey all among the last eight. The Koreans had beaten Spain on penalties after a goalless 120 minutes, but Germany ended their hopes with a goal from Michael Ballack in the semi-final which was another game I saw in the bar where I had originally met Mia. And so, I headed for the Tokyo suburb of Saitama for the semi-final and another game involving Brazil and Turkey who would doubtless have liked nothing better than to kick Rivaldo to high heaven. But sensibly they resisted the temptation and the Turks duly lost to a goal from Ronaldo who was to score twice more late in the final against the Germans. Remarkably the two nations had never previously met in a World Cup which was all the more a sound reason why they would meet this time, I chided myself, with the rueful benefit of hindsight, knowing that I should have put a bet on. It was even more bleeding obvious, I reasoned, that Germany would go all the way following their 5-1 defeat by England in Munich in the qualifiers. Such is the perversity of football. The final was staged in Yokohama where unbelievably I had gone on the morning of the match fully expecting to find a bed. Which, even more unbelievably, I managed in a guest house within sight of the stadium's floodlights. My bed was in a room with a sunken bath and lurid paintings of enticing, semi clad ladies on the walls. And there was I, all alone and left to reflect on the fact that I had only chalked off six of Japan's nine World Cup Stadiums. Niigata, Sapporo and Ibaraki would have to wait.

The next morning, I took a boat ride round Yokohama's famous harbour before dashing back to Tokyo as a seemingly distraught Yoko was threatening to leave her tiny flat and dump all my belongings on the pavement. So, I returned in haste only to find her and her boyfriend in complete and utter harmony. I bought them lunch during which he asked me if I thought David Beckham would ever play in Japan. "It's unlikely," I said, "because he is completely under Victoria's thumb."

"Ah," he replied, "we don't have that expression in Japan. We would say that he is under Victoria's hip." Which could have been the title of this book had I not decided otherwise.

I left that evening on a flight to Perth in Australia where I had arranged to meet two of my sons, James and Ashley who happened to be half-brothers and who had only met for the first time the previous week. The three of us spent the next few days together during which James met his future wife Angelina in a discotheque in Freemantle. It was now a week since the World Cup final and withdrawal symptoms had already begun to set in. So, it was to Freemantle's Maddington suburb that I took us all to see Freemantle City oppose Athena FC in the West Australian State League. As Athena is the name of Ashley's mother, he took an interest in a football match for the first and only time in his life, supporting the visitors.

No sooner had I arrived back in the UK than Janette was telling me I could go on another BMA flight as her guest and, what's more, I could invite a friend along. The great advantage with BMA was that some of their routes were to weird and wonderful places such as Azerbaijan. I took Neil who was already well advanced in his pursuit of visiting every country on the continent for football. There was no all-night drinking binge this time which was a good thing. The only drawback was the sleeping arrangements. I was told that I must share a twin-bedded room with Neil who, along with Chris, is one of the world's loudest snorers. I was desperate for Janette to vacate her room so I could move in as soon as she had left for an early flight back to Heathrow. By then dawn had broken and I had suffered several sleepless hours. I slept in and then belatedly explored the oilfields on the outskirts of Baku with Neil before we went to the game, a Euro qualifier which Wales won 2-0. The 8,000 capacity Tofiq Bahramov Stadium, named after the linesman who had confirmed that England's controversial third goal by Geoff Hurst in the 1966 World Cup final was over the line, was basic. In no way did it resemble the spacecraft-like Baku Olympic Stadium that took its place in time for the 2019 Europa League final plus the delayed 2020 Euro finals.

Neil and I were supposed to be pulling out early the next day, but I don't think either of us minded too much when we heard that our flight had been delayed 12 hours. We got back in touch with the cabbie we had used the previous day for our look at the Caspian Sea. This time he was delegated to take us on an elongated road trip encompassing the delights of the Absheron Peninsular with lunch thrown in at a restaurant of his recommendation. It was a Thursday afternoon, so we were the focal point of the owner's attention. He had time to locate us a table in the long grass of his orchard. That was fine, albeit akin to something out of a bizarre film set but less savoury was his treatment of his handsome Alsatian who had befriended us in the hope of a few titbits. We had been obliging when the owner suddenly re-appeared, kicking out violently at the dog. He relented when I jumped to the dog's defence. But our meal didn't taste so good after that.

Chapter 26:
The scrapbook survives

For some reason, I hadn't been able to get Mia out of my mind, so I knew I had to go back to Japan. And what better time than the next summer when there wasn't much on to keep me at home. Furthermore, I could maybe chalk off the World Cup venues that I had missed out on in 2002. So, I headed back to Asia in June, arriving the day before Japan's women were to take on Mexico in a warm-up game for that year's World Cup. And the extra enticing bait was the venue which happened to be Tokyo's Olympic Stadium which I had yet to visit. But it was there on a brilliant sunny afternoon that I saw Japan's girls win 2-0 before I headed back up to Sendai on the Shinkansen. As soon as I saw Mia coming towards me at the pre-arranged meeting place, I wondered why I had been so pre-occupied with thoughts of her for the previous 12 months. Maybe she thought likewise when she saw me approaching. Perhaps it had been the romance and heady excitement of the World Cup that had thrown us together. But now there was no World Cup so our relationship fizzled out fairly quickly after that.

My immediate consolation was a journey to Ibaraki, one of my three missing World Cup stadiums and a Kashima Antlers home game. It was one of the most intoxicating atmospheres I have ever experienced with a torrent of noise and a sea of red forming the backdrop to a dazzling 3-3 draw with Vissel Kobe. You just couldn't get a bad game in those conditions. The background was far less atmospheric when I took in another J-League game at Chofu, the home then of Tokyo Verdy, soon after they had appointed Ossie Ardiles as manager. Two days after their 3-1 win over Kashima Reysol, he gave me an interview that World Soccer used. He seemed to have the weight of the world on him and wasn't riveting company. His time with Verdy came to grief in 2005 following defeats of 7-1, 7-0 and 6-0. The rest of my schedule consisted of lower league games, all meticulously planned beforehand by a conscientious lady who worked for the J-League and got me press passes. When we came to part, I attempted to kiss her on both cheeks as a farewell gesture. She turned away, very embarrassed. Apparently it's not the done thing in Japan, let alone on a station platform.

Much as I would have liked to have fitted Sapporo and Niigata into my schedule, they just couldn't be done. I did, in fact get to Sapporo 13 years later after meeting my son James in Tokyo to view the Japan ATP tennis tournament. Taking my leave of him and my grandkids, Sally - who I had met at a Beatles evening in Kings Road - and I took the Shinkansen up to the end of the line on what proved to be a costly and wasted trip. We had arrived in the city the night before with tickets for Hokkaido Consadole Sapporo's game against Mito Hollyhock that Yoko had procured for us. But alarmingly there was no sign of fans or scarves on the local train to the Sapporo Dome. There was just no match fever. Luckily the couple I turned to in a panic spoke English. After inspecting my ticket, they politely informed me that the stadium we needed was not Sapporo's World Cup stadium but the Atsubetsu Stadium some distance away. The Sapporo Dome was hosting a baseball game featuring the Hokkaido Nippon-Ham Fighters that weekend, so the footie had been shifted. They told us to carry onto the end of the line and take a cab. We raced out of the station and found an obliging cabbie who got us to the ground just before kick-off which was just as well as the only goal of the game came in the fifth minute from the Brazilian, Jonathan Reis. I could hardly blame Yoko this time for the mishap, but it was frustrating to think that we had travelled half the length of Japan for a game when we could have stayed near Tokyo and the family, spent quality time with them and seen a game nearby. So, Sapporo will have to wait as will Niigata.

Returning to 2003, I hadn't been back from Japan long before I was bringing to fruition the plans Neil and I had made to occupy ourselves during the next international break. It was a crazy caper, starting with a drive from Lyon Airport to Gueugnon for a Friday night second div game. The hosts defeated Rouen 2-1. As we were then going east into Switzerland, I had arranged for our overnight stop to be with Agnes, my parents' former au pair whose family reside in the small town of Lyss, 240 miles away. That would have been no problem but for Neil's map reading which left much to be desired. It was therefore well into the early hours before we arrived. To give her enormous credit, Agnes was waiting up for us with a much-needed snack. Thankfully we had some time to relax the next morning as we could hardly go wrong on the Swiss motorways in broad daylight. Our destination now was Vaduz. I had deliberately given Liechtenstein's Euro qualifier with England a miss six months earlier as I calculated that it would be far easier to obtain tickets for any other game such as another Euro qualifier, against Turkey. We saw the Turks win 3-0 after which we embarked on the maddest diversion of all time. It was to take us a total of 600 miles out of our way, a lengthy drive down the Adriatic coast, all for an Italian Serie C game at Teramo. We holed up at a cheap hotel in enough time, I reasoned, for me to go on a run. "You are not going for a run," Neil insisted, on noticing that I was stripped and ready to go. "Watch me," I said.

I did a few miles and was showered and dressed in no time, but I began to regret my craving for exercise when we got bogged down in heavy traffic. The game was a local derby with Sanbenedettese and the local cognoscenti wanted to be there in numbers judging by the massive snarl-up. Knowing of Neil's need to be there for the start, I began to feel guilty. He was quiet, obviously sulking. We parked precariously and dashed into the ground, getting in just as the teams kicked off only to find that we could hardly see a thing over all the heads. So we hurried round the terraces to find a better vantage point. "I'm sorry," I said, "I suppose you can't count it now and you'll have to go back some time."

"It's ok," he said," I saw them kick-off, that's good enough for me." So, much relieved, I relaxed and we settled down to watch an action-packed 1-1 draw. The calibre was good, much better than what we had expected from two mid-table third div sides.

We had a post-match pizza and hurried back for some shut-eye as we had to make an early start for the next leg of our voyage. This was to take us back up the Adriatic coast and into Slovenia for what transpired to be the opening game in the Stadion Z'dezele in Celje. There was only one giant stand, which could accommodate roughly 3,600. Less than half that number saw a goalless draw between the youth teams of Slovenia and France. The stadium now houses crowds of 13,000 and stages some internationals when Slovenia are not using Ljubljana which happened to be the last stop on our tour.

We interrupted our good progress the next day for a coffee in the provincial town of Domzale. We were idling our way round the streets when Neil drew my attention to the handwritten notice on a shop front. "Look at this," he said, "it looks like there's a game on at 4." Looking at our watches, we saw that it was 3.45pm. We found a passer-by and, barely concealing our excitement, managed to stay calm enough to comprehend directions to the ground, such as it was. The game turned out be an early-round cup tie, important enough to qualify for a mention in Neil's scrapbook. There were no programmes, so he spent half-time with officials of both clubs who gave him the respective line-ups. But I think he had to go without a match report which is also part of the ritual that includes the shirts of both teams, appropriately coloured in.

He was at work one day when a neighbour rang to say he had been burgled. He suffered several hours of torment before discovering that his precious scrapbooks were not among the stolen items.

Suitably grateful for our unexpected bonus match in Domzale, we applauded the teams off before completing our journey to the capital.

106

True to form, I found Chris and Haya in one of the city's gastronomic paradises while Neil made straight for the ground as he had no wish for a repeat of the panic of two nights earlier. We saw France beat Slovenia 2-0 with goals from David Trézéguet and Olivier Dacourt. The European champions held out easily enough after having Claude Makele sent off for two yellows. We began our long drive back to Lyon the next day, metaphorically clapping ourselves on the back after seeing six games in six days in four different countries.

Chapter 27:
Sights to behold

2004 had a lot more going for it with the Euros, the Copa and the Asian championship all to be squeezed in. The Indy were giving me work in Portugal or, to be more specific in Faro, starting with Spain's 1-0 defeat of Russia on the opening day which meant that I had to forego England's game with France 24 hours later. That was when Zidane scored twice in added time to cancel out Frank Lampard's opener for Sven Goran Erikkson's side.

Portugal is such a lovely country that it was a joy to travel by train up and down, taking in all the venues. England duly recovered with impressive wins over Switzerland by 3-0 and Croatia 4-2, with the 18-year-old Rooney scoring twice in each game. It was before the Swiss game in the cobbled streets of Coimbra that a group of about a dozen of us met for a sumptuous lunch in a Michelin Guide restaurant that Chris had found.

The venues included the northern city of Braga whose stadium contains a rock face and therefore no spectators behind one goal. The scene of Denmark's 2-0 win over Bulgaria which I saw, it still ranks as one of the most remarkable stadiums I have set foot in. Braga is a few miles from Porto which was where my latest flame, Judy was flying in to join me for the rest of the tournament. One of Porto's special attractions is the River Douro on which we took a day trip on a sweleringly hot day. We sat in the back of the boat and I stupidly scorned her offer of suntan cream with the result that I got horribly burnt, the source, I suspected of the dermatological problems I later suffered and skin cancer I developed which required two operations to suffuse. Judy had a friend near Evora, 100 miles to the east of Lisbon and it was to there that we drove to spend a couple of days between semi-finals and final. She had a beautiful house and gardens and thankfully, a television on which we saw Maria Sharapova overcome Serena Williams to win Wimbledon at the tender age of 17.

My work had dried up now, so I was able to relax as we headed back to Lisbon for the final in which the hosts were due to meet Greece in a repeat of their opening game which the Greeks had unexpectedly won 2-1. No way would the bubbles win again, us know-alls reckoned, despite their single-goal wins over France and the Czech Republic in the knockout stages. The hosts had followed up their success in the penalty shoot-out against England to beat Denmark in their semi. Under their astute German manager, Otto Rehhaghel, the Greeks surpassed themselves. It was a defensive performance to match Italy's epic defiance against Holland in that semi-final of four years earlier. No matter what Ronaldo and co threw at them, they could not break through the barrier either before or after the headed goal from Angelos Charisteas that was decisive. It contributed to probably the biggest football shock of all time. Greece had only qualified for two previous tournaments, the 1980 Euros and 1994 World Cup in which they failed to win a single game. No wonder there were bemused looks on the faces of every blue-scarved Greek I encountered in Lisbon's airport the next morning as I headed for Lima.

The football calendar couldn't have worked out more conveniently with the Copa America refusing to overlap the Euros. But if that was convenient the choice of venues in Peru was far from it. There are 2,211 miles between the northern outpost of Piura and Tacna in the south but some members of our small group, including yours truly, managed to get to all of them which was no simple task. We were travelling from the morning after the opening day's double header which was rounded off by the hosts' 2-2 draw with Bolivia after Colombia's 1-0 win over Venezuela. We either took arduous bus trips or internal flights. It was while queuing up for one long coach ride that Ross Clegg, a banker from Nottingham who happens to support Leeds, and I got talking to another passenger. With Ross and I seated some way from Gabriella, I thought no more of this chance meeting when the coach pulled out. Gorgeous that she was, the anticipation for games in the towns and cities of Piura, Chiclayo and Trujillo got the better of me. They were all venues north of Lima. And this was to be a proper Copa with no intruders such as Japan to join in the fun as Mexico and the USA were making up the numbers.

Rocio was still some days away from joining me from Houston and her work teaching English when Ross suddenly announced that Gabriella had got in touch with him because she wanted to meet me. Unbeknown to me, the two of them had swopped numbers but the outcome of that exchange was still bizarre, I reflected. Ross handed me her number and I phoned up and conjured up all sorts of fantasies about her in the hours before our planned rendez-vous at a coach stop on the outskirts of Trujillo. There was no sign of her, but I heard my name called by a gent hovering there. He turned out to be Gabriella's husband so I naturally wondered what the evening might have in store for me on the drive back to their expansive home. And to this day I am still wondering. They cooked me a delicious steak but over dinner and after the meal, I was never left alone with Gabriella for long enough to discover what our date was all about. Maybe Claudio had come back suddenly from a trip - and

109

she had had to own up about my invitation - or perhaps they had planned a threesome and he simply didn't fancy me. Nothing was clarified as he drove me back to my hotel while she cleared up the dishes. We promised to stay in touch but, of course, we never did. I met up with the lads later that night and regaled them, amid much hilarity, with my tale. There had been no seduction, but it transpired that I had enjoyed a much better meal than they had.

As the games unravelled, we found ourselves heading south of the capital whose Mira Flores district had been our magnet with its array of distinctive shops, full of ethnic artefacts, and inviting restaurants. Leaving Lima, we flew to Arequipa where pilots face the hazardous task of steering their planes between the snow-clad mountains of the Andes for safe landings. Group C was calling, especially its final game involving Brazil and Paraguay which had been on our radar for some time. But, alas, the group's final fixture was something of a let-down as both nations went into it knowing they were sure to qualify. Paraguay won 2-1 to top the group. With no game the following night, we had all decided on an obscenely early start of 2am in order to go to the famous Colca Canyon which is where a flock of Condor birds hang out. Chris went to bed early, but Martin and I went out for a late-night drink with the result that we had hardly got to our beds before our tour guide arrived. As his minibus negotiated the unkempt roads on the three-hour drive and I tried unsuccessfully to get some kip in the back, I found myself questioning my sanity. Why I had bothered to do without a precious night's sleep just to see some sodding birds of prey flying around. But the journey proved worthwhile. The first light of dawn coincided with our arrival at an Andean tourist village staffed by indigenous tribesmen who persuaded me to purchase a woollen beanie hat. And then we drove on towards the best vantage point to spot the Condors who greeted us over the next few hours with frequent forays from their nests. They are a legend among Incas who reckon that the old birds, close to death, withdraw their wings and plummet like stones from their nest. They hit the ground and die only to be reborn. Immortal or not, they were indeed a sight to behold.

On our return to Arequipa we were reunited with our friend Steve Rolf and his girlfriend Debs. They had taken time off from the Copa to visit the famous city of Iquitos, deep in the Amazonian rain forest, which is only accessible by plane to foreign visitors unless they are from Ecuador. For others there are no roads in or out. They were full of stories about this remarkable place on our drive down to Tacna for the last of the quarter-finals, between Uruguay and Paraguay whose victory over Brazil counted for little as they lost 3-1. Tacna is close to the border with Chile which was a country none of us had visited as we had all been too young to visit the World Cup in 1962. So, of course, Chile beckoned and we headed for the country's northern-most town of Arica only 40 miles away. It was a Saturday so, of course, we had vague hopes of finding a game and headed therefore to the Estadio Carlos Dittborn where there was indeed something of a sporting nature going on. But it was not of the type we craved. It was a veterans athletics meeting but on perusing the stadium's confines, I came across a plaque on which there was a picture of a footballer and the names - in Spanish of course - of Yugoslavia, Russia, Uruguay and Colombia. We had hit upon one of the venues for the 1962 World Cup and a historic one at that as it was where Colombia's Maros Coll had scored the Mundiale's only ever goal direct from a corner, beating the great Lev Yashin in the process.

The stadium had been named after the president of the 1962 organising committee who had done a fantastic job in getting the tournament staged on schedule just two years after Chile had suffered a massive earthquake. But alas for his efforts, Senor Dittborn had died a month before the World Cup opened.

The sight of that plaque helped us over our disappointment at not finding a game.

While the others dallied the next day, I took a bus back to Arequipa as I had a date with Ana Maria, a lady I had met during my night out with Martin. She was a dish and fiery with it but just about worth the perils of that bus ride. That road had seen its share of fatal accidents over the years which was not a fact I cared to dwell on as we sped along its various precarious edges, hundreds of feet up. After dinner, Ana Maria put me up in her spare room having made it clear that she didn't fuck on first dates. Not to worry. I wanted to see her again. With her captivating looks and such an evocative name, she had a lot going for her.

It would be hard to find any tourist in Peru who was not there to include the ancient Inca ruins of Machu Pichu on his itinerary and we were not about to become the first. But that meant missing both semi-finals in Lima. Sacrilege, I hear you saying. But there was no other way for it, so tight was our schedule. So, Argentina's 3-0 win over Colombia and Brazil's 5-3 victory on penalties after Uruguay had held them to 1-1 over 90 minutes, both had to go by the board. It would have been a bonus if we'd had the time to take the four-day trek from Cuzco to Aguas Caliente, the town at the foot of the hill which accomodates Machu Pichu. But we didn't want to miss out on the Copa final as well as the semis, so the decision was taken to take the train there which is a pleasing enough journey in itself with the River Urubamba running parallel with much of the railway track.

111

Aguas Caliente is a fun town full of tourists resting tired limbs in the hot springs of thermos-medicinal water, so it was an appealing overnight stop. But it is some 400 feet below Machu Pichu which I found to my cost after a perspiring trudge up the road and around a score of hairpin bends. It was my punishment for taking too long to file a story to the Telegraph on the semis - which I had seen on television - thereby missing the designated bus to the top. I arrived at the entrance to the heritage site with sweat pouring from my brow. But my efforts were not in vain as Machu Pichu was every bit a wonder of the world and certainly worth the sacrifice we had made. We took in the architectural delights of Ollantaytambo on the way back to Cuzco.

In normal circumstances we might have given the third place final a miss but seeing as Cuzco was staging its one match of the Copa, Uruguay v Colombia became a must-see. Uruguay won 2-1. Cusco's focal point was its charming town square and adjoining arcades, but we couldn't linger there long as our flight to Lima was the next morning. It was just as well that we hadn't opted out of the final as well as that game in the Estadio Nacional will live long in the memory. It was one of the finest matches, if not the best I have ever seen. Argentina who had not won anything since their 1993 Copa triumph in Ecuador, were favoured by us Brits. And twice in front, they were within sight of winning a tumultuous game until Adriano came to Brazil's rescue with their second equaliser in the 93rd minute. The Copa is a machismo contest at the best of times so for this tournament at least, there was no extra time. The game went straight to penalties. With Argentina missing their first two efforts, the second by Gabriel Heinze - who was soon to join Manchester United - the onus was on Brazil who didn't let down their legions of fans, winning the shootout by 4-2. We couldn't help but feel desperately sorry for the Argies who were to spend several more years in the international doldrums.

112

Chapter 28:
Three disappointing gorges

There was no time to lament Argentina's latest failure as I was off again, this time to China via a swift stop-over in Auckland. The Asian Championships were well advanced by the time I arrived in Chengdu for that evening's quarter-final. My first taxi broke down and on getting in another, the driver soon made it clear that he couldn't go any further because the police were only allowing cars containing VIPS to pass. With kick-off beckoning there was nothing else for it but to complete the last few miles by rickshaw which to this day remains the weirdest mode of transport I have ever used to get to a game. I egged on the poor driver who pedalled furiously, eventually getting me to the stadium just on time. But as bad luck would have it, my accreditation was awaiting me on the far side of the ground. But then as good luck would have it, I missed only a few minutes but none of the goals in the 2-2 draw between Uzbekistan and Bahrain. The Uzbeks eventually prevailed in the shoot-out.

The next morning, I boarded one of the Silor minibuses that were the most popular means of travel in Asia. They go as soon as they fill up. A bit like the average hooker, I couldn't help but think. My destination now was Chongquin which was, depending upon who you listen to and which guidebooks you read, the world's largest city with a population of over 30 million. Not only was this vast metropolis the venue for another quarter final but handily, it also sits alongside the Yangtze River which had always been a beacon for me. I had a thing about rivers and had always wanted to travel up this mighty waterway. Which was why I stepped onto a sizeable passenger liner the morning after yet another penalty finale, won 4-3 by Japan after they had been locked at 1-1 with Jordan after extra time.

My decision to sail up the Yangtse at the expense of seeing the Japan v Bahrain semi-final in Jinan had been met with incredulity by Dave or Oldham Dave as he was now known, the chap I had befriended in South Korea two years previously. I told him that Jinan would have represented a clean sweep of venues for me at the Euros, the Copa and now the Asian. "The Yangtze will always be there, but you'll probably never get to Jinan," reasoned Dave who was aghast at my decision-making. But I had few regrets even after learning that I had missed a seven-goal thriller, Japan's 4-3 extra time win. I had booked a comfortable cabin which looked over the water and the food on board was acceptable if nothing else. I got chatting to a well-spoken young English couple who were sleeping on benches with the proletariat down below. One hot morning as we stood talking on deck, I told them they could make use of my cabin for a while if they so wished. They must have been dying for a shag, but they were perhaps too shy to accept my offer.

As the voyage progressed, the boat pulled in at some cities and floated serenely over others which had long since been submerged by the river's rising flood waters. Thousands of people had been relocated in the cause of a hydroelectricity project and the distant dam. I was engrossed by all this and looked forward to the famous Three Gorges but so high was the water level now and so dusky the evening when we approached, that disappointment lay in store. The subsequent dam meant that the boat could go no further so all its passengers disembarked near the city of Sandouping which meant that after three days aboard, I faced a further four-hour bus ride to Wuhan from where I would catch the overnight train to Beijing. As I killed time in Wuhan, little knowing what a global landmark that city would become for all the wrong reasons 16 years hence, I went to an internet café. I happened to glance at the screen of the person next to me and saw that he too was studying the website for the Combined Counties League back home. It was such an amazing coincidence that I just had to pluck up courage to speak to him. While I was looking at possible fixtures to occupy me on August Bank Holiday Monday, he was a referee wanting to know his appointments for the new season. See you at Chessington Hook mate.

With Beijing's Worker's Stadium the venue for both the forthcoming games, Beijing was my obvious final port of call. I had booked a room in a guest house in a rather bohemian district where I was initially laid low by a stomach upset. That prevented me from fulfilling all my sight-seeing obligations. The Great Wall would have to wait for another day, but I did get to Tiananmen Square in the days before the tournament's climax. I saw Iran overcome Bahrain 4-2 in the third place final the night before Japan took on the hosts. I might have favoured China in the final had either Fan Zhiyi or Sun Jihan still figured in their starting line-up. Fan's international career was over and Sun only came on as a late substitute. The two Chinese players were pioneers, having been among their country's first players to go abroad. But they had both moved on from Palace so there was no good reason to root for China in that final. Therefore, my soft spot for Japan prevailed and I stayed loyal to them. Their 3-1 win came with goals from Takashi Fukunishi, Koji Nakata, the pin-up boy, and Keiji Tamakai.

With the game crucially poised, the Chinese crowd were incensed when Nakata's handball in the area went unspotted and the more partisan among their supporters sang a patriotic song calling for the decapitation of Japanese people. There was rioting after the game. The two countries never did like each other very much.

I was to see Japan and, for that matter Bahrain again seven months later in a World Cup qualifier in Bahrain's Madinat 'Isa Stadium. Japan's 1-0 win was as dreary as the surroundings. I discovered there was a Crystal Palace Hotel in Manama so of course I had to stay there. But it had seen better days. Its carpets were worn and there was an air of decay and faded opulence.

Chapter 29:
Going Dutch

Hardly had I flown back to Heathrow than I was getting my trusty Ford Mondeo serviced for the next road trip which was to Holland and all over dyke country since the 2005 World Youth Championships were next on the hectic agenda. With distances between the six venues presenting no great challenge, it was a heaven sent opportunity for those of us wanting to visit pastures new.

Ground hoppers from England and Germany were not slow in coming forward but they are entirely different breeds. Whereas the English have bad haircuts, carry plastic bags, wear ill-fitting jeans and are usually the wrong side of middle age, their German counterparts are invariably far more sophisticated, younger and more jolly. And they don't jot every substitution down in little notebooks the way the English saddos do. I was reminded of the occasion when 55 Germans, all non-journalists applied to Wycombe Wanderers for press passes for a match against Leyton Orient late one December, the time of year when German football takes its mid-winter break. Starved of games, the Germans come to the UK in their droves from Boxing Day onwards. There's nothing they like better than to boast of how many of our 92 league grounds they have completed. But now it was the Dutch grounds they had a chance of adding to their lists.

The tournament got under way in Kerkrade's Parkstad Limburg Stadium, luckily for me on a Friday. That gave me a chance to wax lyrical about the performance of a certain Quincy Owusu Abeyie as, fortuitously, I had received a late call from the Sunday Times to do some work for them. I was able to go overboard about the 19-year-old winger who had given a bewitching display on Holland's left wing in their 2-1 defeat of Japan. He was mesmerising which made it all the more surprising that his career never really took off in the manner it had promised that balmy evening. Then on the books of Arsenal who had taken him from Ajax, Quincy became one of football's nomads. Arsene Wenger must have seen the light for Quincy swiftly moved on from Highbury - mostly on loan deals – to Spartak Moscow, Celta Vigo, Birmingham, Cardiff, Portsmouth, Al-Sadd in Qatar, Malaga, Panathinaikos, Boavista and then back to Holland with NEC. On that tournament's opening night, he had looked like an all-time great in the making but that kind of mantle will always be reserved for the likes of Lionel Messi who do fulfil their potential. Messi finished as the event's top scorer with six goals. His two penalties in the final in Utrecht's spectacular Stadion Galgenwaard gave Argentina a 2-1 win over Nigeria and the feel for silverware with which Messi became so accustomed. Argentina had beaten Brazil in their semi-final. Nigeria had ousted the hosts in the quarter-finals with a remarkable 10-9 success in the penalty shoot-out after the teams' 1-1 draw.

Apart from Quincy's outstanding initial contribution, the group stages were noticeable for some peculiar scorelines such as those of Chile who slaughtered Honduras 7-0 only to lose by the same scoreline to Spain next time out. With Anya, a lady I had met on a swift dating evening in Richmond, joining me for the competition's later stages, we hurtled round Holland, taking in games at Emmen, Enschede, Utrecht, Tilberg and Kerkrade. Tilberg where we based ourselves for a couple of days, had the benefits of a track alongside a tributary of the Meuse River which proved good running terrain for both of us. The only disappointment from my point of view was a failure to see a game at Doetinchem which remains unticked off to this very day. For as long as De Graafschap, de Vijverberg Stadion's usual occupants, loiter in the Eerste Divisie, the Dutch second tier, I won't be rushing there.

Anya and I survived just long enough for her to accompany me on my first ever visit to the West Indies during an international break five months later. Luckily her best mate who was in the travel business got us cheap flights to Barbados which we used as our base. I had clapped myself on the back for spotting that France and Costa Rica were due to play a game in Martinique in aid of the dependants of passengers who had perished in a Colombian air disaster. France were still newsworthy as recent world and European champions, so I got some work. A charity game it may have been, but it proved a full-blooded tussle with the Ticos taking a two-goal lead before Les Bleus roared back to win 3-2 with Thierry Henry getting their final goal. Martinique was an all too short stop-off for both of us. Returning to Barbados, I barely had time for a swim and a run before returning to its airport for a whistle stop trip to the Port of Spain where Trinidad and Tobago were opposing Bahrain in a World Cup qualifier which fortunately for me was another game deemed of sufficient interest to English readers chiefly because the Soca Warriors had in their line-up, a Port Vale player by the name of Chris Birchall.

I had come across and indeed met Birchall four months earlier when I was in Miami officially for the Concacaf Gold Cup but for the real purpose of being reunited with Ana Maria who had flown in from Arequipa. I was more preoccupied with her than the game against

117

Honduras when I suddenly noticed that Trinidad and Tobago had in their central midfield, a white man. I looked him up in the squad list and started to take more of an interest in the proceedings. Even more so when the white man scored, burying a shot into the roof of the net from Jason Scotland's pass. Ana Maria was not the most patient of souls, I was soon to discover to my cost when I asked her to hang on after the game as I just had to go to the bowels of the Orange Bowl for an interview with the marksman whose goal had given his side a 1-1 draw.

Apparently Birchall's grandmother had been from Trinidad and word had reached Dennis Lawrence among others that he might be eligible for selection. Lawrence was a Wrexham player when, during a lull in a match against the Vale, he suddenly asked the opposing right winger if he had "Trini blood in him." The upshot was that Birchall was chosen by the national team whose Dutch manager Leo Beenhakker converted him into a goalscoring midfielder. The Observer took my feature on the first white man to score for Trinidad and Tobago and the Indy accepted my match report of the game against Bahrain when Birchall scored again. His stunning equaliser gave Trinidad and Tobago a dramatic 1-1 draw for an aggregate 2-1 win that took them to the 2006 World Cup finals. With England among their group stage opponents in Germany, Birchall became even more of a celebrity than he might ever have envisaged. He went on to play for Coventry, St Mirren, Carlisle and Brighton before winning two MLS Western Conference titles with LA Galaxy. where David Beckham was among his teammates. Birchall was last heard of playing non-league football for Kidsgrove.

It was not long before I was swopping the warmth of the Caribbean for the drizzle of Bucharest. For a while I had been saying to Maryan, "'wouldn't it be great if we could find a midweek when all three Bucharest clubs were at home in the Uefa Cup?'" It was in the days when Uefa saw fit not to impose Draconian sanctions and permitted two clubs from one city to play at home on the same day, albeit preferably with different kick-off times. The entire trio of Bucharest clubs were in the perennial habit of qualifying for Uefa's secondary competition, so now all we needed were the dates of the group games to come to our aid. Every year, I would scan the ties as soon as they were announced but invariably one Bucharest club would be at home and the other two away or vice versa. But ultimately the fixtures unravelled exactly the way I wanted. I rang Maryan who had just seen for himself the opportunities presented by matchday four. So, in late November we both flew to Eastern Europe. I was astonished on arrival at the airport to find Maryan asking me for a loan of 100 euros. It was a sign of things to come. He had gone to Romania with hardly a euro to his name.

118

Steaua Bucharest, who had been allowed to bring their match forward a day, therefore had the Wednesday all to themselves for their Group C home tie with Halmstad of Sweden, which they won 3-0. The next day was a hectic one as, before our two games, Maryan wanted to see the Stadionul National which was in the process of being renovated. I had seen England draw 0-0 there in a 1985 World Cup qualifier in the days of late-night curfews as the regime of the communist dictator, Nicolae Ceausescu neared its grisly end.

The cost of cabs in the capital was not excessive so Maryan and I hurried between the various stadiums in taxis. We saw Dinamo gain their first and, as it happens, only victory in group F when they beat fellow strugglers, CSKA Moscow 1-0 and from there, at breakneck speed, we moved onto Rapid's Giulesti-Valentine Stanescu stadium for another 1-0 home win, this one over PAOK who were accompanied by a surprisingly large contingent of boisterous fans, from Greece, all of them soaked to the skin after standing in the rain. Rapid, who finished top of group G, and Steaua progressed to a quarter-final confrontation, won on away goals by Steaua whose semi-final opponents were Middlesbrough who won 4-3 on aggregate only to lose the final 4-0 to Sevilla in Eindhoven. Rapid, incidentally, later went bankrupt and were eventually replaced by Academia in the top flight. Their eventual plight was worse than ours as it had been a brilliant trip and I even got my 100 euros back from Maryan.

By now I was accustomed to lower, even freezing temperatures which was just as well since I was soon to be heading for the Arctic Circle on what was an emotional stay in northern Norway. For it was while I was there that I learned of the death of George Best. They say that everyone remembers where they were when informed of the deaths of John Kennedy, John Lennon and Princess Di. So far as I was concerned Best had to be added to that list too. For some reason, more than any of the great individual goals he scored, I still treasured the memory of the piledriver he had swept in, left footed with the minimum of back lift, against Real Madrid at Old Trafford many years earlier.

I had flown to Trondheim for the Champions League group game between Rosenborg and Olympiakos and was still bemoaning the fact that the odious Rivaldo had scored the Greek club's goal in the 1-1 draw when my travels took me onto Tromso. As the plane flew into land on a runway that seemed to be the only part of the landscape not under several feet of snow, I wondered how they could possibly play football anywhere in the vicinity. But play they did and it was the morning after Tromso's 3-1 win over Red Star in a Europa League tie that I rang Ben Findon on the Telegraph's sports desk to ask him what my commitment might be

119

for the following day. He told me about Best. The news was inevitable, but it was desperately sad all the same.

Chapter 30:
Ticket palaver

There was a Machiavellian sub plot to my involvement in the 2006 World Cup finals. It developed from the day, some two months before the tournament when Jurgen rang to ask if I could name 25 people who would be interested in receiving tickets for the finals which would be passed onto to him via me. In other words, I had to find 25 acquaintances who weren't interested in football or, at least, could be trusted not to use the tickets for themselves. That was no easy task since the vast majority of my friends have some connection or other with the game. Anyway, I delved into my address book and eventually came up with 25 names which I gave him. As someone who was fast on the way to becoming the world's biggest ticket tout, Jurgen's idea was to bypass FIFA's stringent regulations on ticket quotas. He would offer 'my tickets' and others he had sourced by similar means, utilising his world-wide contacts, for re-sale in Germany at inflated prices. My reward was an offer to buy at cost price whatever tickets he still had available for early-round games. As I had been struggling for tickets myself, I accepted his conditions although they were not exactly the height of generosity.

As time went on, more and more of my friends rang to say they had a FIFA embossed envelope sitting on their hall table. Others rang to say that they had returned from work to find a message from DHL telling them where to collect their packages. Which of course they were not willing to do. So, it was left to me to trawl around the Home Counties to blessed DHL depots. Instead of waking up in the mornings wondering what non-league stories I might do for the Telegraph, I was waking up thinking which sodding DHL depot do I have to visit today. I told Jurgen in no uncertain terms that this was not what I had envisaged or how I wanted to spend my days. "This is ridiculous," I said. "I want more tickets." To which he invariably replied: "we will talk about it. We talk about it." But we never did talk about it, so I decided to withhold one of the envelopes which was addressed to my good friend Janette who I regarded as my surrogate sister. I would have preferred to have had her as a sister than the one I ended up with.

Janette duly handed over the envelope which happened to consist of four tickets for the final. Whoopee! I sent Jurgen 20 of the 25 envelopes and he duly delegated his identical twin Bastian to fly to London to collect the five remaining ones. I handed over four envelopes telling him that one was still missing. "Okay, I'm only the messenger," replied Bastian who had flown into Stansted and caught a train to Liverpool Street where I met him in a café on the concourse. He asked me what might have happened to the missing envelope and I said that it had probably been retained by Janette's boyfriend because he had caught us in bed together. It was a ludicrous fabrication, but Bastian seemed happy enough with my tale of woe and headed back to Stansted to catch his return flight to Karlsruhe/Baden-Baden. Jurgen was on the phone within hours wanting to know about the missing envelope. "Give me my extra tickets," I demanded to which he continued to answer: "We talk about it." But we never did.

Arriving in Germany for the games, I started to get text messages from Jurgen that were becoming increasingly fraught. "Where are the four final tickets?" he demanded. And then: "You are a bad person. FIFA will cancel those tickets. You will be arrested if you try to use them. FIFA will give me duplicates." It was a bit like two criminals falling out over their share of a bank heist, but I knew that Jurgen was in no position to ask any favours of FIFA. So, I carried on but, getting a trifle nervous as the final approached, I did wonder if he might be awaiting me at the entrance to my block in Berlin's Olympiastadion. So, the only thing for it was to exchange those four tickets for four others. I travelled up to Berlin two days after the second semi-final in Munich to find the station swarming with Italians eager to see their team in the final. Some of them were keen on a swop that suited me down to the ground. I was offered four cat 2 tickets plus 1,100 euros in exchange for my four cat 1s. Deal done.

All I had to resolve now was the lucky recipients of those four tickets. There were five takers. I was going to get one, of course and so was Rieko, my Japanese girlfriend who I had left behind in Munich while I sorted out the mess. And then there was Oldham Dave, my Belgian friend Maryan Mahieu and Yann Tear, a fellow journalist who was becoming a good mate. I had to eliminate one person. It was no easy task, but Yann hadn't exactly helped his cause two weeks earlier when I had asked if I could borrow his German rail pass for the week when he was going back home. My son Ben was coming out to Germany for precisely the same period of time. I would hand Yann back his rail pass when Ben returned home. But Yann was not keen. He predicted - wrongly - that I wouldn't be at Dusseldorf's Weeze Airport - which is nowhere near Dusseldorf - to meet him. So that was it. No rail pass equates to no ticket for the final.

The tickets were in two pairs, so Rieko and I took the ones which were in a slightly better position - albeit behind the goal - to the ones which Dave and Maryan used. But everyone was happy and in a mellow mood when we all met up for a post final drink. They were doubly grateful as I hadn't asked them for any money as I considered the 1,100 euros from the Italians as a suitable reimbursement.

But Jurgen was anything but happy. Our row festered for years. Sometimes when we met up, I thought he was over it. But, at other times, it was obvious that he still wanted his pound of flesh. Or cash. He had wild mood swings. We had one nasty meeting at the Gulf Cup in Abu Dhabi in 2007 and another, much nastier, at the 2010 South Africa World Cup after I had climbed Table Mountain. I was planning to climb down again after taking lunch in the café on the summit when Jurgen turned up. He seemed nice enough on arrival and asked me what I was eating as he liked the look of it. He went up to the counter to get himself the same dish and then started up again with the usual: "Where's the £4,000 you owe me?" Once again, I told him that I owed him nothing of the sort, so he started jabbing me in the ribs with his fork. At which point I thought I should beat a hasty retreat so, rather than climb back down the mountain, I made for the cable car.

Things were now openly hostile between us. By the time our paths crossed again at the final a week later, he had made the front pages of South Africa's daily newspapers by getting himself arrested on one of the many flights from Cape Town - the venue for the first semi-final - that never made it on time to Durban for the second semi. My flight was so late that I missed the first 40 minutes of Spain v Germany. Jurgen's plane was diverted to East London. It was all because of FIFA's desperation to accommodate their extended family of sycophants at the game. Their private jets clogged up Durban's King Shaka Airport to the point of suffocation with the result that regular aircraft had no space to land or park. So the kind of people who go to a football match once every four years which happens to be at a World Cup, were inside at the expense of many genuine fans. They were doubtless all still knocking back their free drinks and canapés in the hospitality lounges when the second half resumed.

Meanwhile and with 16 tickets to sell for the Durban game, Jurgen was obviously not best pleased when he heard news of his plane's diversion over the tanoy. He went berserk. There was a skirmish with a steward who suffered a broken wrist. Jurgen was arrested. He saw the game in an East London police station after which he paid a fine and was released. When I found myself sitting uncomfortably close to him at the final, I couldn't resist a little dig. "Did you attack the steward with a fork?" I asked him to which he replied: "For you next time, it will be a knife." The conversation took place in the hearing of Chris who, much amused, forever referred to the German thereafter as "Jurg the fork." Funny that may have sounded but I knew I had to make peace before Jurgen carried

123

out his threat to knife me. I was told that he would be "doing tickets" at the 2012 Olympics in London so I asked him two months before the event if he would like to save himself at least £4,000 in hotel accommodation by staying at my pad for free for the duration of the Games while I moved in with Sally. He gladly accepted my offer but although he rather abused it by inviting all his cronies in to kip on the floor of the lounge in my one-bedroom Wimbledon flat, all was well between us again. They departed leaving a two-foot-high pile of dirty plates stacked up in my sink. The clean-up operation was a small price to pay for the outbreak of peace. And I was alive.

Jurgen had done me no great favours with the tickets he had sold me for Germany. Most of them were for the games I least wanted to see including all three Saudi Arabia group fixtures which, with all due deference to the Saudis, were not on my most wanted list. So, I sold all three tickets onto Oldham Dave who, for a seasoned groundhopper, was not great when it came to thrusting himself into the midst of a heaving throng clustering around a tout. He had been wizzing around the dozen German venues, hurrying from the early game to the afternoon game and onwards to the evening game without having enough readies at his disposal to get into any of them. I couldn't bear to hear any more of his sob stories so I knew that he would, at the very least, see three games. That left me free, would you believe, to concentrate on the Dutch Amateur Cup final in the picturesque hamlet of Ijsselmeervogels Echt. The local club, EVV were staging the final against Voetbalvereniging Altid Sterber Worden Hendrik-ido-Ambacht (which must be one of the longest mouthfuls in global football) so I had an alternative to a World Cup tie even if some would claim that it wasn't much of an alternative. But since I had already sampled one Dutch amateur cup final, I knew that I wouldn't be disappointed by the quality of football. And nor was I. ASWH (for short) were the winners by 3-1.

It was almost time to welcome my son Ben who had flown out for three games for which I had somehow managed to get us both tickets. Berlin was full to bursting with not a single spare room to be had in any hotel, guest house or back packers' hostel until we were directed to a youth hostel which offered us accommodation in addition to swimming facilities in the lake nearby. We saw Brazil beat Croatia 1-0 in the Olympiastadion and then the next day, we drove down to Leipzig for Spain's 4-0 victory over Ukraine on a boiling hot afternoon. We had good seats but on the umpteenth occasion that our view was impeded by a bunch of Australian girls standing up to take selfies of each other, I finally lost my cool to yell at them: "why the fuck can't you watch the game like everyone else?" They promptly sat down and stayed seated thereafter while I earned the gratitude of those nearest us for having the temerity to speak out. World Cups are full of people who just want to tell their mates they've been there with the photographs to prove it. Back in Berlin the next day we took in Sweden's 1-0 win over Paraguay.

Helped by the acquisition of a few tickets I had bought from Maryan, I continued on a tour round Germany's new tech stadiums, most of which I had, of course, visited before. The arguments raged among the hoppers as to whether we were visiting new grounds or not. Some of these stadiums had been renovated and moved slightly with the result that behind-the-goal was now on the side or vice versa. Those debates were similar to those who would nit-pick about Bournemouth's Dean Court ground after it had been turned about face. Were they visiting a new ground or not. Who cares?

There were no such arguments concerning Gelsenkirchen's Veltins-Arena where I was lucky enough to get a ticket for Argentina's group game against Serbia and Montenegro which ended in a 6-0 win for Jose Pekerman's team. Messi rounded off the rout, but the highlight was Esteban Cambiasso's goal, the second, which completed a 24-man passing move - sheer poetry. It was voted goal of the tournament. Argentina looked like possible winners but, alas they were beaten in a quarter-final penalty decider by Germany. Another quarter-final ended with England's customary defeat in a penalty shoot-out at that stage, beaten again by Portugal. I didn't get to any of our games.

Soon after that Rieko was at my side, having taken her annual vacation from her work as a salesgirl in a Japanese store in Hanover Square. I had met her on the party circuit and taken her to a game at Aldershot on our second date when she well and truly got the bug. She had never been to a game before but when I returned from solo trips abroad, I was often told that she had been seen at such and such a non-league match. In true Japanese fashion she liked everything to be neat and tidy which was why she was in her element when it came to dealing with my clutter. She was a godsend when it came to collating thousands of my programmes and memorabilia which had been scattered around what Lissi referred to as "Nick's dirt room" at the top of the former marital home.

Lissi had given me a deadline to clear them out which I just kept, storing them in bin liners that Rieko retrieved from me at her Tooting flat. Ever so diligently she then stacked them in order so that I was left with a separate pile, neatly strung together, for each year dating back to the 1950s when my father's hairdresser had given him his latest batch of unwanted Chelsea programmes every time he came in for a trim. My dad would pass them onto me and so my collection began. I often joke with Lissi that I'll leave her all my programmes in my will.

Rieko's reward for her painstaking hard work was to be treated to the latter stages of the World Cup so I looked forward to welcoming her in Munich when she flew in for the second semi-final. I got off lightly for it was absurdly cheap and easy to purchase tickets outside the Alliance Arena which I was visiting for the first time, for the France v Portugal game. That was a relief after the expense of obtaining a ticket the night before in Dortmund for the Germany v Italy blockbuster semi-final. But in the end I could have few complaints as I was seated over a corner flag at the end where Italy scored their two late goals.

With a free day on the Thursday, I was indebted to Ian Seymour for finding us a pre-season friendly - or testspiel -even if we did have to take the train 175 miles to the delightful city of Wurzburg whose Oberliga team, the Wurzburger Kickers were hosting Mainz 05's Bundesliga giants. The visitors could have come by boat as a lovely stretch of the River Main flows behind the stadium. Glancing at the river from time to time, I was periodically distracted from the game which Mainz won 2-0.

In the need to keep costs down, I told Rieko to retain the outward half of her train ticket from Munich for use on her subsequent 5hr train journey from Munich to Berlin. I urged her to proffer the Munich to Wurzburg ticket to the inspector when he came calling, plead ignorance and pretend not to understand a word when he demanded an extra payment. Good girl, she did as she was told with the result that the exasperated inspector finally gave up on trying to extract any extra euros out of her and permitted her to stay on the train. I knew that wasn't the most chivalrous gesture on my part but needs must ...

By then I was in Berlin too, having found the perfect solution to our personal ticket dilemma regarding entry to the final. I went to that France v Italy denouement disguised under an Argentinian baseball-type cap for fear of being spotted by Jurgen. Even if our seats had been the best, I doubt that we would have noticed the game's most controversial moment, the one when Zidane headbutted Marco Materazzi in the stomach. Even the referee missed it but an eagle-eyed linesman had seen the incident which led to the 14th dismissal of Zidane's illustrious career. Along with Cameroon's excellent defender Rigobert Song, he became the only player to be sent off in two World Cups. I often wonder how a player with a record like that can become a successful manager when, among other duties, he has to tell his men to keep cool and avoid provocation. However, Zidane hasn't done a bad job as Real Madrid's coach. And yet on the field, he hadn't exactly set a good example.

126

Coincidentally both players had scored the game's only two goals, Zidane putting France ahead from the penalty spot, Materazzi equalising with a header from Andrea Pirlo's corner, all within the first 20 minutes. And so, for the second time in four World Cups, the winners had to be decided by the lottery of a shoot-out. Italy had, of course, lost this way in 1994 but now they were triumphant as Trezeguet hit the bar with the second French attempt to thereby suffer the nadir of his career so soon after its zenith against the same opponents. For years afterwards there were conflicting accounts of what exactly Materazzi had said to Zidane, but the most credible version was that the Italian had made a derogatory remark about Zidane's girlfriend rather than his sister or mother.

Chapter 31:
Suzie one frock

With three major tournaments to squeeze in, 2007 was going to be every bit as hectic as 2004. I had not really warmed to the Middle East, but the Gulf Cup had nevertheless still been jotted down in my new diary. The possibility of a trip materialised when I discovered that the United Arab Emirates hosts were using only two stadiums, both in Abu Dhabi. Furthermore, the schedule permitted me to get to both of them and not miss a Palace match. Or so I thought. I flew to the UAE after Palace's 1-1 draw with Hull knowing that I could take in two double headers at the Zayed Sports City Stadium and the Mohammed bin Zayed Stadium. Thanks to my previous trip to Muscat with Judy, Oman had earned a place in my affection and I was therefore pleased to witness their 2-1 win over Yemen. UAE overcame Kuwait 3-2 in the next game. With Judy continuing to make use of the hotel swimming pool the next day, I took in Bahrain's 2-1 success over Qatar and Saudi Arabia's 1-0 victory against Iraq. With the weather now overcast and the prospect of a day by the pool much less appealing, I was doubly grateful to Markus Linke - one of a host of German hoppers - for finding an alternative to sight-seeing. Markus can always be relied on in such situations. He had discovered that one of the local league clubs, Al Ain had a game on the Thursday afternoon. It was a desultory encounter in the almost deserted Khalifa Bin Zayed Stadium, but a game is a game is a game, we consoled ourselves as we helped ourselves to more of the goodies intended for dignitaries in dishdashas.

My plan then was to hurry back for Palace's FA Cup fourth round date with Preston which I was due to cover for the Observer. But thanks to our connecting flight from Bahrain being delayed by 12 hours, I had to ring Brian Oliver, who was now the Ob's sports editor, to tell him that I was stranded in another continent. Frustration kicked in. And it didn't go away. There is nothing worse for a football addict than to arrive back in Heathrow on a Saturday night and get on the tube to see fans in scarfs returning from games, knowing that you have missed out on the action. It is even worse when you have missed your favourite team's match. Worse still when you could have made money out of it. Brian had to delegate someone else to cover Palace's 2-0 exit from the Cup. At least I hadn't missed us winning.

As a prelude to the Copa America, I had gone to almost the opposite geographical extreme by flying to the Faroe Islands with Rieko on making the joyful discovery that the hosts were using both their national stadiums for a double header of Euro qualifiers against Italy and Scotland. This was manna from heaven as the Faroes are a tricky and expensive place to reach once, let alone twice. In those days you could only travel via Copenhagen as the Faroes, midway between Scotland and Iceland, are under the external sovereignty of Denmark.

Torshavn's Torsvollur Stadium, the scene of Italy's stumbling 2-1 win, is a pleasant enough ground but it doesn't compare for incredulity with Toftir's Svangaskard Stadium, constructed on a hilltop overlooking a fjord. It's a revelation, as spectacular as Alesund's former home in Norway. The sight of hundreds of Scots in their kilts, carrying their wee drams in one hand and clinging onto tufts of grass with the other as they took short cuts by ascending the steep slopes, was another one to behold. We had got to the island of Eysturoy on a boat buckling under the weight of its extra cargo of booze that had been transported on board by the visiting clans, most of them clad in their tamoshanters. With a 2-0 win to celebrate, those fans were in even better spirits on the homeward boat ride.

One bonus of the whole escapade was the charming bed and breakfast abode, just walking distance from the centre of Torshavn, where Rieko and I spent those four nights. The other bonus was the match we hit upon to occupy us on the Sunday, also in Eysturoy, one of the 18 islands that form the archipelago. I could hardly believe our luck when we were informed of that friendly in the Surpugeroi Stadium in Nororagota which is home now to the Vikingur Gota club, a product of a merger involving G Gota and Leirvik IF. The backdrop was of Eysturoy's forbidding hills, half obscured by clouds. On this occasion we took the bus to reach the island. With time at my disposal, I think I'd always prefer that winding, scenic route of over an hour, to the 12-minute journey that can be undertaken now through the recently completed Eysturoy Tunnel.

We spent one of our spare days on a tourist boat jaunt circling the islands, gawping at the gravity-defying ability of the sheep grazing on the mountainous slopes. If those creatures weren't so nimble, they would tumble into the waves. No wonder the Faroes derived from old Norse terminology of Foroyar which means Sheep Islands, a name chosen by Viking Age settlers. With a six-hour stop-off in Copenhagen on the way home, we found a restaurant on the water's edge for a traditional Danish lunch.

The climate and arenas of the northeastern tip of South America three weeks later were quite a contrast to those of the north east Atlantic. Rieko

129

joined me in Venezuela for what turned out to be her one and only Copa. She was travelling extremely light, carrying only the bare minimum of clothes. She had a favourite dress which she would don so often that Martin dubbed her "Suzie one frock." She liked nothing better than to shock her audience. On the frequent occasions when she got down to breakfast first, she would, unbeknown to me, regale the lads with tales of what kind of a night we'd spent. If it was not "nice fuck last night," it was "no fuck last night, Nick too tired." So, invariably there were smirks all round when I descended for my first meal of the day.

From the first time they met her in the car on the way to Selhurst Park, my kids were certain that Rieko was on some drug or other. I rubbished their notions, but they were proved right when she eventually owned up to weekly visits to her supplier in Islington for pills. For all that she was engaging company. When my Dad was in his dotage she asked me if she could do a striptease for him. I deterred her for fear of a heart attack pushing him over the edge. When we began to fall out because her friend Yuki had taken a shine to me, Rieko would tell anyone within hearing range, especially those she had never met like the doorman at the Spurs club shop: "He fuck my friend." The doorman stood there with a bewildered look on his face.

With a record nine venues spread far and wide, Venners as it became known, represented quite a challenge. As did the various sights we wanted to take in. On a visit to the Bolivia v Uruguay (0-1) and Venezuela v Peru (2-0) double header in San Cristobal near the Colombian order, we stopped off on the way back for Peru v Bolivia (2-2) and Venezuela v Uruguay (0-0) in Merida, a city celebrated for its famous cable car. I have never been so terrified as I was that day on the Teleferico de Merida especially when our car stopped for no good reason for about ten minutes when halfway across the 500-yard divide which is 5,380 feet up. It was spectacular alright, but it must also provide the kind of thrill usually reserved for those of us with a death wish.

On the other side of the country was another attraction which we linked to the Mexico v Chile (0-0) and Brazil v Ecuador (1-0) double header in Puerto la Cruz. That port also just happens to be the gateway to Margarita Island. A two-hour ferry ride away, it's a resort high on any intrepid traveller's list of essential places to see. Colombus had discovered the island in 1498 and the wonder was that he ever moved on from its golden sandy beaches.

Among our party was an old friend, Danny Murphy, a Millwall fan who had suddenly stumbled upon us from out of the blue. He is a lovely bloke, a bit of a lost soul who often scrapes together the funds to go to the other side of the world for a game, fortified by drinking the day away with

130

the locals. Whatever the temperatures in Venners, he usually wore a scruffy, baggy suit that had seen better days. He is prone to sleeping rough or extremely cheaply so there were times he had to be led to the nearest bathhouse before his suit walked there for him. He hardly ever saw Millwall play as he preferred the obscurity of the lesser lights. The last time I saw him was at a Boodles Cup tie at Brighton College.

Danny regaled us with his latest tales on the boat ride to Margarita and joined us for a few games before disappearing as suddenly as he had appeared. By then we were heading for the semi-final at Cuidad Guayana where Messi held us spellbound with a goal that was not only voted goal of the tournament but was surely one of the best in the catalogue of great Messi goals. It came with an audacious chip over the head of the Mexican goalkeeper Oswaldo Sanchez from a position where it seemed impossible to score. "Only a genius could do that," said Argentina's coach Alfio Basile. Messi's goal helped Argentina to a 3-0 win which put them into another Copa final with Brazil who had improved drastically after starting out with a 2-0 loss to Mexico. Brazil reached the final by beating Uruguay in yet another penalty shootout after they had finished level at 1-1.

Cuidad Guayana was only a short stop from Puerto Ordaz from where we caught a light plane to view the famous Angel Falls, another place high on the list of Venezuela's tourist hot spots. The waters which spill from the top of the Anyan-tepui mountain, were discovered, so rumour originally had it, by Sir Walter Raleigh when he was searching for El Dorado. Aren't we all? However, the locals weren't ever convinced about Sir Walter's claim to fame so a certain American aviator by the name of Jimmie Angel is credited with the first sighting in 1933. Four years later, after landing his Flamingo monoplane on the plateau at the top, he was unable to take off again because the plane's wheels were stuck in marshland. It took his party a week to get down to civilisation. His plane was finally retrieved by helicopter in 1974. By then the Falls had long since been named in his honour but I did wonder what all the fuss was about as those Falls certainly weren't in the same league as Iguazu which we had visited eight years earlier. Still, it made for a pleasant day out.

With the final approaching, Rieko and I joined the main party heading back to Maracaibo for the final. Chris, Steve and Martin - who was by now known as 'dos metros' for his height of 6ft 5ins - decided to risk a visit to Caracas for the third place final. Rieko and I had stopped off there often enough for connecting flights to the various venues but the capital - which was staging its one game of the Copa - has such an unenviable reputation as a haven for muggings, murders and general criminal activity that I thought I could afford to depart this Copa one short of a maximum nine ticks. The lack of any flight back to Maracaibo in time for the final was a further persuasive factor not to join the intrepid trio. They were faced with an overnight 11-hour coach journey if they were going to make it. As soon as I saw them in the foyer of our hotel on the morning of the final, I knew that I had made the right decision. They looked like death warmed up. Of course, they were quick to inform the rest of us what a treat we had missed and how brilliantly Mexico had performed to beat Uruguay 3-1 and what a great evening they had enjoyed in Caracas. Pull the other one.

After the majesty of the 2004 final to which Argentina had contributed so gallantly, the 2007 version was a distinct disappointment. The 20-year-old Messi was a subdued figure and with an early goal from Julio Baptista, an own goal by Roberto Ayala and a third from substitute Dani Alves, Brazil cruised to a comfortable 3-0 win. Even with six starters from 2004, Argentina were inexplicably awful. After the game, we returned to the hotel. I dallied in reception saying my farewells. I got back to our room to find Rieko systematically going through the contact list on my mobile phone which I had left charging up on the floor. Our days were numbered after that.

Chapter 32:
Getting my dong out

I had to fly from Maracaibo to Santiago at the start of my marathon journey to Vietnam for the Asia Cup. It was while I was in the departure lounge in the Chilean capital that I got involved in a needless row with a fellow passenger that culminated with him being removed from the flight. I had been at the desk asking about meal times on board or some such nonsense when an obnoxious Aussie behind me started telling me to get a move-on. Departure time was still an hour away, but his impatience escalated and he blew his top with the result that, I too, lost my cool. Witnesses took my side as the innocent party so, he very much the instigator, was led away by burly security staff. So far as I was concerned, the saving grace to the altercation was that I could now get my mind off worrying about the inevitable repercussions to Rieko's scheming.

It seemed like I had been travelling for days when I eventually pitched up in Hanoi, one of two Vietnamese venues for the event which, for the first time, was being staged in four different countries, the others being Indonesia, Thailand and Malaysia. As previous lesser tournaments had already led me into the main stadiums of Bangkok and Kuala Lumpur, I had decided to give Thailand and Malaysia a miss and concentrate this time on the ensuing games in Vietnam and Indonesia. As it happens, it was an easy decision as the competition was by now at the quarter-final stage. The Indy, who were among those giving me work, took my report on Japan's 1-1 draw with Australia who were making their bow in the championships after leaving the Oceanic Federation, primarily because they had little to beat apart from, perhaps the Kiwis on a good day. But with Japan prevailing 4-3 in the shoot-out, Australia - who had already lost a group game to Iraq - were quick to discover that there would be no easy pickings this time.

Eva, a German flautist who had tempted me from the moment we had met over the breakfast counter in an Austrian hotel a few months earlier, flew in to join me. Luckily she was, like Rieko, a decent runner, so for a couple of nights we completed a few swift circuits of the Hoan Kiem lake which is the focal point of Hanoi's old town. To do so, we virtually had to take our lives into our own hands as Hanoi's scooter drivers seem to target every foreign pedestrian as if he was an American soldier who had served in the War in Vietnam. But, having survived, we could fulfil our plans to take a bus up to Hon Gai from where we had booked a three-night, two-day stay aboard a boat in Halong Bay which is surely one of the most idyllic places on earth. I will forever treasure memories of its enchanting beauty. We swam from the boat, ate delicious fish cooked by the boat's chef and on one occasion disembarked on an island where bicycles were awaiting us for a 6-mile ride inland. But saddle soreness has always been my enemy so, along with one of the Australian brothers we had befriended on board, I elected to run to the café which was our lunchtime rendezvous. He was a much younger man, so I was delighted to leave him trailing in my wake.

Returning somewhat reluctantly to Hanoi, I reported on Japan's 3-2 defeat in their semi-final by Saudi Arabia in the impressive Mi Dnih Stadium before Eva and I rounded off our Vietnamese adventure by travelling south of the city to a complex offering rides around its narrow waterways in boats the size of large canoes. Our navigators were a mother and daughter crew who became ardent saleswomen the moment they paused for breath at the halfway stage. They were intent on selling us a tablecloth from the pile that had been secreted at the front of the craft. Eva was incensed by what she saw as a cheap stunt. But the mother wanted payment, so I got out my dong. I sensed that it would be unwise to give Eva the tablecloth the next Christmas. Maybe we had fallen into the same tourist trap as every other passenger on every other boat on this quaint canal system but with signs of poverty all around us, I was happy to part with some Vietnamese currency. Her anger had subsided by the time we left the next day for Indonesia where we hired a driver who took us on an extended tour that included a visit to one of the nation's main tea-producing plantations. As an avid tea drinker of many years standing, I was fascinated.

Eva was a sweet natured girl but alongside Athena and Christine, she must rank as one of my life's loves who least liked football. One balmy night in Odense she had walked away from a Europa League Cup tie against Motherwell at half-time to explore the Danish city. On another occasion when I had gone to see her in Cologne for a long weekend, I was dismayed by her fierce objections to my plans for Bundesliga div 2 and 3 games on the Friday, Saturday and Sunday. The last two would have been afternoon matches leaving the evenings free for me to wine and dine her. In the end I gave in and we compromised on just one game, the Koln v Borussia Mönchengladbach derby thriller in the Rhein Energie Stadion with which I was already acquainted. I defy anyone not to be moved by the tune of 'Mer ston zo dir, FC Kolle' (we stand by you, FC Koln) which is a direct lift of the Scottish folk song, 'The bonnie banks o Loch Lomond.' It greets the players as they emerge. Koln's players should feel ten feet tall and yet their record over recent years has not been impressive.

With Eva's grumbles in Indonesia starting to mount up, I was not too upset when the time came for her departure from Jakarta. I was bound for Palembang which was the venue for the Asia Cup's third place match. Such games are usually expendable but not when they're taking place in such exotic locations as the capital of Sumatra. Japan versus South Korea was no great spectacle but the penalties, resolved 6-5 in the Koreans' favour, were dramatic. I returned to Jakarta on the same flight as an old pal, John Bethell, a hopper who was in the midst of putting us all to shame with his feats of endurance, many of which took him the length of Siberia for games. He seemed to have a particular liking for the fragmented USSR.

However, the destiny for both of us that Saturday night in 2007 was Jakarta's massive Gelora Bung Kamo Stadium where Iraq were taking on the Saudis in the final. As my first misguided loyalty was still towards the Telegraph, I offered them a report which they seemed happy enough to accept. Imagine my fury then when I bought the paper on my return to London to see that my carefully scripted 400 words had been reduced to a measly caption underneath a large action photograph. Considering that Iraq was at war and that their footballers had been unable to prepare at home, I thought that they had done well to qualify for the tournament let alone win it. Under their Brazilian coach Jorvan Vieira, their shock triumph was on the same scale as Greece's uprising three years earlier. Vieira's men dominated the final, succeeding 1-0 with a header from Younis Mahmoud. I thought they were worth decent coverage. I could, I told the Tel, have given my report instead to a paper with a better news sense such as the Indy or Guardian had they told me what they had in mind. I had to battle to get my match fee. The weird and sometimes not so wonderful machinations of newspaper editors are something which confound us all. Some hacks react better than others when their painstaking efforts are abused or spiked.

My anger had long since dissipated by the autumn when my spirits soared on spotting an Italian midweek league programme. It meant sacrificing Palace's Monday night game with Watford but as Palace appeared to be going nowhere in the championship following the recent sacking of Peter Taylor, I set forth with Rieko for Sicily. Our relationship was in its dying embers, but she was still enthusiastic company, never more so than when games beckoned. She had, after all, accompanied me to a match at Aldershot on our second date. This guy certainly knows how to treat a girl! So we flew to Palermo and with a combination of buses and trains, made our way to Catania for their Serie A game in the evening with Sampdoria. Catania's ultras had been blamed for the death of a policeman when he tried to break up a battle with their Palermo counterparts. Football in Italy was briefly suspended and now, less than nine months later and despite the hosts' 2-0 win, a negative atmosphere still hung over the Stadio Angelo Massimino, a disappointing arena surrounded by a running track.

The next day was sadly devoid of a live game, so we made our way up the coast to Messina. The idea, on the recommendation of Jurgen, was to take a look at the local club's former inner city Stadio Comunale Giovanni Celeste. It was all chained up and there was no one about to let us in, so using our initiative, we found a residential building with an open front door. We took a lift up to the top floor from where we had a fine view of the empty 12,000 capacity ground. How I wished we could have seen a game there. I could understand why Jurgen had raved about it. Hemmed in by apartment blocks, this tight stadium seemed so much more conducive to a lively contest than the modern Stadio Comunale San Filippo where we saw Messina Peloro lose 2-0 to Vicenza in a desperately uninspiring Serie B match the next evening.

We took a ferry to the mainland the morning after as the fixtures had certainly come up trumps. Reggina, based in the port of Reggio di Calabria, were at home that evening in another Serie A game, to Livorno who were 3-1 winners. Reggina's stay in Serie A was not to last and the Sicilian pair have since fallen on hard times too. Catania were relegated following proven charges of match fixing and Messina's descent, all the way to Serie D came after the club went bankrupt. It all seems par for the course in Italy, the land of footballing scandals.

With no apparent game to fill our time on the Thursday, we were killing time over breakfast in one of Reggio di Calabria's coffee bars while I perused the pink un, or La Gazzetta dello Sport to use its proper title, which is the nation's daily sports paper. To my surprise, I noticed a raft of fixtures listed on one of the pages. My eyes lit up. The bar owner spoke no English, but I managed to convey my desperation to him. He managed to confirm that "si" there were indeed games on that afternoon in Lega Pro 2, the fourth tier. Unbeknown to us, it was All Saints' Day, a public holiday in Italy. Which was the nearest "proxima" club to where we were now? He pointed to Vigor Lamezia who play in the town of Lamezia Terme about 110 miles north. There was only one way of getting there. With the bar owner's help, we managed to hire a Fiat in world record time and dash up the A3 autostrada and enter the Stadio D'Ipplito just as the teams came out. The game with Cassino was a surprisingly skilful affair which the home team won 1-0. Mind you, any game would have been a good one in the circumstances. It was my luck that I had Rieko with me rather than another woman who might have insisted that I honour my promise for a day of sight-seeing. The sight-seeing came the next day, when back in Sicily, we took the Circumetnea train on its 68-mile route through the pistachio groves from Catania. It takes three mesmerising hours to inch its way around the base of Mount Etna which was fortunately not spewing forth just then. With more time at our disposal, we would have stopped off for lunch in one of the vantage-point restaurants in Riposto, the terminus. But we had to catch the bus to Palermo for our homeward flight.

Chapter 33:
The enormous shadow

My abiding memory of the 2008 European Championships is not of the football but that they coincided with my dad being on his death bed. I was all for getting shot of my tickets and giving the games a miss so as to stay with him, but he implored me to go to Switzerland and Austria who were acting as co-hosts. "Don't be a mug. Of course, I'll be all right," he insisted. So, with a heavy heart I went, consoling myself with the thought that he was still capable, even at his ripe old age of 98, of flirting with the two decorative black South African girls who were his carers. I flew back three times to see him. But with such a pre-occupation, it was hard to enjoy the tournament even though Spain did their utmost to cheer me up.

England were absentees because they had succumbed to Croatia in a crucial qualifier on the rain-soaked night when poor Steve McClaren earned his "wally with the brolly," tag when it was tipping down. Poor sod, I thought, what's he supposed to do, stand there and get soaked. There's no pleasing some people. I had not been at Wembley to witness McClaren's demise as that fixture had clashed with Northern Ireland's visit to Las Palmas for another qualifier. And I hadn't done Las Palmas. With Sally in tow, we were initially misled on asking directions to the media tribunes in the Estadio Gran Canaria with the result that we ended up in a box reserved for policia and security staff. Towards half-time I received a tap on the shoulder, followed by instructions telling me that we should go elsewhere to watch the second half. Sally was paranoid at the best of times and claimed nonsensically during a blazing row that we would be arrested. She threatened to leave the stadium. I told her that we were locked in. Maybe I should have let her go as she remained full of grumpiness throughout the rest of Spain's 1-0 win even though there were no further taps on the shoulder or suggestions that we should vacate the empty press cabin in which we were now ensconced. Xavi's goal, deflected off the head of Stephen Craignan, led to Ireland's exit.

My devotion towards Real Mallorca had helped fuel my affection for the Spanish national team as Daniel Guiza, the Mallorca striker was now an integral member of Luis Aragones' squad. Guiza was a character. I loved his goal celebrations. He would get down on one knee and aim an imaginary rifle into the middle distance. With Spain based in Austria and me spending the first part of the championship finals in Switzerland, I

138

had to wait patiently for my first live view of them in action. Portugal's 2-0 win over Turkey in Geneva and Holland's crushing 3-0 victory over Italy in Bern, sweet revenge for their 2000 semi-final defeat, were my personal highlights among the early games before I saw Peter Cech's calamitous mistake lead to elimination for the Czechs in a 3-2 defeat by Turkey in Geneva. And all the while EasyJet were benefitting from my custom as I was rushing back and forth to Godstone to see my Dad who was weakening by the minute. But still he insisted that I should return to the football although he had precious little idea now as to who or what I was watching. I returned from one trip back to Surrey to see Guiza's 88th minute goal give Spain a 2-1 win over Greece, the defending champions who thus went out without a single point from their group games. A hero one minute, Otto Rehhagel, their German coach, was now despised in Athens and beyond.

Transport was a simple matter with trains in that part of Europe living up to their reputations for punctuality, speed, tidiness and delicious meals in the restaurant car. Furthermore, those of us with match tickets could travel free of charge. But it was on the one occasion when Chris, Steve and I were forced to rely on a lift from Oldham Dave after that Spain v Greece match in Salzburg that our frustrations nearly got the better of us. Charming bloke that he is, confirmation came then that Dave doesn't take kindly to being given advice or being told what to do. We probably sat in that Wais-Siezenheim Stadium car park for an hour longer than necessary because of his resentment at our recommendations as to how he should ease his way towards the exit without his bodywork getting scratched. With the rest of us fuming in the passenger seats, he refused to budge until there was nothing else for it but to drive out of the car park after just about every other car had left.

The competition was now in its later stages and I timed my arrival in Vienna to coincide with Spain's 3-0 semi-final win over Russia in which Guiza scored again. He didn't add to his tally in the final but no matter, I was delighted to be the right end for a perfect view of Fernando Torres speeding onto Xavi's exquisite pass and bearing down on Jan Lehmann's goal. Torres slotted away and Spain resisted all Germany's subsequent pressure to herald a six-year domination of world and European football.

Ideally, I would have rushed straight back to my father's bedside, but I had long since promised Ben that I would help him transport his luggage from Bologna where he had been at university. So I took the overnight train from Vienna, collected my son's remaining bags and caught a flight from Forli to Stansted. For fear of hearing the worst, I dared not ring home so, in a panic I recovered my car and dashed to

Godstone to find that my Dad had died earlier that morning. I was comforted by Jackie, one of the careers who told me that the conversation I'd had with him a few days previously had been the last meaningful one he'd had with anyone.

Two days after my father's funeral, Sally and I set forth for the European Under 19 championships. England, under Paul Simpson's tutelage, were competing so I got some work. With the Czech Republic acting as hosts, there was an extra bonus as I had done few grounds outside of Prague. Group B was going to be centred on the twin towns, barely eight miles apart, of Jablonec and Liberec, both homes to top league clubs. There was something rather forbidding about Liberec which was, geographically, our first point of inspection so after a brief look around on a rainy Sunday afternoon, we drove onto Jablonec. The need for a base near a decent place to run was uppermost in my mind so Jablonec got an immediate vote as the town was altogether more appealing and what's more, we happened upon a pension overlooking the Mseno reservoir which had paths encircling it, perfect for running.

England's performances were less than perfect, however. Simpson's team lost the opening game 2-0 to the Czechs and a goalless draw against Italy in the next group fixture meant that a big win was required against Greece in Liberec if we were to progress. England did win 3-0 with goals from Ben Mee, Freddie Sears - who was soon to join Palace - and Daniel Sturridge but it was not quite enough to earn a semi-final place as the Czechs had only lost by 4-3 to Italy, giving them an identical goal difference to us but, crucially they had scored more goals.

I didn't let our elimination and subsequent loss of work depress me too much as Slovakia's Superliga early-season fixture list was throwing up all kinds of intriguing prospects to bridge the gaps between semi-finals and final. Both Bratislava clubs, Slovan and Inter, who are less than a mile apart, conveniently staggered their home games one hot afternoon but with the road map I had purchased focusing mainly on the Czech Republic's historical points of interest - such as castles which we had visited - I had little idea of how to get us to a small town staging another game. The cabbies at Bratislava Station seemed unduly reluctant to help until I found one wanting - and getting - a larger than usual fare for the 30-mile drive to the stadium belonging to newly promoted Dunajaska Streda. As the previous season's western league champions, they had suddenly found themselves thrust among Slovakia's elite through a merger with FC Senec.

The choice of Plzen as a venue for the Italy v Hungary semi-final was also an enticing one so far as I was concerned as the stadium represented virgin territory as did the club's famous sponsors. The brewery and visitors' centre is a must for anyone with a taste for ale. Italy won the game by a single goal but they, too, had to return to Jablonec for the final which they lost 3-1 to Germany under a brightly setting sun.

There was barely time to acquaint myself with Palace's early season fixtures before my travels resumed in earnest. Utilising an international weekend free of a Palace fixture, I took off again for Australia for my other son James' wedding to Angelina, the girl he had met in the Fremantle disco. As I had always wanted to see the Kakadu National Park, Sally and I flew via Darwin to Melbourne. We also visited a war graves cemetery but, alas, the Northern Territory is not a hotbed for football so no games in that state could be streamlined into our programme. Fortunately, that was not the case when we carried on south for the wedding as the Victorian State League was in full season. There was an incredibly helpful guy behind the information desk at Melbourne's Flinders Station where our hikes to the likes of South Melbourne, Altona East and Heidelberg United invariably began. So frequent were our requests over the next couple of weekends that he labelled us "the socceroonies." Many of those clubs were, like Floreat Athena in West Australia, of Greek origin. But then there was Albion Rovers who had been founded by Albanian immigrants and Dandenong who were started by Croats.

We headed almost straight back to the UK after James had married Angelina as, alas, there was not a single midweek game in Asia to tempt me. I got back in time to see Palace lose at home to Plymouth. Typical.

Chapter 34:
A controversial sleeping remedy

The 2009 Gulf Cup in Oman had been inked in for a while. It could be neatly woven around a visit with Judy to her best friend, Jan who was based in Muscat with her ex-Army colonel husband, Mikey who had also been at Westminster School, albeit after me. That was about all we had in common since he was not a football man, more of a whisky drinker. I had the odd glass while he downed several. He had been in the Argyll and Sutherland Highlanders before being delegated to train the Omani forces. Manik, the couple's talkative houseboy, regaled me with stories from his native Bangladesh while I ate the dinner's leftovers that had been kindly left out for me on my returns from double-headers in both the competition's venues, the Sultan Qaboos Sports Complex and the Royal Oman Police Stadium. Not for the first time in my life, I then saw a final go to a penalty shoot-out. The hosts overcame the Saudis 6-5 after a goalless 120 minutes.

The rest of 2009 proved the fallowest of fallow years with no major tournaments catching the eye. Which left the way clear for a trip to Dublin which is home to a handful of clubs in the League of Ireland who do, thank goodness, play their games during the summer months. Fitting in visits to the likes of Dundalk, Drogheda and Bohemians around a couple of weekend visits to Sally's friend Mary, we ventured forth, even across the border to Dungannon on one occasion. But still the rest of the summer yawned ahead and with my resurrected interest in cricket yet to surface, Australia beckoned once more as I had only seen Ashley, my youngest son, briefly at James' wedding.

Sally's friend, Hicham was now living in Singapore so where better than there for a stop-off, I surmised, especially if the S-League could oblige me with a fixture. As I was by now a slave to the Soccerway website, I scanned the possibilities and found that Geylang's home game with Woodlands would coincide nicely with our planned itinerary. While Sally and Hicham gossiped away the evening, I traipsed most of the way along the city's Mass Rapid Transit system to find a nondescript stadium where I joined a sparse crowd who saw a 4-0 home win.

Flying onto Melbourne the next day, we based ourselves in the city's lively St Kilda district, which is a decent run away from Albert Park, the home not only of Australia's grand prix races over the years but of South Melbourne FC, another club with Greek origins. Most of the games in the

Victoria State League take place in front of dilapidated stands on what are known as Reserves in the middle of protected areas for nature. But the Lakeside Stadium that I ran past every morning on my daily sorties from our cheap hotel was a class apart. I knew I had to take in a game there as well as sampling the atmosphere of an A-League fixture at Melbourne Victory who were captained by the former Palace full back Kevin Muscat. They also had in their attack the legendary Archie Thompson who once scored five goals in a game.

Taking our leave of James and Angelina, we flew onto Sydney for some quality time with Ashley whose girlfriend Alexandra had decidedly expensive tastes. I treated them to lunch at Criniti's Italian restaurant on the edge of Darling Harbour where she went the whole hog, ordering without any apparent qualms an aperitif, appetiser, the most expensive main course on the menu, a desert and a liqueur. She clearly regarded me as a wealthy prospective father-in-law with a much fatter wallet than the one I actually carried so I was not too dismayed when he ditched her a few years later although she was extremely easy on the eye.

The fixture secretary of The New South Wales State League had not seen fit to greet my visit with a flurry of midweek games, let alone a single one, so I could now concentrate on starting my journey home alone as Sally was flying off to Malibu to see her sister. I was embarking not by plane but by train as it was now seven long years since my last marathon rail voyage on the Trans-Siberian. For train buffs like me, The Indian Pacific is as much an essential part of life's rich tapestry, so it was around the sacrilegious hour of 3pm on a Saturday that I boarded the express at Sydney Central station. Once again, I was lucky enough to be told that I had a two-berth cabin to myself, so I sat down to enjoy the first leg of the marathon trek taking us past the resort of Katoomba which I recalled fondly from an earlier visit to its famous Three Sisters rock formation at Echo Point in the Blue Mountains.

However, with nightfall coinciding inconveniently with the approach of those peaks, the route was not conducive to a decent night's kip. The train rattled slowly up and down every incline, creaking and groaning its way round each agonising bend as I struggled in vain for some much-needed shut-eye. I vowed that the scenario would not be repeated on nights two and three of my passage towards Perth. The train's bar sold only beer and wine, not strong enough I reckoned to induce a peaceful night's sleep so when we stopped at Adelaide the next day for four hours, I made for the nearest bottle shop. I bought a small bottle of my favourite Glenmorangie whisky which I smuggled aboard as I was aware of the house rule that only the train's grog could be drunk on board.

I am not a great one for knocking back neat whisky so that evening I ordered some ice at the bar. They didn't have ice, so I asked for a Coca Cola which was forthcoming. As I sat down with my meal, one of the train's supervisors asked me what I was drinking. I told him "Coke." A little later a lady in uniform came along and asked me the same question. "Coke," I said "but why does everyone want to know what I am drinking?"

"Let me smell it," she replied, which she promptly did, pressing my glass to her nose. "There's whisky in there," she said. "You are only allowed to buy the alcohol we sell on the train and we don't sell whisky. Where's the whisky bottle?"

"You're too late," I lied. "The man collecting the rubbish has just been along and taken the empty bottle." The empty bottle was, in fact, nestling between my shoes. She went away tut tutting furiously while people around me were getting merry on the train's cheap booze. And there was I sitting quietly. The next morning as I enjoyed a cup of tea with my breakfast fry-up, she entered the restaurant car again only to studiously blank me when I waved my teacup at her, asking if she wanted to sniff the beverage. I kept the whisky bottle well concealed in my cabin after that episode which reflected sadly, I thought, on my expenditure on the trip which was not a bargain.

There are some people who think that endless views of the Nullarboor Plain are monotonous, especially if a train is required to go 297 miles in a straight line across it, which is a world record, but I found the panorama riveting, all the more so when I spotted camels in the distance. There was a fascinating halt for re-fuelling at Cook, an outpost in the Outback which once boasted a population of 50 until nationalisation of the railways reduced it to a paltry quartet. The Western Australian goldmining centre of Kalgoorlie was, like Adelaide, another obvious choice for a city tour on our last night. And so, the train rumbled on towards its terminus of East Perth. Taking the specially inscribed Indian Pacific bedspread with me as recompense for the pathetic scene in the restaurant car, I flew home with my souvenir the next day as there was nothing in the West Australian State League to detain me.

There was still plenty to cram in before the season started. The venue for the NatWest Island Games was the intriguing tourist resort of Aland which belongs to Finland though it is much nearer Sweden. Aland was a tempting enough spot for Eva to get over her aversion to football, so I met her at Stockholm and we took the bus up the coast to the ferry port of Kappelskar which serves Mariehamn, Aland's capital. We stayed in a shack in the woods owned by a chap who, Eva was convinced, was spying on her when she took her morning showers in the outside unit. We

144

surmounted that hurdle to enjoy the rest of the week, helped by the island's rich mix of restaurants and, for me, its six football venues, including the stage for the final, the modest home of IFK Mariehamn, a top Finnish League club. It was there that I saw Jersey beat the hosts 2-1 in a game that I reported for the Non-League Paper. Jersey have since, of course, been admitted to the Combined Counties League where they swept aside all their first division opponents until Covid19 dashed their hopes of a record-breaking 100 per cent opening campaign.

Exhausting all Aland's football possibilities must have got the better of Eva for she never joined me on another football caper. We went our separate ways at Berlin. She was heading back home to Cologne while I was flying south to Sardinia for a make-it or break-it holiday with Judy with whom I had come to a deal. I would get divorced if she gave up smoking. I had kept my side of the bargain, but she failed miserably. She wasn't best pleased when I rang her to tell her I had missed my flight to Olbia thanks to being told by the check-in girl to join another queue because I was over the luggage allowance. After being turned back at the departure gate I went back to remonstrate with the check-in girl, little caring at that point that she was a real looker, blonde and curvaceous. "You might have told me that I'd miss my flight by getting in the other queue," I said angrily. She was probably more used to softly spoken Brits buttering her up and saying "can I have your number sweetheart" so, suitably impressed perhaps by my admonishment, she came to find me when her shift was over. I was calming down over a glass of orange juice and croissant in one of the airport's cafes.

"What are you going to do now?" she asked in an incredibly husky, sexy voice which turned out to be her Ukranian accent. I told her that I had booked to fly the next day after which she asked for my number. "I ring you in two hours," she said, taking her leave of me. She didn't ring me in two hours, but she did ring me while I was on a run in Sardinia with the result that I quickly got over the cost of my missed flight.

Judy overcame her fury at my late arrival for us to enjoy a harmonious few days which were enhanced for me, not only by Nadiya's call, but the anticipation of AC Ajaccio's home game with Guingamp after we had taken the boat into Corsica (which belongs to France) since the Italian Serie B and Serie C seasons were a month away from resuming. That French second division game was no great shakes, but my eyes lit up the next morning while perusing the sports pages of the island's main paper, the Var-Matin. My linguistic skills were only of French O-level calibre, but I could decipher enough of a certain article to comprehend that there could be a game for me that Saturday afternoon after all. An annual cup fixture between the reserve sides of Ajaccio and Bastia would be taking place in neutral Venaco, which I had never heard of. With Judy happy enough to bask by the hotel pool for the afternoon, I set forth in our hired Renault on the 40-mile journey towards Corsica's ancient capital of Corte. There was no sign of a ground in Venaco but leaving the town, I almost knocked down a group of pedestrians. And then, glory be, there were more and more walkers, all striding out with that unmistakeably purposeful gait of fans hurrying to football. They were making for a clearing high up in the woods from where there was an unobstructed view of a beautifully manicured lawn beneath with goalposts that had quite literally been carved out of the forest. I was astounded. It was one of the most extraordinary grounds I have ever stumbled across. There were no seats apart from the odd bench, but I was happy enough to stand and take in the action and the surroundings which were absolutely surreal.

My ticket for the 1966 World Cup Final

A lifetime of lanyards competes for space

Mascot duty. Nick with company at the penultimate game at Swansea's Vetch Field

South Africa 2010. Where the oceans meet. Mark gets the best view above Chris (L) and Nick

Halfway up Table Mountain. The author stops for a well-earned respite in 2010

On the summit. Nick and Martin Scott reach Table Mountain's peak

Relics from the past. Nick and Chris visit the 1962 World Cup stadium in Arica, Chile during a diversion from the Copa in Peru

Get a grip. Two pairs of hands are required to keep hold of the Copa America. Nick and Martin with Brazil's cup in 2004

The Bombonera Stadium, home of Boca Juniors. L to R: Mark, Steve, Chris and Nick take a look at South Anerica's most intoxicating ground on a non-match day

Our intrepid group take in the Igazu Waterfalls during a break from the 1999 Copa America

Argentina and Lionel Messi await the presentation of the World Cup in Doha - 2022

Who pays what? Chris and Nick debate bill in Cape Town - 2010

Chapter 35:
Parrot lost for words

The 2010 World Cup finals in South Africa were preceded by the kind of drama I could have done without. Sally and I were in Spain, taking in a few games and admiring the scenery. Noticing that Girona were at home to Levante on the Friday night in the Segunda division, I planned to see the game and catch an early-morning flight from there to Stansted, giving me enough time to get to Derby for Palace's crucial game in the championship. That was when Sally took a phone call from her sister Annie, asking how we were planning to get home. "By plane of course," said Sally completely unaware, like me, of the travel chaos throughout Europe, caused by the ash cloud, the product of the eruption of Eyjafjallajökull, the Icelandic volcano. Twenty countries closed their air space with the result that ten million passengers were affected. Planes were being diverted or not flying at all.

If it hadn't been for having to dump the hire car at Girona Airport, I would have put my foot down there and then, sacrificing the Girona game. We spotted an English car outside our hotel with the owners pottering around outside it. I brazenly introduced myself to the couple and asked when they might be going home. "First thing in the morning," he replied. "Any chance of a lift?" I asked him. They readily acquiesced as long as we didn't smoke (which neither of us did) and shared the cost of petrol, toll fees and the Shuttle from Calais to Folkestone. Maybe I should have plucked up the courage to ask why we couldn't leave that instant, but my good manners spared him the need to answer such an impertinent question. And so the two of us went to the game, witnessed Levante's 4-0 win, found a decent restaurant for our paella dinner and retired for an early night.

For the first few hours of our car journey from northern Spain the next morning I entertained the crazy idea of getting to Derby but of course that was out of the question. With our hosts not in the least bit interested in the fortunes of Palace and therefore reluctant to engage the sports stations on their car radio, I had to be satisfied with goal flashes on my mobile from friends at the game who, much too late for my peace of mind, eventually gave me the good news that Stern John had hit a late equaliser, giving Palace a 1-1 draw and a point that subsequently proved essential in our survival battle. A couple of weeks later we went to Sheffield Wednesday, needing another point to stay up at their expense.

147

It wasn't just relegation that Palace feared but oblivion. We had been deducted ten points for going into administration. If we had gone down, the club might have folded. The suspense was unbearable but ultimately, after five desperate minutes of added time which seemed like an eternity, we got the point we required from a 2-2 draw. I have never known a day of such heart-sapping emotion. I was on the top deck of Hillsborough's infamous Leppings Lane stand while my son, Ben was below. I had exchanged a few words with the guy next to me. I didn't know his name but as the final whistle went, I am embarrassed to relate, I hugged him. I hugged Ben too when we met up after cheering our heroes from the pitch as some of Wednesday's fans sought retribution with a set-to against our own heavies. There was hostility in the air so, while Ben had a beer or three with a Wednesday fan mate of his, I went with Hy Money and a long-lost cousin of hers to nearby Rotherham for a celebratory ale.

Palace's salvation enabled me to fly to South Africa for the World Cup in a more light-hearted frame of mind than might otherwise have been the case. Much as I like travelling, it had never occurred to me to follow the example of my German friend, Markus Linke who spent four months going overland the length of the continent to get there. He had taken buses, trains, a motorbike, a boat from Egypt to Sudan and hitchhiked and seen matches enroute. He did well to reach the tournament on time considering that he had been arrested for criminal trespassing in Uganda and detained for three days near Kampala in a police dormitory housing petty criminals. He had been suspected of espionage while spotted taking photos of a football pitch on wasteland at Bombo which happened to be in front of army barracks. The authorities needed some convincing that his dubious photographs weren't the cover for some spying mission he had been sent on. The whole escapade cost him 1,500 euros in legal fees. "Everybody wanted a piece of the cake," said Markus who had to wait another four days, following his release, before being reunited with his camera and passport.

All of which made me glad I taken the more conservative route by air. But with South Africa's transport system way short of perfection, it was quickly evident that access to all ten stadiums would be no easy task. My dislike of overnight bus journeys didn't help either. So, I was doubly grateful to Chris and Brian Clarke for collecting me at Johannesburg's Tambo International Airport. Our destiny was Nelspruit 210 miles away, the venue for the group game between Honduras and Chile. We would have had no problems but for the hire car breaking down. Brian managed to get it started again but our stuttering progress persuaded him to give me his match ticket while he spent the duration of the game getting the vehicle sorted. Which he managed. I was full of gratitude. I would

148

probably have got into the match anyway for a pittance, but I was indebted to him now for being able to see Chile's 1-0 win.

Organisation had never been my forte so I had gone to South Africa ill prepared, booking no hotels in advance, thinking that it would be a doddle to find cheap abodes. No such luck. Chris and I spent the first few nights forking out on expensive hotels close to Joburg before we went our separate ways. From the recesses of my mind, I remembered that Vanessa, one of my parents' former au pair girls had come from Pretoria. Helped by a few phone calls and emails, I managed to track her down. Vanessa proved to be a godsend. I spent 19 nights of that World Cup based in the spare room of her lovely, gated home which doubled up as an aviary. She and her boyfriend Wynand collected rare birds. The guest of honour was a gorgeous colourful parrot by the name of Jessica which I partly adopted as that is also my darling daughter's name. But try as I might, I could not manage to get Jessica to speak though I did believe there was a certain chemistry between us. I was so smitten that Vanessa said I could take her home. At a price. But bearing in mind my lifestyle, I thought that would have been unfair on both of us. I was sorry to hear a few years later that she had died.

One other bonus of my stay in Pretoria were the lush grasslands to be found a couple of streets away, perfect for my almost daily bouts of exercise from the house. And yet another bonus of my new residence was its proximity to so many other stadiums which could be reached either on the desperately slow train that creaked its way out of Pretoria bound for Joburg or on the match special buses to the other venues within easy reach. The train took us to within a bus ride away from Joburg's Soccer City and Ellis Park grounds and the buses conveyed us fans to the likes of Polokwane, Rustenburg and Bloemfontein. Pretoria's Loftus Versfeld Stadium which had been converted from a major rugby ground, was but a cab ride distant.

On the way to Rustenburg for the USA v Ghana round of 32 game I bumped into Mark from Edinburgh who I had met before though neither of us could remember where. Now known by all and sundry as Scottish Mark, he is a big events person who forsakes the nitty gritty of non-league or lower league football for the showpieces. It is the same with every sport he watches. No way would he be seen at a tennis challenger tournament or a minor golf competition when he can do the grand slams and the majors. Chacun a son gout as the French would say. But for all our differences, we became firm friends. Mark's home which I have often visited on expeditions to Scotland's second and third div grounds is a monument to all the world's huge sporting events he has graced over the years. There are cushions, bedspreads, glasses, tankards, all souvenirs

149

relating to his predilection for games or sports which will make headlines the next day rather than the small print. He is a big one too for having his picture taken with celebrities. We were at the Copa America, one year when I said, "oh there's José Pekerman."

"Who's he?" asked Mark.

"The manager of Colombia, of course," I said, with which Mark promptly scarpered, camera in hand, to get Pekerman to pose for a selfie.

On the way back from Rustenburg's impressive stadium which lies uncomfortably close to the city's most poverty-stricken neighbourhood, we talked about the game which Ghana had won with a goal in extra time from Sunderland's Asamoah Gyan. The next day I got a lift with a few Germans in their minibus to, would you believe, the Germany v England game, five hours away in Bloemfontein. The driver was Alex who told me a few days later that I had been the subject matter of his daily column on the World Cup for a newspaper in Berlin. He told his readers how weird it was to be facilitating an Englishman's transport to such a game. I got to Bloom as we called it, in time to meet up with Chris for a meal after which we surveyed the scene and the surprising number of tickets in the hands of touts and general punters.

Alex and co needn't have worried about me crowing all the way back to Pretoria as Fabio Capello's England were well and truly trounced notwithstanding the shot from Frank Lampard which bounced down over the line via the crossbar. That would have given England an equaliser at 1-1. I sympathised with the affable Mathew Upson - who I had met in Malaysia - for the amount of stick he took afterwards from the English press for he was just one of a number of beleaguered defenders and he had, after all, scored England's goal in reply to one apiece from Miroslav Klose, Lucas Podolski and two late efforts from Andreas Muller that gave Germany a 4-1 win.

The nutcases among us managed a round of 32 game-a-day as Brazil's 3-0 win over Chile at Ellis Park and Paraguay's win on penalties over Japan after a fascinating yet goalless 120 minutes in Pretoria both fitted snugly into our schedule. Likewise, the quarter-finals. Ghana's great run had taken them to a tie with Uruguay who faded somewhat from my affections with the handball from Luis Suarez that denied the Africans a late winner as Gyan's subsequent penalty struck the bar. Gyan made amends in the shoot-out, but Ghana still went out, Wondrous footballer that he is, Suarez has never been uppermost among my favourites because he behaves in the manner of the street urchin he resembles. If he is not biting opponents, he is forever diving or in the ear of the referee. "The hand of God now belongs to me," he boasted senselessly, making even more enemies after his red card. Spain, fast approaching their first

150

World Cup final, won the other quarter-final we took in, beating Paraguay with a goal from David Villa.

And then it was down to the south that we flew with my room in Pretoria now exchanged for one in the apartment owned by Chris' friend Eric who worked for an organisation in Cape Town that was supposed to be a sanctuary for prostitutes. But Eric's failing was a tendency for sampling the goods. He loved telling us his stories. He was good company. He met us at Cape Town airport and drove us two hours out of town to a garden centre which had a restaurant with food to die for. Chris and I treated Eric to lunch as we did when Mark escorted us to Africa's southern most point at Cape Agulhas on another idle day. It's where the Indian and Atlantic oceans converge. We had gone via Hermanus which is supposed to be a vantage point for whale-watching, so we felt somewhat cheated at seeing nothing more than the vague outline of one of the great mammals followed by a spout of foam.

My narrow escape from Jurgen's fork at the top of Table Mountain was another adventure on the eve of the first semi-final which was the five-goal thriller between Holland and Uruguay who were without the suspended Suarez. Holland's 3-2 victory took them into their third World Cup final. The chaos caused by Fifa's acolytes wanting to get to Durban dominated the angst of the next day. My flight finally arrived three hours late causing me to miss the first 40 minutes of the second semi-final, so I remained suitably grateful to Puyol for waiting until the 73rd minute before notching Spain's winner against Germany. Returning to the Moses Mabhida Stadium - which looks more like a spacecraft - the next day and in a mood for revenge, Mark, Chris and I took a lift to the empty hospitality suites to find to our joy some distinctive inscribed rugs that had been overlooked by inebriated guests the previous night, doubtless after they had swallowed too many glasses of free champagne. The scenario was similar at the final, so I have a different 2010 World Cup rug on each of the sofas in my living room.

My plan had been to take in the third-place game at Port Elizabeth to complete the full set. Easier said than done. PE as they call it, lies between Cape Town and Durban but there were either no seats on flights there or no seats on flights from PE to Joburg which I needed if I was to see the final. To go by train required an elongated journey via Joburg and buses were of the overnight variety which I didn't fancy. So, reluctantly I had to give Germany's 3-2 win over Uruguay a miss, promising myself a visit to PE at the African championships three years later. We flew back to Joburg instead in plenty of time for the final which gave me just the outcome I craved; a win for Spain curtesy of Iniesta's goal in the 116th minute against Holland's aggressive provocateurs. Howard Webb, our

151

esteemed referee did well to keep control despite handing out 14 yellow cards including two for Holland's John Heitinga. Spain thus became the first European nation to win on another continent.

Within a month of my return, I was watching England again and suffering a needless altercation with the law. I had applied for three tickets for the friendly against Hungary at Wembley and, besides myself, was giving one each to Sally and her mate Caz who had never been to a game before. Arriving early for once, I had been whiling away the time in an internet café before our rendezvous. Upon meeting them, we were sauntering up Wembley Way when I realised that I had left my spectacles in the internet café. I handed Sally the tickets at which point an aggressive young constable pounced, accusing me of being a ticket tout. I sometimes think the police deliberately provoke an innocent person into screaming obscenities at them in the hope of totting up their required number of arrests. Sally was taken to one side and asked to verify my name and address, which she duly did. During the ensuing heated exchange, I suggested that the copper should go and arrest a few real touts. "And where may they be?" he asked. If the guy was not on his first day on the beat and a complete and utter dunderhead to boot, he was giving a very sound impersonation.

"They are hanging around Wembley Park tube station where they always are," I told him as if he didn't already know. "Do I look like a tout?" I asked the imbecile who was naive in the extreme.

"And what might a tout look like?" By now he must have qualified for promotion to Scotland Yard's forensic crime squad.

"They all look like spivs, unshaven, bad haircuts, unpleasant." I nearly added: "A bit like you, in fact," but thought better of it as that would probably have given him the excuse he needed for having me locked up for the course of the match. I was eventually allowed to go and retrieve my glasses and see the game which England won 2-1.

The prospect of combining a visit to Nadiya with the Germany v Turkey Euro qualifier in Berlin was too enticing to dismiss. Like me, she had a thing about lakes, rivers and the sea so I didn't need much persuading when she urged me to take her for a few days to a hotel on the shores of Lake Tegel to the north of Berlin. We hadn't been there long when she asked me if I could loan her - which meant give her - £700 towards some dental work she required. She lapsed into a sulk when I suggested that her dentist should ring me in London at her next appointment and I would give him my credit card details over the phone for the surgery.

By the time I returned from my next run along a path hugging the lake, she had disappeared. She wouldn't answer my calls or texts. So, I

152

thought 'sod it' and rang Steve or Berlin Steve as he came to be known. He is a little balding chap, a veritable football nut who talks for both his native Luxemburg and Germany, his adopted home. He is an authority on everything and everyone whether it is politics, the history of the clubs, great and small, around Berlin or a myriad of topics in-between. He had already told me he was going to the Czech Republic for a midweek cup tie that for Nadiya's benefit I had decided to sacrifice. But not anymore. If she was giving me the cold shoulder, then why shouldn't I occupy myself by joining Steve on his excursion which he had researched would only cost a pittance if we bought a particular concession ticket and travelled on certain trains. He was an expert at this kind of thing which he needed to be as he was forever pleading poverty despite travelling huge distances to feed his football habit. We had to change trains four times on our journey along most of the length of the former East Germany, but Steve got us to the town of Sychrov in good time to complete the rest of the journey by bus to the village of Hlavice. We devoured a tasty Czech version of wurst mit brot before kick-off.

SK Hlavice's opponents were the mighty Ceske Budovice. The whole village plus all its grannies had turned up for the game which took place in the afternoon as the third division hosts possessed no floodlights. With a slightly sloping pitch, the game had all the ingredients for a shock. But the first division side rode out a considerable storm and eventually showed their class to gain a merited 3-1 win which we watched from seemingly the last two remaining unoccupied seats in the tiny stand.

Our only problems now were getting back to civilisation and locating a hotel as there was no way we would be able to return to Berlin that night. The last bus for Sychrov had long since departed and we had confirmed that Hlavice was far too humble a community to accommodate a taxi service. After we had asked around for lifts to no avail, the last resort was the first aid team making their reports on a casualty-free match. Plucking up courage, I went up to them and explained our predicament. They were our saviours. They probably broke all the rules by permitting us to sit in the back of their ambulance for the 12-mile journey. It was the one and only time I'd ever ridden in an ambulance to get to or from a game. But needs must. Steve and I found the cheapest hotel in town and celebrated our good fortune over a Chinese meal before heading back to Berlin the next day.

There was still no sign of Nadiya on my return to the hotel by the lake, so I killed time that night over a desultory meal on my tod. I always think that people eating on their own in restaurants resemble 'Billy no mates' so I found the furthest corner of a Greek diner away from prying eyes and pretended that I didn't have a care in the world over my retsina and

Kleftiko. I met up with my German journalist friend, Alex for a beer early the next evening before the big game for which I had procured a press pass. Germany's 3-0 win came with the help of two goals from Miroslav Klose and one from Mesut Ozil which was apposite revenge for the abuse he suffered throughout the game from the Turkish fans for having the effrontery not to represent the country of his parents' birth.

Back in the UK, I made the grave error of regaling various friends with the story of Nadiya's vanishing act. For years afterwards I was asked, "How are Nadiya's teeth?" whenever her name cropped up in conversation. I met her once in Gatwick's arrivals hall, holding up a bit of cardboard with the words 'Prima Donna' on it. She saw the funny side of my joke as she emerged.

As for Berlin Steve, I continue to bump into him on our respective travels. For a man not boasting enormous wealth, he has a knack of reaching the major tournaments. Emerging from Lyon Gare at the 2016 Euros, I was astonished to hear the shout of "Crystal Palace" when he spotted me. And then two years later in Moscow, I found myself sitting a few seats away from him at a game during the Russian World Cup. But it was on the occasion of another Germany international in Dublin that he asked Sally if we had a sofa in our bedroom where he could kip. There was indeed a sofa there, but we didn't fancy him giving us marks out of ten for our performance so, instead, he elected to sleep in the Fiat Uno we had hired. When Sally woke Steve up the next morning, she took a photograph of him curled up in the front passenger seat.

The plan following breakfast was to head for Sligo for an Irish League game v Galway. In lieu of petrol money he handed me a dog-eared Roy Keane ghost-written autobiography that was hardly my choice of reading material. On arrival at Sligo where we stopped for pre-match refreshments which he said he couldn't afford, he asked the waitress for a spare glass so that he could consume the milk she had brought to accompany our tea. Other people were also subjected to his impoverished lifestyle. Oldham Dave was hunkering down in his Hamburg hotel after Fulham's Euro League final against Atletico Madrid when there was a knock on the door. "It's very cold out here," said Steve who was trying to sleep on the landing. "It's nice and warm in here," said Dave slamming the door shut.

154

Chapter 36:
Tracks in the sand

Judy and I were still hanging in there, so she accompanied me to one of her favourite parts of the world, the middle east for the next edition of the Asian Championships which were to be in Qatar. It was a month after the country had been awarded the 2022 World Cup which was a topic that naturally stimulated most of the conversation. The competition took place in four of Doha's stadiums, all of them pretty soulless - except the Khalifa International Stadium - plus Al Rayyan, less than ten miles away. With Al Rayyan's Ahmed bin Ali Stadium staging its last game on a Monday in Group D between Iraq and North Korea (1-0), I was able to get to all five venues even though the need to be back for Palace's re-arranged league game against Norwich was paramount. It meant that I had to sacrifice Japan's 1-0 win over Australia in the final.

We holed up in a five-star star hotel which cost a fraction of what the same hotel might charge in 2022. Fortunately, neither Jurgen or Bastian were ensconced there. I had been dismayed from the moment I arrived to see a dozen Germans occupying the press seats including the twins. Since my disagreement with Jurgen was far from settled, that was the last thing I needed. Bastian buttonholed me during one half-time break to argue his brother's case with the result that we both missed most of the second half. I minded far more than he did.

Feelings were still running high when I encountered both of them in Argentina a few months later at the next Copa America though, fortunately we did not all have exactly the same schedules. After a frantic dash to the CONMEBOL's media headquarters on arrival in Buenos Aires, I hurried by train down to La Plata to see Venezuela gain a surprising goalless draw against Brazil. One of the highlights of the second half was provided by Scottish Mark dashing down a steep flight of stairs from the press box to have a selfie taken with a bikini clad Miss Venezuela beauty queen who was strutting her stuff. It was the kind of thing that happens only in the Copa.

The plan then was to fly to the northern most venue of Jujuy which is famous for its "hill of seven colours," a kaleidoscopic rock formation on the outskirts of the city that has seven different shades. According to geologists, each colour represents a different geological age. It is truly a sight to behold and Steve - who had joined me - and I marvelled at these sensational slabs of rock. I also purchased an ethnic coat which is still in my possession and which I would wear more often but for its faulty zip. We saw Costa Rica beat Bolivia 2-0 and then, on the bus heading south the next day, we got talking to an attractive English girl. I was disappointed to find on arrival at Salta that she belonged to the journalist, Jonathan Wilson who was waiting for her. Along with Chris who had belatedly turned up, we all enjoyed a disappointing pre-match meal before seeing further confirmation of Venezuela's drastic improvement. They beat Ecuador 1-0.

The cost of hefty internal air fares was a persuasive factor in our decision to hire a car the next few days which were spent undergoing long trips between the provincial venues of Cordoba, Santa Fe, Mendoza and San Juan. The car was at the centre of all our subsequent adventures from the moment I came desperately close to a head-on collision as we raced to make kick-off in Cordoba for Argentina's game against Costa Rica, a 3-0 win. I hadn't allowed for traffic lights being well above the line of vision. And then in Mendoza for the Uruguay v Chile (1-1) and Peru v Mexico (1-0) double header, after leaving the vehicle in a parking lot outside the stadium, we returned to find it gone. Mark and Steve looked on in disbelief while Chris and I had a furious argument as to the car's whereabouts. He was convinced that I had confused the place where we had left it until I turned detective to follow what I believed to be our car's tyre marks in the sand leading from where I was certain I had parked it. The tracks led us towards another car park nearby where the police had towed it. We drove off in it without further ado except for me gloating and telling all and sundry "I told you so" over and over again. They must have got fed up with me.

By now we had in our company, Luke, a young rascal of a West Brom fan who could have been straight out of a Dickens novel. He had made his way to Argentina for the Copa. Steve and I got talking to him one night in a bar with the result that he quickly became a member of our merry band who were sitting down to dinner one night when the former QPR chairman Nick Blackburn joined us. Blackburn was regaling us with a story which included an anecdote about a woman he had met on his travels. "Did you fuck her?" Luke piped up mischievously. You could have heard a pin drop. Here was this pipsqueak with a rich Brummie accent asking a public school-educated, top football man if he'd had sex. Blackburn, to his enormous credit, replied: "No, I didn't actually." Hilarity followed. Luke was such a wit that we wanted him along, so we let him off with minimum contributions towards petrol costs as he was short of pesos.

Leaving Cordoba after Peru's 2-0 quarter-final victory over Colombia, we made sure that our stop for dinner would coincide on television with

Argentina's epic quarter-final, a 1-1 draw with Uruguay which ended with a 5-4 exit on penalties. It was yet another blow to Messi's hopes of collecting a senior trophy on Argentina's behalf. We stayed the night nearby after which I had to rely on Chris' map-reading for the journey to San Juan. Big mistake. Chris decided to considerably reduce the length of our journey by following "the red squiggly line" on the map which took us up a steep and windy road onto a 2,000 feet high plateau from where the views were stupendous so long as I kept half an eye on the road. The drops onto the floor of the desert below to which we eventually descended were precipitous. A squiggly line it may have been on the map but what masqueraded for a route through the sand for the next 30 miles was far removed from a decent strip of tarmac. With my foot pressed down on the accelerator I just had to keep our wheels in the ruts formed by all the vehicles containing drivers foolhardy enough to have attempted that hazardous route before us. Judging by the very few other cars we encountered, not many were risking it now. We got the map's small print translated later to find that red routes were for four-wheel drives only and our gallant Fiat was no four-wheel drive. No wonder its poor sand-caked wheels took time to adjust when we found ourselves on terra firma again. We got to San Juan in time for Venezuela's shock 2-1 win over Chile.

This was proving a strange Copa with neither Brazil nor Argentina making it to the last four. Uruguay beat Peru in the first semi-final while we returned to Mendoza for Paraguay's goalless draw with Venezuela and a 5-3 win on pens. Overcoming my usual reluctance to go overnight by coach, I dumped the Fiat and went coche cama class back to Buenos Aires, returning to the cheap hotel I had found near the station. We had a few days to spare before the final. Six of us sat down one lunchtime in one of the city's most fashionable restaurants where, uncomfortably for me, Jurgen was among our group. That afternoon we inspected the artistic murals on a tour of La Boca which had to include a visit to La Bombonera, home of the famous Boca Juniors. It was the first time I'd ever been inside a stadium without seeing a game. But what an intoxicating place it must be on matchday, I thought, making up my mind that some day I would see a game there. Somehow it seemed more impressive than the Estadio Monumental which belongs to Boca's great city rivals, River Plate. It was the scene of Uruguay's 3-0 win over Paraguay in the Copa final, assisted by an early goal from Luis Suarez and two from Diego Forlan.

Chapter 37:
A boat ride like no other

Eastern Europe has always held a certain mystique for me which is why I looked forward to the 2012 Euros in Poland and Ukraine as much as any tournament although I was familiar with most of the grounds. With England based in Ukraine and in group D, the obvious incentive was to see some games in Poland before heading towards Donetsk via the delightful Ukranian city of Lviv which did, in fact once belong to Poland. It was the scene of Portugal's 2-1 win over Holland, helped by two goals from Ronaldo.

I hired a Skoda that did us proud, pounding along the motorways between the two countries. Some distances were too great so we came to rely on the excellent albeit infrequent train service between Kiev and Donetsk which was the stage for England's 1-1 draw against France and the 1-0 victory over Ukraine. With its ornate park that runs most of the length of the city, Donetsk is an attractive place that has since fallen into Russian hands. Less attractive alas was the once winsome receptionist who had flirted with Chris when we had stayed at her hotel three years earlier on the occasion of a Spurs defeat by Shakhtor. She gave him her number but when we looked her up again, she had ballooned outwards. That original visit to Donetsk incidentally was the culmination of a double-header that had started with Dynamo Kiev's game with Valencia in Dynamo's own humble yet picturesque Valeriy Lobanovsky Stadium. We had travelled between the two Europa League ties on a sleeper through the chilly February night.

Ukraine looked so utterly different when it was not knee deep in snow, which was our experience the first time. Now it baked for the most part under a scorching sun. The day after England's win over the co-hosts, the trains were fully booked so I elected to travel by coach back to Kiev. I found myself sitting next to a body slumbering alongside me. When he awoke from a deep sleep that had been assisted by copious amounts of alcohol to celebrate England topping group D, he turned out to be another Tottenham fan. Stefan proved to be good value, so we became buddies until a petty fall-out at the next Euros in France. He told me of his amazing lifestyle. Based in Nice as Panini Stickers' south of France representative, he still managed to fly home for just about every Spurs game, home and away.

The way the Euro fixtures were panning out, the journey between Kiev, Donetsk and even further east to Kharkiv for Portugal's 2-1 win over Holland, became increasingly well worn. There were stops for refreshments at Poltava within tantalising sight of Vorskla Poltava's floodlights.

With Chris in the passenger seat, the Skoda was eating up the miles on Constitution Day, a Ukranian public holiday when we were without a game. We had just passed one scantily dressed lady standing at the roadside in the middle of nowhere - which brought from Chris the comment "ah a lady of the afternoon" - when we turned a corner to find another shapely woman wearing not much more. To our great delight she was in skimpy black attire and about to put her afternoon to more legitimate use. She was, we quickly discovered, the lineswoman at a match that was just about to commence, not on a pristine surface but in a grassy and rut-strewn field that would have been more suited to cattle.

Someone had done his utmost to mark this apology of a pitch with white lines. But we were not complaining. Indeed, we could hardly believe our luck. We thought the only action was in Warsaw, hundreds of miles away. The delectable lineswoman had all our sympathy after she was ticked off by the referee when, without his approval she had ushered on a player who had been receiving treatment. Considering the bumpy, uneven surface, the quality of the skills on show was remarkably high.

Carrying on after our bonus game, we found the road was not festooned with hotels. We eventually hit upon a ramshackle inn which also had a none too inviting restaurant with a pixelating television where we saw what we could of the Euro quarter-final in Warsaw which was Portugal's 1-0 win over the Czech Republic with Ronaldo adding to his two goals against the Dutch to be his team's matchwinner once more.

With Kiev now our destination, Nadiya came out to join me. For becoming the catalyst in the demise of my relationship with Judy she had earned the wrath of my former girlfriend who referred to her as either "knickerova" or "slutvana." Pleading poverty, Nadiya was in the custom of expecting me to pay for all her flights. Over the years she managed to miss four of them for such trivial reasons as my failure to text her the night before. Stupidly I tolerated this behaviour for a while despite remaining firmly of the belief that every Russian or Ukranian baby girl is barely out of the womb before she is taught by her mother to milk the western man for everything he is worth. I couldn't get her a ticket for England's quarter-final with Italy but no matter, she was in her cousin's cramped apartment to see our latest defeat on penalties after 120 minutes had produced no goals.

The outcome was exactly the same in the first semi-final, a 0-0 followed by a 4-2 outcome on pens in Spain's favour against Portugal. Italy edged past Germany 2-1 in the other semi in Warsaw but must have wished they hadn't when Spain took them apart 4-0 in the Kiev final to capture their third successive trophy. Xavi and Iniesta were at their peaks.

Nadiya had returned home to Berlin by then so, in a need to fill my time I replied to an advertisement in an English language-speaking newspaper offering boat trips on Kiev's Dnieper River. Boat rides come a close second to long train voyages in my list of hobbies. I texted the number and was answered by someone saying that the price of the boat ride would have to be negotiated. I assumed that the cost would depend on the number of other tourists on a pleasure craft. A further few texts ensued during which I was told the captain was trying to get his precious boat ready. Getting a trifle exasperated by now, I awaited the next text. To my astonishment when it arrived, it asked me, "do you like nice massage?". Silly me for not twigging that the boat rides were a front for rides of an alternate variety. So, I never did get my boat ride on the Dnieper, but I did get to fraternise with the text sender who turned out to be absolutely gorgeous. Business must have been booming as Ulyana was the proud owner of a top of the range Mercedes in which she was happy to give me a free ride to Kiev Airport on my last morning.

"You're a sucker for any East European babe who mangles the English language," texted my mate, Yann when I told him the story.

That was all highly entertaining but Palace's subsequent promotion-winning season from the championship included a needless off field drama. In late November we had successive away matches in Leeds on the Saturday and Hull, the following Tuesday night. There was doubtless a more stimulating way of filling the gap than by watching a Scottish third division game but that wouldn't have been for me. So, I took the train onto Edinburgh following our 2-1 defeat at Elland Road. Scottish Mark, ever the perfect host, was waiting for me although East Stirling's game against Berwick on the Sunday in their adopted home of Ochilview Park, the home of Stenhousemuir, was certainly not on his agenda. But for me it was an opportunity not to be missed. I saw Berwick's 1-0 win in front of 327 hardy spectators and carried onto Hull after a further two-night stay with Mark.

I had treated Mark to an expensive meal, so I was short of readies which was why, somewhat misguidedly I tried to enter Boothferry Park, or the Kingston Communications Stadium as it is now known, with an out-of-date Telegraph press card. That was ill judged on my part, but I surely didn't deserve what was coming next. After I had been stopped

160

from going in, the club's petty jobsworth of a chief steward followed me round to the away end and prevented me paying £10 to enter. In fact, he wouldn't let me go in at all. And yet a policeman on horseback said he would have no objections to me entering the stadium, but he had to abide by what the steward wanted. So, I faded from view and changed my appearance with clothes plus a cap that were in the bag I had brought along for my five-day trip.

I went round to the home turnstiles where stewards were ganging up. They recognised me, refused me entry and reiterated that I couldn't go into the stadium. How pathetic, I thought. By now the game had started so, pressing up against the glass-fronted reception area, I started to watch the action on a television monitor there. It was then that I felt the heavy hand of the law on my collar or, rather several heavy hands as there were three police officers, all reminding me that I had been ordered to stay out of the ground. But I was outside the ground, I told them. Try making a pig-thick copper understand that little nuance. No matter. They were adamant that I would be arrested if I didn't budge. I knew they would have liked nothing better than to detain me in a cell overnight, so I beat a reluctant retreat. If the match had been televised live, I would have made for the nearest appropriate pub, but it wasn't, so I found an Indian restaurant and killed time over a curry while I waited for the guys - who had promised me a lift back to London - to come out of the ground. All I missed was a goalless draw.

I wrote to the chief constable of Hull's police force telling him how heavy handed I thought his officers had been. The correspondence back and forth lasted three months. It was a fruitless exercise and eventually, I gave up in exasperation. After Hull had subsequently won promotion, I was delighted to see them chuck away a two-goal lead and lose the cup final to Arsenal two years later. Even better, 12 months further on, was the sight of Palace sealing Hull's second relegation to the championship in three years by thumping them 4-0 at Selhurst Park in 2017. It wasn't as if I had an axe to grind or anything but ...!!!

Further satisfaction came when Hull dropped into League One.

Chapter 38:
A bumpy ride

I felt there was some unfinished business in South Africa after 2010. Not only had I enjoyed a lovely, hitherto unconsummated flirtation with Wynand's mum Arina who had been staying in the next room to me in Pretoria, but I had not visited one of the World Cup venues at all and had only seen 50 minutes of a game at another. So, with both Port Elizabeth and Durban among the five host cities for the 2013 African (CAF) Championships, there was an urgent need to return. Palace helped my scheduling by getting knocked out of the FA Cup in a third-round replay at Stoke which meant that I could go to SA, see a handful of games there and not miss a single Palace fixture.

The meticulous planning also led to Arina and I getting off, quite literally, to a flying start. She boarded the same plane that I had taken from Heathrow when it stopped off in Joburg. Our destination was Port Elizabeth or more, specifically the Nelson Mandela Bay Stadium which was to be the scene of Mali's 1-0 win over Niger. We explored PE during our three-night stay in a guest house which should have only been a two-night stay as there are some 570 miles between PE and Durban over undulating roads. And it was on that long drive that the rot quickly began to set in. We should definitely have left the previous day in our hired Cavalier. The scenery was fantastic but with time against us, I could not enjoy it. Traffic was heavy and there was a certain amount of risk-taking by those drivers with a deadline. Even so, I felt that my driving fell short of being reckless. But after coming to a stop at roadworks the guy behind us jumped out of his car to take umbrage with me over the line of cars I had just overtaken. Other cars were being driven in a similar manner, but it was obvious, judging by the ensuing stony silence, that Arina was in total agreement with the chap who had challenged me.

Matters did not get any better when she asked me to halt for a coffee and I got talking to a group of black guys sitting at our table. She was certainly not a racist, but she made no attempt to join in the conversation although they were friendly enough. As soon as we were back in the car, she did somewhat huffily take me to task over my apparent willingness to conform to Nelson Mandela's idealism. It wasn't the done thing apparently for the likes of her, a dishy blonde and with a gilded existence, to be seen chatting to black men. Things did not improve on arrival in Durban where we had to dash to the hotel I had booked, to dump our bags, from where we had to dash again to the stadium for the double header, South Africa and Angola (2-0) plus Morocco v Cape Verde (1-1). Nor was there any rapprochement after I had waited for her to get ready one evening. I was in the hotel bar where some lively ladies engaged me in discussion over a drink. Even so, I was somewhat surprised when I woke one morning to find Arina half-dressed and packing her bags. She was going to fly back to Joburg and she wanted me to give her a lift to the airport which was not forthcoming seeing as I felt she had made little effort to make ours a happy reunion. So, off she went in a cab, leaving me in a state of shock and rejection. I tried to look on the bright side. I could now talk freely to the girls in the bar without having to check the lift every time I heard the doors slide open. With Oldham Dave in town and some tasty matches still in store, namely the game between the hosts and Morocco (2-2) and Congo and Mali (1-1), the tournament still had plenty going for it.

I could not leave South Africa without saying hello to Vanessa, so she met me when I flew into Joburg and drove me to Rustenburg for Nigeria's 2-0 win over Ethiopia. She took me to a nature reserve the next day where we admired two devilishly handsome lions, brothers parading around their pen. I was devastated to hear that they were due to be split up and have ever since chastised myself for not doing anything about it such as, at the very least, a letter of protest to the owners. Back in Vanessa's gaited home where thankfully there was no sign of Arina, there was just time to resume my love affair with Jessica, the lovely parrot, before flying home. For once Palace greeted my return with a win, 2-1 over the dreaded Charlton.

With no World Cup or Euros to contemplate, the rest of the year promised little in the way of overseas trips unless I counted my frequent forays to Spain to see Real Mallorca. But the one possibility of a tournament on the horizon meant going against all my principles as I have always considered the Confederations Cup a needless addition to an already overcrowded calendar. So, I had given it little attention. But this time there was a case for going. Brazil would have 12 venues for the World Cup the following year and I did, of course, want to visit them all besides seeing something of this vast country. So, with the prospect of extra relaxation at the World Cup, I hit upon the bright idea of doing half the venues one year and the other half 12 months later. The notion looked all the better when my mate, Frannie asked if she could come along too. There's never been anything between us except friendship, so we agreed to share twin bedded rooms as she does not snore which had always been a problem when I was travelling with Chris or Neil.

Our first mission on landing at Rio was to get a connecting flight to Brasilia for the opening game, Brazil v Japan in the Estadia Nacional Mane Garrincha which has since become a gigantic bus terminal. My main memory of the next game in Recife, a two-hour flight away, was not so much Spain's 2-1 win over Uruguay but the journey to the city's out of town Arena Pernambuco alongside Jurgen with whom, of course, I was now back on amicable terms. As must be the case for someone who once threatened me with a fork, he is prone to flashes of rage and bursts of impatience. That much was evident when we were stuck in match traffic. He suddenly got out of the hired car to swear furiously in German at the Brazilian driver of the car in front who had taken a split second longer than necessary to merge with ongoing traffic, thereby delaying us. The poor sod didn't know what manner of Teutonic tempest had engulfed him.

With a room 14 floors up overlooking the Atlantic Ocean, Frannie and I had some slight consolation for the drizzle of the next couple of days before Jurgen and I allowed rather more time to spare for our next drive to the Arena Pernambuco. This time we saw a thriller in which Italy beat Japan 4-3. Recife is a bustling city, but we found the more gentle pace and rhythm of Salvador to the south more to our liking. We had booked a room in a pousada which Frannie complained, smelt of mothballs. No matter, our hosts were hospitable and the view of the city's ramparts and the sea from their breakfast room compensated for that slight hiccup.

Salvador's Arena Fonte Nova provided the stage for a high-scoring two-games-in-three-days fest. Nigeria and Uruguay shared four goals before Frannie was overjoyed at the acquisition of a ticket from Jurgen for the other game which wasn't a bad one for a girl watching her first ever match. Brazil beat Italy 4-2. From the next stop of Fortaleza where I saw Spain beat Nigeria 3-0, Frannie's research had deemed it essential for us to spend a few of the Cup's rest days in the unique resort of Jericoacara, unique because it is a town constructed on foundations of sand and also because it bans vehicles which must be deposited in a car park on the town's outskirts.

The plan would have been a sound one had we hired a car with the minimum of fuss but the company nearest our hotel invented one little hitch after another to delay our five-hour slog up north by 24 hours. But what a jewel Jeri - as we renamed it - turned out to be with its pedestrianised heart which is full of tastefully designed white buildings accommodating galleries, shops, restaurants and small hotels, one of which put us up for a single night. The highlight of our stay, probably everybody's stay was to climb to the top of the highest sand dune at the far end of the beach to watch the setting sun dipping beneath the

164

horizon. A large crowd gathers there every fine evening for this momentous sight. We were devastated to be leaving Jeri after so swift a stay. It will prove one of my life's regrets if I never get back there.

We drove back to Fortaleza in time for me to have a late-night drink after Frannie had retired. As I approached our hotel, I was aware of a motor bike suddenly doing a U-turn to swerve right in front of me. I sensed that the pillion passenger was not getting off the bike to ask me the time of night so, with a helmeted thug in swift pursuit I ran diagonally across the road, yelling "help, help". Luckily the hotel door swung open immediately and my would-be mugger disappeared back from whence he came. Frannie asked me what all the commotion was about when I got back to our room. That little mishap filled me with apprehension for the World Cup which, as bad luck would have it, was fully justified. And I had not even been near a favela. We stayed in Fortaleza for the following afternoon's semi-final, won 7-6 by Spain in a penalty shoot-out after 120 minutes of play against Italy had produced no goals and precious few shots. But I was naturally relieved to get out of town pronto and in one piece. We departed the following afternoon for Rio de Janiero. With time not on our side, the tourist trail led us only to Rio's equivalent of Kew Gardens before the final beckoned. It was hot and we felt extremely lethargic which was how the Spanish team looked in the final when they succumbed 3-0 to Brazil who thus exploited their extra day's rest. It was my first experience of the much-vaunted Maracana Stadium. Missing only Belo Horizonte, I had done five of the six Feds' venues. Roll on the World Cup.

My plan after a final is usually to get the hell out of the host country the next day and head for home but this time with no good reason to hurry back, Frannie and I headed north to Manaus which was to be England's first stop 12 months hence. No Brazilian League games were scheduled but that wouldn't stop me looking for one. And yet myopic that I am, I knew that I couldn't go to Brazil and not sample the Amazon. We spent the first night in a boutique hotel which was so quaint that I lived to regret my failure to book it again for the following year. The next day helpful travel agents directed us onto a boat which took us to an Eco hotel on the waters' edge. There can be few more dramatic places to stay than on the banks of the world's greatest river, so Frannie and I lapped up the next four days. There was a tour into the jungle, another into a crocodile-infested tributary and a third into the swollen waters of where the River Negro and the River Solimoes converge. One has black water and the other's contents are of a pale, sandy hue. For about four miles the two rivers run side by side without becoming a cocktail. This remarkable phenomomen is down to differences in temperatures, speed and density.

Our various rides on the Amazon took us past the river's floating petrol stations which were an extra source of wonderment. Not that the guidebooks cared to mention them.

The postscript to each tour found me chilling out under the veranda back at base watching the later stages of Wimbledon on one of the hotel's televisions. The need for a television set was even more pressing when we landed back at Heathrow at 3pm on the Sunday. With a peculiar lack of foresight, I had not allowed for Andy Murray's possible appearance in the Wimbledon final so, delegating a grumbling Frannie to collect my bags, I raced around the airport's various terminals in search of a lounge where I might watch his match against Novak Djokovic. I found one in time to see the last set and a half of his straight sets triumph that made him the first Briton since Fred Perry in 1936 to capture the men's title. That brought a happy climax to my trip which was not really shared by Frannie, herself a Scot. She had little interest in the proceedings. Sacrilege.

Chapter 39:
No Justice for Hodd

With no football for two weeks, withdrawal symptoms were beginning to set in when Scandanavia came to my rescue. How many of us addicts have, I wonder, blessed the fact that the football seasons of Norway, Sweden and Finland stretch right through the summer months, thereby filling empty pages in our diaries. They don't play between late November and March because their grounds are usually under several feet of the white stuff. If they are in the European club competitions, they have to clear it away as was my previous experience with Tromso. So, it was that Sally and I flew off to Haugesund on the third Sunday in July with me cursing the Ryanair schedule that would, if on time, bring our plane in only 50 minutes before kick-off. It is the custom in such instances for panic-stricken hoppers to seek seats at the front of the aircraft so they can be first down the steps and first through passport control. Invariably their hopes are dashed by the plane landing on some far-flung spot on the airport's periphery, thereby forcing them to wait for every other passenger boarding a coach bound for the terminal. Thankfully, that wasn't the case this time, so we were first in the taxi queue. With the help of a speedy, albeit costly cabbie, we made kick-off for the Tippel igaen game with Alesund who won 2-1.

The next morning, we took the express boat from Haugesund to Bergen after which I had my first - and hopefully my last - experience of a sea cruise. Sally had liked nothing better than to accompany her mother on "cruises of a lifetime" but my 24 hours on board the Hurtigruten liner that swept us up the North Sea to Alesund were probably 24 hours too many. We sailed about a mile offshore, parallel to the coast which was hardly visible because of the constant drizzle. The rain kept us passengers inside where there's not much else to do than eat or sink endless cups of coffee or a surplus of exorbitantly priced beers. Or make small talk with couples you never want to see again despite promising to do so. The mind blowingly beautiful Geiranger Fjord which was a diversion before Alesund provided much needed solace from the boredom.

All being well in these circumstances, the early rounds of the European club competitions fit in conveniently with other scheduled games. This time the Europa League and Champions League draws could have been fixed by my good self. I had been intrigued months earlier on noticing that a club called Hodd had won the Norwegian Cup. So, of course, I had checked up on Hodd who had almost been relegated from the second division just before their cup final win over Tromso. Hoddvoll is so tiny that it's not found on most maps They played in the almost equally small community of Ulsteinvik, a few miles south west of Alesund, so it was to Ulsteinvik that we headed by bus after booking a room in the picturesque and largely rebuilt town of Alesund which had been devastated by fire in 1904. Hodd's Europa League tie with Aktobe had captured the imagination of the locals who turned out in force to fill their prosaic ground for their 1-0 win which was not enough, alas, to take them through another round as they lost the second leg 2-0 when under strength.

The early evening kick-off was conducive to a post-match dinner in the only restaurant in the vicinity. A Russian oligarch connected to Aktobe invited himself onto our table along with his driver. They must have found us satisfying company as he picked up the tab and ordered his driver to drop us off at our hotel. I did wonder for a long time afterwards if the oligarch also had links to immigration headquarters in Kazakhstan when I heard of Hodd's fury at being deprived of the services of their two best players for the second leg. Both Akeem Latifu and Sivet Heitie Nilsen were refused visas "for no good reason," according to Nilsen's father Lars Arne, the club's coach. Welcome to the vagaries of European football lads. It may be some time before Hodd return bearing in mind their subsequent descent to Norway's third tier.

With the rest of my itinerary on the relentless side, I had no real objections to Sally taking off for her sister in Malibu. I did the decent thing by escorting her back to Bergen from where she could catch a flight. But with Bergen's top team, Brann away from home, the only other option that Saturday afternoon was second division Nest-Sodra, a bus ride away from Norway's second city. The large open terrace where we sat down to watch a decent 0-0 reminded me of The Valley at Charlton in ages past. With the pop group Red Hot Chilli Peppers in town, Bergen was full to busting so we did well to find beds in a dormitory at a youth hostel. We were in the bar next door thanking our lucky stars for that small mercy when we got talking to a lovely couple who took pity on us with an invitation to dinner the next evening.

The scenic Flam to Myrdal railway had to be fitted into my itinerary. Just as the Amazon is to Brazil, this 13-mile stretch of steep standard gauge track is a must for every tourist to Norway. The train lingers along its short route between mountain slopes, farmhouses and waterfalls, one of which is adorned by the dancing waterfall women or Huldra who, as folklore would have it, tried to seduce young men by luring them into the nearest forest. A magical myth for the women are, in fact, girls from

168

Norway's ballet school. But in the sunlit spray of one of the train's stops, they are an exotic image all the same.

Moving onto Voss from where I could catch a much faster train, I travelled back up north towards Molde. My bed for a few nights was a pupil's study at the local university which had been turned into tourist accommodation for the summer months. Molde's Aker Stadion, perched on top of the Romsdalfjord, was the scene of the club's 2-0 win over Sligo in a Champions League qualifier. I stayed on for Ole Gunnar Solksjaer's press conference. If anyone had told me then that he would be Manchester United's manager within another six years, I would have scoffed. It was fortunate perhaps that there was nothing more to tempt me that midweek as the weather was ideal and the tiny island a boat ride away offered perfect bathing facilities. I got talking to a friendly couple there who let me share their barbeque.

Alesund's home game with Sandnes the following Saturday made for an obvious stop. Alesund's original Kramyra Stadion which I had visited with Jurgen a few years previously would have been well worth a second visit. Built on top of a fjord, the so-called terrace opposite the main stand was more like a cliff face, covered in grass and rocks with chunks of it chiselled out to accommodate benches for hardy spectators if they didn't fancy standing on the slippery, stony surfaces. I was so astonished that I successfully persuaded Brian Oliver to take a piece on it for The Observer. Like the ground in Corsica and Toftir in the Faroes, it contained a backdrop so utterly compelling that it was hard to concentrate throughout on what was happening on the pitch. But it was on the bus to Alesund's modern new Color Line edifice that I caught a glimpse of their former home which was now overgrown and unkempt. It was sad and with a fondness for the home club largely because of where they had once played, I was sad to see them lose a thrilling game 3-2.

I defy anyone who has ever been tempted to tour Norwegian grounds without a car to plot a path to Sogndal without serious headaches. English Northerners complain about finding Palace just as southern fans decry the complications in getting to Middlesbrough. They don't compare with Sogndal which has no train station anywhere near it. As I was travelling solo now without anyone to share petrol or car hire, I had to rely on public transport to keep costs down in this land of expensive living. Kick-off was not until 6pm the next day but getting there was no simple task. I set off on my 165-mile trek as soon as Alesund's game was over and had changed buses three times before finding the gazebo-like dwelling that I had booked for the night in someone's garden just outside the town of Stryn. That still left me three more bus connections the next day and a good deal more anxiety before chancing upon the small town of Sogndal near the end of the Sognefjord. Remarkably I still had time to see most of the women's European Championship final between Germany and Norway in a bar before Sogndal's 1-1 draw with Haugesund. I felt I had accomplished one of my life's great feats by seeing a game at the Fosshaugane Campus, but I need not have fretted. I should have realised that everything in Scandanavia runs like clockwork.

One of the delights of travelling in Norway is the frequency with which the buses must board boats so as to cross the plethora of fjords. And there were plenty more of them to traverse. Most passengers stay put in their seats for the short crossings, but I was like a kid with a new toy, forever disembarking the buses to watch the ripples of the fjord's waters and the oncoming ports if you could call them that. More like hamlets in the middle of nowhere with mooring posts. In the safe knowledge that the hard part was over and that nothing would be more tricky than getting to Sogndal, I left the next morning, little caring if I made it to Oslo on time by a combination of buses and trains. For the only option that Monday night was a game at Fjellhamer's nondescript third division ground from where I travelled on the next day into and across Sweden by train.

Chapter 40:
Hitching a lift

The raison d'etre of my trip was to get to grips with the Veikkausliiga (Finnish League) but to reach Finland via the northern Swedish port of Umea I had to go via Uppsala whose fourth-tier club Gamla Uppsala happened to be at home. I must have been desperate. I took a bus out of town to a ground which would barely have graced the Combined Counties League and I stood in a rotting wooden stand where a combination of overhanging tree branches, none too sparkling floodlights and rainwater trickling down my neck failed to enhance the entertainment on offer. I dried out in the town's railway station waiting room before the sleeper arrived. Maybe I got out of the wrong station in Umea at an unearthly hour but the cab ride to the port seemed endless and once again, costly.

The saving grace once more was the convenience of the games. If I had been the fixture secretary responsible for the whole of Scandanavia I couldn't have done a better job. For boats from Umea serve Vaasa, a port on the western coast of Finland whose local club VPS, believe it or not, were at home that Wednesday night, not that their game with Lahti had much going for it. Vaasa were dismal and Lahti, who won 3-0, not much better. The standard seemed better at the weekend when adjacent to Helsinki's woody suburbs, lies the picturesque stadium of Vikingit where I saw Haka, the Ykkonen (second division) promotion contenders win 3-0. By now, Susan who worked for a satirical magazine and who I had met at swift dating, had flown out to join me. She was a part-time Chelsea fan.

I had honoured Susan's arrival by booking a decent city centre hotel, but we couldn't stay for long as the games were coming round thick and fast. Next stop was Espoo who sit among Helsinki's western outskirts. Since their visitors were Inter Turku and since I have never been accused of looking a gift horse in the mouth, I utilised a sudden stroke of ingenuity to tell Susan before the game that we would wait for the Inter Turku supporters club coach. Knowing that they would be heading back to Turku where we needed to be the next night for TPS Turku's game with Lahti, the obvious ploy was to try and hitch a lift. The visiting supporters duly arrived and I asked their leader if they might just have two spare seats for us. He seemed happy to comply and let us off with a token payment for our one-way 100-mile journey. Luckily the Inter supporters were in a mellow mood after their club's 0-0 draw which was not the case with their city rivals 24 hours later since Lahti were 2-1 winners in the Veritas Stadium which both Turku clubs share. Our room for the night had been over a launderette, astutely booked by Susan when we were on the supporters' club coach. Whatever my many gripes with booking.com, they certainly came to our rescue on that occasion.

On our tour of Turku between the two games, Susan and I followed the obligatory boat trip around the harbour by exploring the city's Paavo Nurmi Stadium named after the Flying Finn whose 3,000 metres world record in 1922 was one of 20 athletic world records set in that arena. A plaque in Nurmi's honour adorns the stadium. With complicated journeys ahead of us from our wooden chalet on the idyllic farm we had booked for the rest of our stay, we hired a Volvo which conveyed us to Haka's 4-0 win over Oulu. Any visit to a Haka match just has to be supplemented with a visit to the football museum in the industrial town of Valkeakoski. It was just as well that Mikko, my Finnish mate who supports Palace - despite being based in Congleton, near Manchester - had recommended that fascinating museum or it might have escaped our attention. I am sure Susan would have been mortified.

Through Mikko's contacts, we had company on our next and last stop. Two of his pals, both big Man City fans were proud to show us their pictures in the local paper which had done a story on their forthcoming excursion to Helsinki for City's pre-season friendly there. But on this occasion, we were all going to watch the Tampere club, Ilves beat Kajaani 3-0. That ended my Scandanavian adventure of 14 games in 25 days. I was back home in time to accompany Neil on our first ever visit to The Hive, the new home of Barnet who overcame Chester 3-0.

3-0 scorelines certainly seemed to be the order of the day as that was also the outcome when I ventured to Morocco for the semi-finals of the World Club Championships in December. Bayern Munich trounced Guangzhou Evergrande of China in Agadir and Raja Casablanca were shock 3-1 winners over the Brazilians from Atletico Mineiro in Marrakesh the next day. The games were far from memorable so the highlights of my four days away were provided away from the football stadiums. The goats who nibble away at the vegetation while they balance precariously on the branches of trees were one incredible sight. And then in the company of Scottish Mark who had long since jumped on the Bayern Munich bandwagon, plus the usual phalanx of Germans, there was an excursion incorporating a lunch of lamb stew in a restaurant that was completely surrounded by Atlas Mountains. It was difficult to concentrate on what we were eating.

Chapter 41:
Tension at the turnstiles

The need to see Mallorca's must-not-lose segunda div game in Cordoba - which finished 0-0 keeping them up - meant that it was from Spain that I flew to Brazil for the second summer running. I had accessed some tickets for the 2014 World Cup through the Fifa ballot and conducting swops where necessary with Chelsea Ian. With a ticket for the final in my grubby mitts, the other priority was to visit the only stads with which I had not already acquainted myself during the previous year's Confederations Cup. Even with only seven grounds on my to-do list, I was on such a hectic schedule that I didn't get to see much of the cities I was visiting. I remember little for instance of Natal where I saw Mexico beat Cameroon 1-0 but I was at least a little familiar with Manaus where Roy Hodgson's England team succumbed 2-1 to Italy. Cuiaba, the scene of a 1-1 draw between Russia and South Korea was also a new one to me as was Sao Paolo where England went down 2-1 again, this time to Uruguay. That meant we were effectively out. I wouldn't have been so indifferent as to our plight had I suspected then that Hodgson would become Palace's manager in years to come.

I wasn't remotely envious of the likes of Chris who had a dozen venues to tick off so I was happy to chill out for a week in the southern city of Curitiba where conveniently there would be three group games evenly spaced out. But inconveniently I had tickets for none of them. The first one, Honduras v Ecuador took me by surprise as it was a remarkably hot ticket. Or was it really that remarkable that I could not get one for love or money bearing in mind that both countries were well supported. Try as I might, I could not find a ticket for sale as I approached the heavily populated entrance to the Arena da Baixada. There was nothing else for it but to jib my way past the guards with sleight of hand. Breathing heavily and shaking terribly, holding a ticket from previous games in each hand, I somehow deceived the uniformed personnel to find myself inside. My nerves were in shreds, but I was in. As anyone who has ever crashed a game without a ticket will tell you, their problems are as good as over when they're inside the blessed gates. There is always a spare seat somewhere, no matter how significant the game is, world cup final or premier league title decider. Someone has been taken ill before the game or someone else has had an accident on the way to the stadium. Or far more likely, Fifa have fucked up with their ticket allocation for hospitality. If the steward at the top of one gangway is a jobsworth inspecting every ticket studiously, be sure that the steward on the next gangway is a more relaxed individual with his eye on the players warming up or on a pretty girl wanting directions to her seat.

The smartest move is to always find an aisle seat away from the steward's line of vision just in case he spots the ticketless intruder moving on every time the late-arriving rightful ticket holder demands his seat. Most of the women who have joined me at football have hated the occasions when I have exchanged lousy seats low down behind the corner flag for superior ones on the side. This frequently means stumbling past rows of occupied seats once the game is in progress. But needs-must I tell them. Sometimes they refuse to budge. Anyway, I digress. Honduras and Ecuador did me proud with a splendid game that the south Americans won 2-1 though to be honest any calibre of game would have been fine by me, such was my overwhelming relief at being inside rather than outside.

Curitiba wasn't a bad place to hang out. There were decent restaurants and cheerful bars on whose televisions I could view the other games. But with no wish for a repeat of my previous escapade or to test my nerves again, I made doubly sure that I had a ticket for the next game which was Spain v Australia. This, too, was a surprisingly popular match given that the two teams were playing only for pride as they were both on nul points, having lost their first two group games which was half to be expected in Australia's case, much less so where the defending world champions are concerned. In normal circumstances I would not have countenanced such a fixture as there's nothing I dislike more than meaningless sporting events. But I was stuck with this one so, wandering through a shopping centre the day before the game towards a ticket collection point, I spotted a Russian couple seemingly at odds with the salesperson over the extra ticket they had unexpectedly found in their envelope. I put them out of their misery by offering them the cost price which wasn't to their liking. So, I offered them a quarter as much again and the ticket was mine. With Mile Jedinak, my all-time favourite Palace player - just in front of Mark Bright - captaining Australia, I was sorry to see the Socceroos go down 3-0.

With my newly acquired weekly membership of a gym near my hotel where I could exercise more safely than on the busy roads, I was chuffed. Extra confirmation of my wisdom in selecting Curitiba as a stopping-off place came with the ensuing exodus of thousands of Aussies. The Russian couple I had encountered earlier were clearly in town primarily for the next game which would be their country's clash with Algeria which word had it, would be of less appeal to the masses than the two previous games.

174

There's no predicting how things materialise on the tickets front. Spain v Australia had been a nothing game and yet it was packed out whereas fewer people wanted to see Russia versus Algeria though it had far more going for it on paper. I'd hate to be a tout in such circumstances. Thankfully, I had evaluated the market correctly as the number of people selling tickets outnumbered the punters wanting them. I got one for under cost price, much to the grumbling tout's irritation. The 1-1 draw was good enough for Algeria to progress but not Russia.

I took a flight to Rio the next day where my fortunes changed for the worse. A group of us got to within a short walk of the Maracanã early enough for a pre match drink and lunch on the top floor of a lively looking establishment. I was wearing shorts with my ticket for the second-round game between Colombia and Uruguay safe in one of the pockets. Or so I thought. I was also carrying two tickets for the forthcoming Brazil v Colombia match which I needed for a possible exchange. Such was my paranoia that I checked my pocket every few moments. And such was the din that at one point I had to dash downstairs so that I could hear who was on the other end of my mobile phone. I went back upstairs after the call and checked my pocket again. The tickets had gone. To this day, I don't know what had happened. Had the tickets flown out on my race downstairs or had some kid sneaked under the table, unbeknown to me, to ease them out of my trouser pocket. I was in a panic but there was no getting past security this time as the police were about five deep outside the Maracana. Along with scores of others who had had their pockets picked on trains to the stadium, I spent the duration of the match in a portacabin outlining details of the theft to an investigating police officer. It was no way to spend a Saturday afternoon. I was even more distraught when I heard that James Rodriguez had won the game for Colombia with a stupendous shot which was later voted goal of the tournament. I did, at least, get to see it replayed on television on numerous occasions but that's hardly the same.

My despair was in danger of increasing tenfold two days later after flying down to the southernmost venue of Porto Alegre for Algeria's second-round tie v Germany, another game for which I didn't have a ticket. On the long walk down an avenue from the city centre to the Estadio Beira-Rio, there were handfuls of people selling tickets including a couple of kids who sold me one at twice face value. I had tried to reason with them, but they were street-wise, probably brought up in the nearest favela. I sauntered on bemoaning the cost but happy nevertheless to have a ticket. My contentment evaporated at the turnstiles where I was refused entry. My ticket had apparently already been used. The kids who sold it, were evidently operating a scam. Four of them go in and one comes out with all four tickets, telling the guy at the turnstile that he is feeling sick or some such tale of woe. He then sells the four tickets. At the end of the day the kids have made a mighty profit and lots of would-be spectators have been turned away after parting with a small fortune. But I was not to be beaten. With time on my side, I circled the stadium until I found one entrance which was manned as there was no turnstile. I waited until after kick-off by when the nearest steward's back was turned. He was engrossed in the action. Choosing my moment well, I hurtled past him and into a clutch of empty seats behind one goal. If the steward was bothered, he didn't show it. Having missed ten minutes, I was glad that the game went to extra time during which there was a flurry of goals, Andre Schurrle and Mesut Ozil scoring for Germany before Abdelmoumene Djabou got one back.

Back in Sao Paolo the next day, the attraction was Argentina's second-round tie against Switzerland, another game for which I did not have a ticket. I had almost given up hope of getting in when a late arrival waving a spare one in the air, sold it to me for half price. I had missed 20 minutes but once again extra time came to my rescue, so I didn't feel too cheated. It was an engrossing game eventually won for the Argies late on by Angel Di Mario's cross shot. It was no way for Ottmar Hitzfeld, Switzerland's manager to end his 31-year career in football management.

I had been more fortunate than Oldham Dave who, looking somewhat distressed, told me his sad story when we met up after the game. He had been hanging around the Itaquera Metro stop on the lookout for a ticket when he was on the point of doing a deal with a couple of shady north Africans who were well aware that they were under police scrutiny. On being summoned onto the station platform, Dave asked: "so where's my ticket?" to which one of the north Africans reached into his underpants and fished out the ticket from where it had been secreted. Knowing that such a souvenir would not add much in the way of fragrance to his shrine back in Oldham, Dave said: "I'm not having that," and missed the match. He was always a man of principles was Dave.

Chapter 42:
Fifa's nasty little scheme

I became aware of Fifa's odious duplicity when I returned to Fortaleza, the scene of my near mugging 12 months earlier. Fifa were obviously within their rights not to offer me a refund for the tickets I'd had stolen outside the Maracanã but then they had them re-issued for sale elsewhere which I thought was despicable. Hundreds of victims must have been in the same boat. I had wondered why Fifa were refusing to issue duplicates which would have been a simple enough exercise until I discovered the extent of their nasty little scheme when Chelsea Ian changed his plans. He offered me one of the tickets I had originally sold him for the Brazil v Colombia quarter-final. It happened to be the seat next to one of the stolen pair so, of course, I was a bit surprised to find a girl sitting in that seat. I asked her how she'd come across the ticket and she told me she had bought it off the Fifa website that morning. I was flabbergasted. When I complained to Fifa, I was airily dismissed. Their policy was not to offer duplicates but to offer the original stolen tickets for re-sale. Incredible. For an organisation with its reputation already in tatters, they were going the wrong way about restoring their image. But what more could one reasonably expect of a firm with a criminal like Sepp Blatter in charge?

Getting to Fortaleza at short notice had been no easy task. I had to find a flight and somewhere to stay. Eventually through the trusty skyscanner website, I discovered a route via Recife where I had to wait for an eternity. Arriving at Fortaleza well past midnight, I got talking to the only other guy in the bus queue who was Steve from Singapore. He was a big Brazil fan who seemed well under the thumb of his wife back in the Far East. She had allowed him to go to South America on the condition that he was back in ten days, which meant that he had a meagre three games on his itinerary. With no hotel booked and Brazil in town, I thought that I might have to make do in my sleeping bag on Fortaleza's huge sandy beach. But thankfully the hotel which Steve had booked, found a room for me too. Unlike Steve though, I was no longer an avid Brazil fan. Memories of Rivaldo's antics in South Korea were still vivid and Marcelo could be a nasty piece of work as Messi found to his cost three years later in El Clasico. So, I couldn't find it in my heart to summon up large doses of sympathy for the whingeing Neymar when he dislocated his shoulder. Brazil nevertheless won a tumultuous match 2-1.

I had never been a huge advocate of fan fests. I would always rather be at a game rather than swilling beer and watching it on a big screen somewhere. But the next evening there was nothing much else for it but to join the throngs on Fortaleza's beach. Conservative estimates suggested that as many as 100,000 people were on that golden expanse by the end of Holland's quarter-final with Costa Rica down in Salvador. Fortaleza was heaving. Where they would all be bedding down for the night, I had no idea. But the whole occasion was absolutely captivating, intensely atmospheric and with screens that were clear and focussed thank God. There was no way I was going to make a habit of this experience, but it was a decent alternative to being at the actual game which was goalless at the end of extra time by when Holland had their substitute goalkeeper Tim Krul on the pitch. Krul who had replaced Jesper Cillesen a minute from the end because he was a better spot-kick stopper, subsequently became his country's hero by saving two penalties in the shoot-out which Holland won 4-3.

All my misgivings about Fortaleza vanished over the next few days until it was time to bid a reluctant goodbye. The semi-finals were upon us and thanks to Chelsea Ian, I had a ticket for the first one in Belo Horizonte in whose Estadio Mineirão England had collected their only point of the tournament a fortnight earlier by drawing 0-0 with Costa Rica. But this time it was Brazil v Germany. Games don't come much bigger than that. Sometimes I groan when I find I've got a ticket for behind the goal as Ian knew only too well from my reactions to the occasions when he had got me a Shed End ticket at Chelsea or one for the Mathew Harding Stand. But this time it was undoubtedly the best place to be as we happened to be behind the very goal where Germany scored five unanswered first-half goals. Brazil were without Neymar, of course, but that was no excuse for their capitulation. David Luiz and Thiago Silva in central defence were little short of pathetic. Germany did not have to be that good to carry out their slaughter. Toni Kroos helped himself to two goals and there were others from Miroslav Klose, Andreas Muller and Sami Khedira before the break brought respite for the hosts. Schurrle added to Brazil's humiliation with two more goals before Oscar got a late consolation in front of us. The 1-7 scoreline was surreal.

Chris and I were ensconced at an Air B and B with a welcoming couple who guided us to the best car hire place for the next day's 315-mile trek to Sao Paolo. He had a ticket for the Holland v Argentina semi-final, but I didn't so my spirits soared when Markus Linke rang me while we were in transit to ask if I wanted to be part of a devious plan to gain entry. He had in his possession tickets for a disabled person and the helper. Did I want to be the disabled person, he asked. Why not, I reasoned, adhering to the maxim that it is always better to try and fail than not to try at all. We met up as planned at the same Itaquera Metro stop where Dave had met his comeuppance only a few days earlier and Markus introduced me to Helmut. The deal was that I would cough up 300 euros if I got in. The plan was that I would stagger and limp towards the turnstiles supported by the German which left us with just two snags. One was the name on the ticket, Gabriella Minosata and the other was that we didn't have a wheelchair between us. So, it wasn't too much of a surprise that we didn't make it past the turnstiles or, at least, I didn't. With little thought for his 'handicapped' companion, Helmut swiftly disappeared. I later learned that he did, in fact, see the game.

I went to the Fifa Help desk which is an anomaly if ever there was one. I might just as well have sought help from a wasps' nest. After my previous experience I felt it could have been renamed the Help Fifa desk. The guy there asked me for my ticket. "But you are not Gabriella," he said, which was very observant of him. "Where is Gabriella?" he asked to which I replied: "She has died so I have got her ticket," whereupon he asked me where my wheelchair was. Sensing that the game was up, I said: "One of the wheels fell off so we could not bring it." With a familiar gesture of his right thumb that suggested he was telling me to hop it, I did as I was told.

Baldric in Rowan Atkinson's Black Adder might have called it a cunning plan but like all Baldrick's cunning plans, it was destined to fail.

There was still time before the game to make one last attempt to get in. Spare tickets were scarce, but I encountered a young American who seemed in two minds as to how much he should ask for one. He kept appearing and re-appearing and had obviously run out of potential takers when he approached me one last time. What he wanted was more than I had on me. We agreed that I would hand over the money in Rio before the final. So, he took my number and I took his driving license to copy down his name and address at which point I was aware of my collar being felt. I was frogmarched away by a burly security chap - who looked like gestapo - before I could hand the American back his driving license. I knew I had to admit defeat then, but it took me to beyond half-time to find space in a bar where I could see the rest of the action. Chris told me after the goalless draw and Argentina's 4-2 success on penalties that I hadn't missed much. It hadn't been a great game, he said. Which wasn't a massive consolation.

Even though I had missed the semi-final, I had no intention of joining Ian in Brasilia for the third-place match. Ian, incidentally, was continuing on what must constitute some kind of record. From the opening match of the 1994 World Cup Finals in the USA, he had not missed a single day's play in world cup finals until the Argentina v Iceland group game at the 2018 Russian World Cup when he baulked at paying £1,000 in Moscow.

Chris and I headed, meanwhile, for Rio in our rented Peugeot. This was a far more leisurely drive, but I was a nervous wreck after all the stress of the past few days, so I did not join him on a sight-seeing trip up Sugar Loaf Mountain. But it wasn't as if I had time on my hands. Eurosport had got wind of my lost ticket saga and Fifa's machinations and wanted an interview complete with photograph of me holding up my ticket for the final. Alas, that story was never going to see the light of day as it was in competition with previews of the World Cup final which meant there would be only one winner. But, at least, through the Eurosport man I was able to reunite the Yank with his driving license. With my ticket for the final safely buttoned up in an inside jacket pocket this time, I went to the game hoping for a German win as I could not warm to the macho men of Argentina despite my untold admiration for Messi. From my seat at a reasonable height over the corner flag, I had an excellent view of the goal from Mario Gotze late in extra time that thankfully prevented yet another final from going to the lottery of a penalty shoot-out.

Chapter 43.
Where eagles dare to dive

With an eight-hour stop-over in Rome on my return to the UK, I had plenty of time to reflect on the World Cup and make plans for the new season or, more specifically, the pre-season. By a remarkable quirk the next game I saw, a friendly, ended Roffey 1, Three Bridges 7. That meant I'd seen two 1-7s in 11 days. This one attracted rather less spectators than Belo Horizonte, just a few of us standing around a pitch in a pleasant tree-lined park just outside Crawley. With the new Premier League season still two weeks distant, Scandinavia called again with Susan once more my companion. The main course of our trip, so far as I was concerned, would be a visit to Bodo-Glimt. Fearing that their stay in the Tippeligaen would end after a single season, I was in a rush to see a game at this far northern outpost. The hors d'oeuvre would be supplied by the second division club, Eidsvold who were a bus ride plus short walk from our Oslo Airport hotel. They treated me to a 4-1 win over Lorenskog. The next day we flew up to Bodo where there was no sign of match day fever among the leafy residential streets where the ground nestles. For all that we saw a thriller, won 4-3 by the visitors, Sarpsborg who were managed by the former Sheffield United striker Brian Deane.

With the early rounds of the European club competitions less helpful than in 2013, I resolved that there must be worse things to do in Norway during a blank footballing midweek than visit the Lufoten islands. With several days to spare, the Lufotens beckoned as did the weather, hot albeit quite breezy. People who eschew northern Scandinavia as a summer holiday destination because of a belief that the weather will not be to their liking, are severely mistaken. The sun shines brightly more often than not. And yet here we were inside the Arctic Circle. We were advised to get to the islands via a bus ride to Narvik, sparing us a costly boat trip from Bodo. In an ideal world that meant taking a car which meant less than ideally, parting with hundreds more Norwegian kroner to hire one. There was nothing else for it. But those spectacular islands merited such an outlay. Animal lover that I am, I couldn't take my eyes off the sea eagle that swooped into the foam to grab a fish when we went on a boat trip. The eagle's dinner was similar to ours on the occasions we dined out on the islands' speciality of salted cod and Arctic Char. With Palace in mind, I bought a t-shirt emblazoned with "where eagles dare to go.'"

Dumping the car on our return - via several bridges - to the mainland, we took buses and trains 320 miles into Sweden for an overnight stop at Lulea from where we continued the next morning to Tornio whose Finnish second div club, TP47 were at home that Saturday afternoon to TBK. One of the Tornio players caught my eye in the half hour before he was substituted, presumably because of his arrogance on the ball which had always been an admirable trait so far as I was concerned. I sought out the player afterwards and asked him why he had been taken off. He had no real explanation but, even so, I made sure that I would recommend him to the Palace chief scout, Tim Coe for whom I was now doing some unpaid work. I never did find out if the player made it as far as a trial.

From Tornio we took a lengthy train ride the next day to Seinajoki where we relished a remarkable welcome in SJK's hospitality tents before, during and after their entertaining 2-2 draw with Inter Turku. Resisting a temptation to ask Inter's fans for another lift, we boarded our next train the following morning. Susan was heading home from Helsinki and I was bound for Germany where the Bundesliga div 2 fixtures had come to my aid along with my Bahncard rail pass. Two matches at Regensburg and Hallescher ended in 2-0 away wins for Unterhaching and Fortuna Koln respectively. I felt as if I was blazing a trail for Michael Portillo as I stepped onto yet another train, heading east this time, into Austria. Like Hodd in Norway the previous year, St Polten were surprise winners of the Austrian Cup which led them into the qualifying rounds of the Europa league in which they had pulled a big one in the shape of PSV Eindhoven whose 3-2 win gave them an aggregate 4-2 victory.

One of the culinary bonuses of watching football in Germany are the wursts mit brot on sale around the confines of the grounds. So, I was delighted to be returning forthwith to Germany, to FSV Frankfurt this time where the appetising aroma wafting around my nostrils simply begged me to sample the local sausages which turned out to be among the best I have ever tasted. Washed down with a Bamburg Rauchbier, a wurst mit brot (bread) and dollops of senf (mustard) sure beats a greasy burger and chips which is the English fan's staple pre-match diet. The game wasn't bad either, another 2-3 in Karksruhe's favour.

I hadn't quite been able to believe it when Pennie, my new Palace girlfriend, told me that Palace were coming to Germany for a pre-season friendly. Not just Germany but Augsburg which was one of two Bundesliga grounds - along with Hoffenheim - I had yet to visit. Pennie had come to my notice several months earlier when she had suddenly appeared in the players bar at Selhurst Park before an Under 23 match.

182

An enigmatic brunette, I had clocked her again three days later on the train back from our 2-0 defeat at West Brom with the result that our first date, a few nights later, was dinner in the Fulham Palace Road after the Italy v Nigeria friendly at Craven Cottage. Talk about spoiling a girl!

Anyway, as a Palace fan who had long since decided that her vocation in life was to see every league and cup game, home and away, she was happy to come to Augsburg although she didn't "normally do friendlies." The German equivalent of a testspiel obviously didn't count so I collected Pennie at Nuremburg Airport from where we sped to the Augsburg Arena for a goalless draw which was remarkable only for the fact that it was the last game with Tony Pulis in charge. The day after collecting a £2million bonus for keeping Palace up and only three days before the start of the new campaign, he resigned, citing a row with the players the previous day. Only it wasn't the previous day and nor did Pulis need the money rapido, as he claimed, to buy some land for his children. The land didn't exist, it was revealed in the High Court where a judge ordered him to fork out £3.7million for leaving Palace in the lurch after promising commitment to the chairman Steve Parish.

The combination of a sumptuous dinner and a therapeutic run alongside the river - for me - made our choice of Neuburg an der Donau as our stop-off for the night, a wise one. Neu as in Neuburg translates to 'new' in English but there was nothing too new about this delightful town which dates back to the tenth century. It lies a few miles outside Ingolstadt whose football club had not long since moved into the modern Audi Sportpark Stadion where we saw a sparkling 2-2 draw with Darmstadt. After that we headed back to Nuremburg for the next night's local derby. For a long time after Gurther Furth's rousing 5-1 win I retained a sense of guilt for taking the only press ticket between us. Well, she did insist that I had it!

We went our separate ways the next day, Pennie back to London, me to Zurich to watch a few days of the European Athletic Championships where, in the distance events, I saw Jo Pavey - at the ripe old age of 40 - and Mo Farah win the first two of a dozen gold medals that came Britain's way.

Chapter 44:
Wedding flashes

Sometimes sacrifices have to be made. If I was to combine the Asian Championships in Australia with visits to my two sons Down Under, it would have to be at the expense of Palace's Premier League game at Burnley and the FA Cup fourth-round tie at Southampton. They would be the third and fourth Palace matches I would forsake that season.

The wedding of Sally's nephew, Charlie in deepest Sussex had already forced me away from the Emirates for the season-opener at Arsenal. There were, at least, a couple of others in similar positions. Andy would have been otherwise engaged, watching West Ham and David was a Man City devotee. Like me, they spent the afternoon fretting and waiting for goal flashes and updates of their clubs' matches on their mobiles. This was nothing new to Andy who was in a constant state of torment. As a big noise with Samsun who were Chelsea's sponsors, he was expected to show his face at most of the club's home games. On one occasion he took his wife, Ruth along to Stamford Bridge. As they sipped champagne, she squeezed his hand and said: "isn't this nice darling? Why don't you give up supporting West Ham and then you could have all this for the rest of your life?" He gave her a withering look.

The thought of 'giving up' his beloved Hammers for the comfort of the hospitality boxes at the Bridge obviously appalled Andy. Telling me the story, he elaborated, "They just don't get it Nick, do they?" I think Andy was much relieved when Samsun and Chelsea ended their sponsorship deal with the result that he could carry on commuting from his Derbyshire home to West Ham's games.

Ten weeks after the wedding came the christening of my grandson, Rex that clashed with our visit to The Hawthorns. Why, I wondered, must people get married in the football season and have their kids christened on Saturday afternoons? But my daughter, Jessica was unsympathetic. At least she chose a date for the christening that didn't coincide with a Palace home game and, furthermore she had decided on a time, 1pm, that meant I could go to the reception and still get to a game even if it was only Colliers Wood v Badshot Lea in the Combined Counties League. I was afraid, all the same, of having to tolerate comments like "what kind of a Palace fan are you?" as I made plans to travel to Australia five months later. But that cup tie at St Mary's in January 2015 was to be the last

Palace game I missed before the arrival of the Coronavirus except for a Carabao Cup tie at home to Colchester.

First stop in Oz was to Sydney for the hosts' 4-0 win over Oman. Thereafter the fixtures had worked out brilliantly. I had only ever been to Brisbane fleetingly for a dreary afternoon's play in a Test match at The Gabba 25 years earlier when Sri Lanka were the touring team. So, I was more than happy to be persuaded to spend a few days there this time. With three Asian Cup group games crowded into four days at the Brisbane Stadium, there was every reason for Sally and I to linger in Queensland's capital city and take a boat ride down the Brisbane River. The usual smattering of Germans were in town plus John Bethell and the two Scots, Ross and Mark so there was plenty of good company. China v Uzbekistan (2-1) and Japan v Iraq (1-0) were the pipe-openers to Australia's shock 1-0 defeat by South Korea. I had done my homework well to find a late-night bar after that game that was showing Palace's match at Burnley. It was a balmy Brisbane evening and yet, on the big screen, I could spot snow on the hillsides beyond Turf Moor. That was a real juxtaposition. And then, even more bizarrely, a chap approached us out of the blue, to ask: "tinder or plenty of fish?" We must have looked as if we were on a first date.

Next stop was Melbourne for the Uzbeks' 3-1 win over Saudi Arabia. The next game was expendable. With Japan 99 percent certain to qualify for the knockout stages, I acted the martyr by giving up their group game against Jordan so as to spend more time with my son James, his wife Angelina and their two kids, Charlotte and Alexander, in Kyneton, a small market town an hour's drive north west of Melbourne. The excitement and bustle of the football seemed a world away on the afternoon we spent riding the Victorian Goldfields heritage railway. But back to the Melbourne Rectangular Stadium I went the next day for South Korea's 2-0 quarter-final victory over the Uzbeks. Taking my reluctant leave then of Melbourne which had coincided neatly with the Grand Slam tennis, we headed for Canberra. It was probably with still vivid memories of the previous occasion I had done this 415-mile journey in a hired car which I had almost written off - plus myself - after skidding on a patch of oil, that the decision was taken to go by air. It was just as well that I arrived in one piece this time as I wouldn't have wanted to have missed that particular quarter-final, a scintillating 3-3 draw between Iraq and Iran which led to the Iraqis winning 7-6 in a tense penalty shoot-out.

The gap between the knockout rounds was an invitation to those of us wanting to embellish the Asian Cup with some A-league games but distances, as ever in Australia, remained a challenge. For instance,

Central Coast Mariners play in the town of Gosford, some 220 miles from Canberra so an early morning start was required in our rented BMW. We made it in time to see Sydney's 5-1 away win which was less of a joke than the hotel I had chosen on the town's outskirts, Bella Vista, the ultimate misnomer. Even without the torrential downpour that greeted us, there would have been no view to brag about. A two-day stay was sufficient after which we drove to Sydney for quality time with my other son Ashley. He is not a football fan at the best of times unless he is handed a ticket for a big game. The semi-final between South Korea and Iraq (2-0) was not deemed big enough for him. Australia's semi-final with the UAE might have got his vote had it been staged in Sydney, but the venue was Newcastle - another new one for me - where the hosts won 2-0.

I was surprised to see a teenager wearing a Palace scarf on the way to the game, so I stopped and questioned him. He had never seen a live Palace game but had decided through watching the Premier League on TV that Palace was the club for him, so he had sent off for the scarf. It was nice to see that Man United, City, Liverpool and the rest had some rivals in this respect.

Suitably desperate for yet more football, Ross and I went along the next afternoon to Sydney's School of Excellence for a game between Western Sydney and the FFA (Football Federation of Australia). I had to suffer some perplexing looks and comments from the others with my decision to fly home two days later. I think they were questioning my sanity. Why on earth was I going back and missing the final just so I could see Palace at home to Everton. Palace, as ever let me down, by losing 1-0. Maybe, after all, I should have stayed in Sydney to see Mile Jedinak lift the Asian Cup after Australia's 2-1 extra-time triumph win over South Korea.

For some unfathomable reason, Brighton's championship fixture with Brentford the following Friday had caught the eye. Susan came with me. As anyone who has ever driven to The Amex will testify, car parking there is a nightmare. Queues to the regular car park I had found were endless, so we made for the press car park. The young steward gave my press card a cursory look and said, "You call that a press card?"

"What's wrong with it?" I asked.

"I could have had one of them mocked up in my local high street," he said. While I opened my mouth to protest, he added: "Anyway, I love a good scam. In you go." But he was right, the card had been designed and perfected for me by an entrepreneurial printing shop in Putney.

Chapter 45:
Friends rally round

Maintaining its four-year cycle, the Copa America was upon us again in 2015 which meant that once more my expedition to south America began from Spain where I had been watching Mallorca as well as a bunch of tercera div fixtures on the mainland. I flew from Madrid to Miami and then onto Santiago. Like Argentina in 2011, Chile was going to present formidable difficulties in my endeavours to complete all the venues. Feeling like an intrepid explorer, I had been pouring over maps and an atlas for weeks beforehand trying to calculate how they could all be done. A further obstacle was the lack of press accreditation until midway through the tournament because of the usual hazards on the CONMEBOL website. That resulted in a near frenzy before the opening game in Santiago's Estadio Nacional until, for the equivalent of about £80, I managed to procure a ticket, enabling me to see Chile's 2-0 win over Ecuador.

Chris Miller, an affable Leeds fan we had met on our travels, arrived the next morning just in time to drop his bags off and drive Spurs Chris and I to Vina del Mar for the goalless draw between Mexico and Bolivia. I could hardly concentrate on the game at all as I had been mugged in the crush to get in. My wallet which was stuffed into an outside pocket in my jacket had disappeared by the time I got inside. I was grateful then for confirmation that my friends were there for me in times of need and great stress. They rallied around. In my panic, I rang Sally who cancelled all my cards while Chris lent me a credit card with which I was able to access cash. I needed this as we were going our separate ways from the northern most venue of Antofagusta to which we had flown to see Uruguay toil to a 1-0 win over Jamaican opponents who were making up the numbers.

After my various expensive mishaps in Brazil, I should have been hating south America by now, but I gradually warmed to the task of travelling almost half the length of Chile's 2,690 miles by the bus route I had mapped out. Much of the country may have a third-world feel to it but its transport system is sophisticated even if it does, for the most part, lack trains. Knowing that the Copa's next two match-days were in venues I had either done or would do, I could take my time now on the buses that conveyed me ever more in a southerly direction alongside the edge of the Atacama Desert.

I had done well to select Caldera for a two-night stay as that small port had plenty to offer in the way of decent paths to run on and the restaurant on the pier in which I could devour delicious sea food when I was not gazing at the colony of walruses snorting and cavorting on the rocks below.

Carrying on the next morning in my semi-kama class (reclining) seat, my reverie was suddenly awakened by the bus pulling in at Copiapo, the town famed for the near fatal disaster in 2010 which led to 33 miners being trapped 2,300 feet underground for 69 days. I got to pondering the fate of the poor soot-stained sod who rubbed his eyes on emerging into the daylight to find both his wife and girlfriend awaiting him. He probably wished he had never been rescued. You'd have thought that one of our enterprising tabloids would have tapped him up for his exclusive story when all 33 survivors were subsequently invited by Sir Alex Ferguson to a match at Old Trafford. That two-timing wretch could, I thought, have been excused for donning a red and white scarf and staying put in Manchester, claiming political asylum.

The city of La Serena was now within reach and it was there that I joined up with the others to see Argentina's 1-0 win over Uruguay. The scoreline was the same when we witnessed Colombia's win over Brazil the next night, in Santiago's Estadio Monumental and yet again for a third night running when Peru beat Venezuela. That game was in Valparaiso. As our bus turned a corner on the mountainous road, we could only briefly marvel at the breath-taking descent towards Chile's biggest port. I momentarily regretted the pace of my schedule that would prevent me from sampling more of what was also the country's culture capital. There were no such regrets the following day in Rancagua, one of Santiago's satellite towns and the stage for Ecuador's shock 2-1 win over Mexico.

With Stefan now my companion, we hired a car to eat up the miles, 425 of them, on the long straight south-bound PanAmerica highway, flanked to our left by Andean peaks peeping through the clouds. These mesmerising distractions contributed to an easing of our disappointment that this was proving one of the lowest scoring Copas ever, a statistic soon to be endorsed by the goalless draw involving Colombia and Peru that we saw that very evening in the southern-most venue of Temuco. Stefan who had been in the habit of travelling everywhere on overnight buses and looking much the worse for wear as a result, was all for staying in hovels so as to continue on his pesos-saving crusade. But that was not for me.

With a few days to spare before the quarter-finals and with Chris' card in my grasp, it was time to hit the tourist trail. But it was in pursuit of a little extra comfort that I settled for a room in the Bellavista Hotel when

188

we ventured further south to Puerto Varas which sits alongside Lake Llanquihue. And this really was a Bellavista Hotel. From my window I could see the twin peaks of the Osorno and Calbuco volcanoes. They were an awesome sight to compare with that of the Sarawak River twisting its way towards the ocean that I'd enjoyed from my hotel room in Kuching 18 years earlier.

Taking the car towards the most accessible of those volcanoes on a free afternoon, we disembarked to get almost hopelessly and fatally lost attempting to scale its forbidding slopes. Amid the near all-white landscape, it was ludicrously easy to misjudge the paths. Sensibly deciding that we were light years away from gaining the expertise required to join the professional mountaineering fraternity, we descended to a more sensible lower level before darkness engulfed us. The relief was twofold. We hadn't paid with our lives for being so foolhardy and the puffs of smoke rising from the crater of one of those volcanoes hadn't mustered the strength of a fully-fledged eruption during our brief ascent. Our stay in the region was all too short. Temuco beckoned once again and this time there were some goals to savour in Peru's 3-1 success over Bolivia thanks to a hat trick from Paolo Guerrero. The schedule had smiled upon us with another quarter-final in the deep south, that in Concepcion between Brazil and Paraguay which ended in a 4-3 win for Paraguay on pens after a 1-1 draw.

With a three-day wait before the first of the semi-finals in the same Estadio Municipal, it didn't take long for us to come to the conclusion that Concepcion was no place to kill time. We were glad of the diversion suggested by Scottish Mark to join him at the ski resort of Nevados de Chillan where it quickly became apparent that he was no slouch in the art of snowboarding. Better leave that to the experts, I decided, declining the opportunity to do likewise. Returning to Concepcion we were treated to a veritable goal feast in which Argentina overwhelmed Paraguay 6-1 with Messi providing three assists though he was surprisingly not among the marksmen. Concepcion was also staging the third place final but as we had long since exhausted the city's meagre temptations, we hit the road back to Santiago. We stopped off halfway, in Curico for a desperate, albeit successful search for a bar with a TV showing the women's World Cup semi-final. Overcoming the dismay of England's 2-1 loss to Japan, we concluded the journey to the nation's capital. With time to spare on the day of the Copa final, I found a third division game just outside Santiago which ended in a 2-1 home win and remarkably, ten players against eight, such was the referee's penchant for red cards. He was obviously out to emulate Mike Dean. For all its lack of goals, the Copa finished with a splendid final, but I couldn't help but feel extremely sorry for the Argies who lost the shoot-out 4-1. Messi scored their lone penalty but the chances of adorning his career with a senior winner's medal were receding by the tournament.

My summer's football was far from over. The bonus of finding a direct flight from Santiago to Dallas could not be ignored. The Gold Cup was in full swing in America and offering a host of venues new to me such as in the little-known Texan community of Frisco, 30 miles up the road, which was masquerading as the Dallas venue. I had assumed that I could just bowl into a hotel in Dallas and find a cheap room but that was far from the case. My usual ploy of going up to reception and saying: "I understand that you've got a special deal for tonight," was obviously well past its sell-by date. As I was to discover quite literally to my cost, it's virtually impossible to find a room anywhere in the States for much less than $200 a night. So, after a frustrating few hours of wandering around this vast metropolis in the heat of the day, buckling under the weight of my luggage, I booked into the most economic hotel I could find.

It was another reason to despise this star-spangled country and everything they stand for. All they had going for it this time was the football or Socca as they insist on calling it. And it's not as if their transport systems have much in their favour either. I eventually found a route to Frisco where I saw a double header (Panama v Haiti, 1-1 and USA v Honduras, 2-1) but that was no simple task. I spent the next day on the city's JFK Assassination Tour, an illuminating insight into the escape route taken by Lee Harvey Oswald after he had slain (their word not mine) the president. I'd always had a morbid curiosity in the drama as I'd been standing next to my mother when she took a call from my Dad at the Sunday Times one Friday night to say he'd be late home as John F Kennedy had just been shot. To this day I even remember who Palace played the next day. It was Hull at Selhurst Park. The game was a 2-2 draw and all the players wore black arm bands.

I took the Greyhound from Dallas the next day down to Houston where I found much cheaper, albeit hardly luxurious digs for my two-day stay encompassing another double-header (Jamaica v Canada, 1-0 and Costa Rica v El Salvador, 1-1). The two group games were so enjoyable and the BBVA Compass Stadium's press facilities so beneficial that I should have stayed put for the women's game between Houston Dash and Chicago Red Stars the next day instead of joining Chris on a Spirit Airlines flight to Kansas City. The intention for both of us was yet another double-header (Haiti v Honduras, 1-0 and USA v Panama, 1-1) but I regretted spending the free day in-between watching the Kansas City Royals versus Toronto Blue Jays baseball match that he dragged me to watch. Maybe it's something that a chap must do at least once in his

190

lifetime but so far as I was concerned, enduring a baseball game amounted to a waste of a sweltering Sunday afternoon.

We were going our separate ways from Kansas. As my onwards journey was by Amtrak now, I had time to admire the incredible Beaux-Arts architecture of the Kansas City Union Station's grand hall complete with its three large hanging chandeliers. The subsequent seven-and-a-half-hour ride to Chicago wasn't the most scenic I've ever undertaken but from my seat on the top deck in the glass fronted viewing gallery, I spied great swathes of the Midwest stretching towards the horizon. That was no great hardship. Chicago Fire's MLS game v Colombus Crew the next night (0-1) was less riveting as was the prosaic Bridgeview venue.

The cost of accommodation was mounting up, so I was grateful to my ex-American girlfriend Linda for her contribution to keeping the rest of my costs down. She invited me to stay in her plush apartment in Hoboken in New Jersey, overlooking the Hudson River. It is a fashionable district of enhanced celebrity status because it was the home of Frank Sinatra. With a five-star hotel next door that was housing the Chelsea team during my stay - as they had a pre-season friendly lined up - it was such a swanky area that Linda's decision to move out years later because she could no longer afford it, came as no great surprise. But for my short stay it was perfect. There were runs along the promenade, a choice of restaurants - all of them adorned with Sinatra memorabilia - where I could treat her to a thank-you dinner, nearby river cruises up to and around the Statue of Liberty and accessibility, of course, to the various stadiums still on my list. The first two quarter-finals (USA v Cuba, 6-0 and Jamaica v Haiti, 1-0) took me to an overnight stay at Baltimore but I was back the next day for the next two in New York's Giants Stadium which both went to extra time, Panama eventually beating Trinidad and Tobago 6-5 on pens, and Mexico winning 1-0 against Costa Rica.

The semi-finals were, I decided, out of reach as they were in Atlanta but, not to worry, there was another MLS game to occupy the vacant midweek slot. I bumped into John Bethell in the grim, soul-destroying suburb of Harrison which is the home of New York Red Bulls. They went down 4-3 in a penalty shoot-out to Philadelphia Union after 90 minutes had found the clubs level at 1-1. They don't do drawn games in the MLS and nor did they, of course, in the Gold Cup's third-place game in Chester - a suburb of Philadelphia - which also finished 1-1 before Panama beat the hosts 3-2 in the shoot-out. Meeting up with Scottish Mark, we recovered from an inebriated lunchtime boat trip on the Delaware River before making our way to Philadelphia's Lincoln Financial Field. With its towering stands, the stadium provided a fabulous setting for a final and

Mexico did the occasion proud with a fine display in overcoming Jamaica 3-1. But I was pleased to see the vanquished Palace defender Adrian Mariappa give a worthy display in Jamaica's rear-guard.

There was still a fortnight before the start of the new Premier League so where better for Pennie and I to spend some of that time than in Finland once more. The idea had been to dawdle through our first afternoon before the evening's HIFK (Helsingfors) v Ilves game (2-2) in Helsinki but on picking up that day's Daily Mail at Gatwick, I had been astonished to read a preview of a pre-season friendly involving HJK, the capital's top club, and Liverpool. It was going to take place in the crumbling Olympic Stadium. I had been there for every day of the 1983 World Athletic Championships but only once previously for football. Could we do both games? You bet we could. So, Liverpool's 2-0 win was included on a somewhat more hectic first day of our holiday than we had originally bargained for. Thanks to VIP tickets laid on by Mikko, my Palace/Finnish friend, we even had hospitality at the HIFK game.

Buoyed by this promising start, things continued on an even keel thereafter. Lahti's 1-1 draw with Jaro the next day just had to be furnished with a boat trip on the Vesijarvi Lake before we headed towards the coast again and the town of Kotka. The guest house I had booked took some finding and when we eventually got there, it was to encounter a glamorous brunette of a Russian landlady with a husky voice - echoes of Nadiya - who showed us to our room. We were on the edge of town which meant that we were close to a forest, a fast-flowing stream, verdant countryside and long grass to be trampled down during a hot picnic. The game we saw, a goalless draw between KTP and VPS had rather less going for it. Making full use of our Finnish rail passes, we bade a reluctant farewell to Kotka before making the near six-hour trip north to Jyvaskyla, the last stop on our five-games-in-five-days programme. The morning after JJK's 2-1 home defeat by Jazz, we flew home. For once Palace obliged us with a 3-1 win at Norwich after which there was yet another new venue on the agenda, the cricket ground at Colchester, in the shadow of the castle, a second home for Essex who were entertaining Surrey in the county championship.

192

Chapter 46:
English cowards in Marseilles

As the 2016 Euros beckoned, I didn't have the usual anticipation for a big tournament. I had already done all the grounds bar two in France and, furthermore I was well acquainted with France as a holiday destination not to mention its autoroutes. But it was a surprisingly enjoyable event, helped by the fact that there was an easy access to tickets through exchanges with Stefan, Scottish Mark, Oldham Dave and my Austrian friend, Wolfgang. With no rush to get to every venue, I could relax, thanks also to my former French girlfriend, Nicole who had loaned me the use of her house in Roanne which she wouldn't be using for most of the month of June. Roanne is conveniently situated about an hour's drive north west of both St-Etienne and Lyon. With tickets for all six games in Lyon and four in St Etienne, I got to know every pothole on the N82 and N7 roads.

My one major miscalculation of the tournament had come after the opening game in Paris, France's 2-1 win over Romania. Instead of taking the TGV to Marseilles the next morning, I agreed, like an idiot to share petrol costs with Oldham Dave on the long slog south. Like me, he had un billet for England v Russia the next night. Typically for Dave, he chose to drive most of the way through the night even though I had a Formula One hotel booked in Nemours, just south of Fontainebleau. Had we stayed there, we would still have had bags of time to do those 480 miles in time for the 9pm kick-off at the Stade Velodrome. I was supposed to be helping him keep awake with idle chit chat but when my head was not dropping into my lap with fatigue, I was cursing myself for not forking out the extra euros on the train fare. But I knew not to keep on moaning as he is of a rebellious nature. The quieter I kept, the more likely he was to stop off for a few hours kip which eventually happened at Villefranche-sur-Saone, just north of Lyon. I bedded down in another Formula One hotel while he stayed in his car for some shut-eye.

There was a hostile atmosphere as we entered Marseilles. It was the prelude to the rioting initiated by the black clad, well trained, muscle-bound Russian heavies who clearly regarded the beer-sodden, overweight English hooligans as easy fodder which they emphasised in clashes between the two factions before and after the 1-1 draw. There were the usual hard luck stories from our unruly mob but as they are basically cowards who liked nothing better than to trash foreign bars and pick on unsuspecting victims, they were beyond sympathy. Diddums. It was about time they were handed a taste of their own poisonous medicine and got beaten up instead of dishing out the punishment.

Dave's ridiculous schedule was taking him back to Paris the next day whereas with a much shorter journey planned - to Nice - I saw Northern Ireland succumb 1-0 to Poland in the Stade de Nice. I'd had the foresight to leave my car in Roanne three weeks before the tournament, so recovering it the next day, I went on the first of my half dozen visits to the Parc Olympique in Lyon for Italy's 2-0 win over Belgium. The bar/restaurant between the most popular parking lot and the stadium proved an ideal rendez-vous point and its barbeque counter did a roaring trade on the hot evenings which greeted every match day. It helped that the Parc possesses an instantly recognisable roof that can be seen a couple of miles away. I eventually hit upon the best route to get there but St Etienne's Stade Geoffroy-Guichard was a different matter. Whichever turn-off I took, I ended up on a nightmarish tour of this industrial conurbation. It was my penalty, I suppose, for being an ill-equipped, old-school dinosaur who did not possess satnav or a smart phone with google maps.

Navigating a way back to Roanne was a simpler task. But I was relieved not to have too many tickets for games in Paris as the 500-mile return trip I took for the 1-1 draw between Romania and Switzerland at the Parc des Princes was an exhausting one that got me back well into the early hours. Frannie, who as ever, had time on her hands between jobs, came out to join me but she did not take kindly to Nicole's petit maison which was perched on top of a hill overlooking the town. She is unusual for a Scot in that she has no time for books which meant that she had more time to grumble on about the basic amenities. But with less appreciation of luxury, the place suited me down to the ground. I liked its rural appearance in the middle of a pasture away from the road. There was a restaurant nearby where we bumped into Nicole and her lover one night but for me, the real drawback was that there was nowhere around specialising in tempting breakfasts of café au lait avec croissants. What I would have given for that. On the occasions I was heading south from Lyon or St-Etienne, I found in Vienne a hotel that sometimes had a spare bed for the night. Alongside the Rhone, the town possesses olde worlde charm that had not gone unnoticed by a group of Germans who had made their base there.

On the one night when everything was fully booked and Nicole was back in her house, Wolfgang invited me to share the Airbnb he and his Austrian mate, Heinze had booked near Valence. I was shocked when I got there to find there were only two beds and no sofas. "It's ok,"

194

Wolfgang said, "my bed is big enough for both of us." He could have fooled me. He is of a plump physique to put it politely but there was nothing much more for it than to thank him profusely and hope for the best. He is not the quietest of sleepers and uses a nebulizer to ease his breathing. So, there I was on my birthday, after a less than restful night's kip, waking up alongside a wheezing Wolfgang. I'd received better presents but I knew he meant well.

Pennie's arrival coincided with a neat trio of fixtures. England's slovenly goalless draw with Slovakia in St-Etienne was followed by Poland's 1-0 win over Ukraine in the all eastern bloc battle in Marseilles. She was lucky to still be in France for the tournament's outstanding game, a dazzling 3-3 draw between Hungary and Portugal in Lyon where we were both delighted to see Palace's former goalkeeper, Gabor Kiraly - in his trademark grey tracksuit bottoms of course - performing heroics for the Magyars at the ripe old age of 40, three years before he decided to finally call it a day. Ronaldo still managed to beat him with the last two of Portugal's three equalisers. After three draws in their group games, Portugal had only qualified for the knock-out stages as one of the best third-placed teams.

But, somewhat fortuitously maybe for Pennie she had gone by the time England took on Iceland in the round of 16 game in the Stade de Nice. Hodgson resigned immediately after our 2-1 defeat and it was easy to castigate him and England, but Iceland have beaten better teams since and, indeed, they took France all the way at Saint-Denis before running out of steam and losing their quarter-final 5-2. I had been hurtling between, Roanne, Vienne, Lyon, St-Etienne and Marseilles but the need to see a game in the new Nouveau Stade de Bordeaux took me way off piste for the Germany v Italy quarter-final which Germany - typically for them - won 6-5 on pens after the teams had reached the end of extra time, locked at 1-1. Lacking the stamina to trek to Lille for the Wales v Belgium quarter-final between the ones in Marseilles and Bordeaux, I missed my only match day of the championships. A sad lapse perhaps but compensation was soon to be found among the lesser echelons. The day after France's 2-0 win over Germany in the Marseilles semi-final I met up with Chris. To our mutual delight, we had found among the small print of France's daily sports paper L'Equipe details of a pre-season amicale in the not-too-distant village of Langlade. Chelsea Ian and his clan had got wind of this tasty morsel as well, so we all celebrated our good fortune over a drink before Nimes' 3-0 win over Beziers.

The tournament's bonhomie was interrupted on my return to Paris following a needless spat with Stefan who had been a worthy cohort in the various ticket exchanges. I wanted to settle up over a lunch involving a group of us. "Can I please have the 41 euros you owe me?" I asked him. "Get it from Chris," he said," he owes me money."

"It's easier to get blood out of a stone," I replied. "Give me my 41 euros," I screamed, the worse for a few glasses of vin rouge. He took umbrage and refused all my subsequent invitations to make up once we were back in the UK.

The final at Saint-Denise the next day had to be worked round the Wimbledon men's singles final between Andy Murray and Milos Raonic. I managed to see most of Murray's straight sets triumph in a convenient bar before heading for the football. I was sitting next to Chris who gave me the moral support I needed in my various tirades at an imbecile who wouldn't sit down. With stewards coming to our aid, he eventually desisted, enabling us to observe the action without further ado. With an unobstructed view now, we could only marvel at Ronaldo's courageous attempts to battle on after a challenge from Dimitri Payet had left him hobbling. Twice Ronaldo went off and came back on before finally succumbing to his jarred knee. When he might have been expected to sulk on the bench, he spent most of the rest of the match cajoling his teammates alongside the Portuguese manager, Fernando Santos. Their efforts on the touchline were rewarded 11 minutes from the end of extra time when Eder, a late substitute, hit Portugal's winner from 25 yards, a fine goal astonishing for the fact that he hadn't scored in 15 appearances for Swansea the previous season. It went some way to compensate for Portugal's ignominy of 12 years earlier when they had lost the final at home to Greece.

A chance phone call during the championships had led me not to fly home the next day but to Dubrovnik, of all unlikely places. Pennie's daughter, Siobhan had wanted me to give her Mum a surprise belated birthday present by joining their family holiday in Croatia. I must have trudged the entire circumference of the walled city on a sweaty evening before locating the restaurant where they were having dinner. Taking little notice of the fact that Siobhan was forever staring out of the window on the lookout for a scruff with bags, Pennie was completely unaware of my impending arrival until I staggered inside. I was honoured by her happy smiles. But there was no time to savour the delights of this ancient port. I had already noticed that Zrinjski Mostar would be at home the next night in a Champions League qualifier so, of course, we had to be there. Luckily, Siobhan and her brother Jonathan are football fans even though Pennie had brought them up badly, to support Chelsea and Man United. My suggestion to travel into deepest Bosnia for the game did not, therefore, meet with too much resistance.

Jonathan's driving got us to Mostar in time to inspect the famous Stari Most (old bridge) from which divers will hurl themselves 100 feet into the Neretva River if the watching tourists fork out enough for them to risk their lives. I can think of several better ways to make a living. From the cobbled entrances next to the ethnic clothes shops that precede the bridge, we then found our way to the stadium. My bank notes were of denominations too high to gain entry through the turnstiles, so I had to get change outside by buying a Zrinjski club mug which was a souvenir of a 1-1 draw against Legia Warsaw that didn't live long in the memory. Nor was the spectacle much better on the Saturday when Pennie and I took leave of her family to speed 145 miles up to Split. Hadjuk weren't at home in the Croatian League but the city's other top club, RNK were hosting Rijeka in their ramshackle stadium. As we awaited kick-off among scores of diehards, I told Pennie that a late rush of spectators would contribute to, at the very least, a decent quorum. How wrong I was. The official attendance was 467. I couldn't believe that so few fans would come out on a Saturday evening to see a game in what was formerly football crazy Yugoslavia. With most of Croatia's clubs based in the vicinity of Zagreb, hundreds of miles to the north, there was nothing else for it but to spend the Sunday on the beach. We took the car back to Dubrovnik the next day and then flew to Lyon where I had, with astute planning, left my car to convey us the rest of the homeward journey.

Chapter 47:
Beckhaaam gets lucky

It may have only been mid-July now but there were still jaunts galore to be fitted into 2016. I hadn't been back from the Franco/Croat expedition for 48 hours before, in Susan's company, I was off again, this time to Bulgaria on the suggestion of Neil who was taking his wife Maria and daughter Anna for a holiday there. The raison d'etre so far as Neil and I were concerned were games. A spacious hotel on the outskirts of Sofia was our base, only a short cab ride away from the city centre park where lies the Stadion Bulgarska Armiya, home of CSKA who, ever so conveniently, had arranged a pre-season friendly with Udinese which ended in a goalless draw.

That left Neil and I looking forward to the next day's excursion across the border to Serbia which was why I couldn't believe it when he wimped out of the trip, presumably because his Portuguese wife had said something along the lines of: "I would prefer it if you didn't go." Maria is a good Catholic and probably thought that I would lead her hubby astray or that we would get locked up for abusing the speed limits. Whatever it was, he looked suitably sheepish when he gave me the bad news on coming down to breakfast that Sunday morning.

With Susan declining the escapade as she had made a new friend in Maria, that left me to go it alone, contending with map-reading and all the complications of the border crossing at Gradina of taking a Bulgarian Capri into Serbia which I knew would be no picnic. But the lure of Radnicki Nis v Cukaricki in the Super Liga could not be ignored. The distance was only 85 miles but with hundreds of trucks hogging the trunk road, progress was slow both sides of the border which I crossed after protracted form-fillings, signatures and stamps in my passport. The difficulty in making myself understood didn't help. I think they eventually came to the conclusion that I was law-abiding and not set upon flogging the car in Serbia. On finding Nis I drove around for 15 minutes before spotting the Gradski Stadion's floodlights. There was time for a decent meal before the game, a 2-1 home win after which I braced myself for the homeward trip. I was much relieved that the lorry drivers in that part of the world were no longer taking their lives - and everyone else's life - into their own hands by driving without headlights on in the mistaken belief that they were saving energy and electricity. On my first road trip to the old Yugoslavia in the late 70s I had been terrified by the trucks looming out of the darkness without lights on. I was glad to get back to the UK in one piece.

Now, thankfully, there were headlights emerging from the gloom and the border would present me with slightly less difficulty. Taking a Bulgarian car back into Bulgaria left me with fewer questions to answer. I didn't exactly sail through, but I was eventually waved on. That left the Sofia ring road as the sole concern ahead. Fortunately, I had done my homework well and knew which slip roads to take in order to find our hotel.

Midweek threw up the temptations of Champions League qualifiers at Razgrad (Ludogorets) and Giurgiu in Romania but with each one requiring a round trip of over 400 miles, we settled instead for exploring the sights of the ancient city of Plovdiv plus countless frolics in the swimming pool near the hotel. However, it was not as if Ludogorets would remain unchartered territory for long, thanks largely to Ivo, the Bulgarian friend to whom I had been introduced by Neil. Paying for his flight to Sofia two years later, on condition that his Mum would put me up - as well as him - I sat back in her car while he drove us through a snowbound landscape to Razgrad for a Europa League tie. The frustration of watching AC Milan's 3-0 win in the unattractive surroundings of Ludogorets' half renovated stadium was almost as bad as that earlier in the day when we had stopped at a roadside snack bar on catching the whiff of sausages cooking on a hot slab. Mine amounted to lumps of gristle that were woofed down by the nearest ravenous feral dog, leaving me with a hole in my stomach. The sausage-makers could learn a lot from their German counterparts, I reckoned ruefully.

With still a fortnight to go before the Premier League opened up again, Finland beckoned for the fourth year running. The fixture secretaries had excelled themselves, enabling me to complete the Veikkausliiga which would take me to within reach of a clean sweep of all Scandanavia's top leagues. The first stop on a baking Saturday for Pennie and I was the northern town of Kemi which we had reached via an overnight stop at Oulu following our flight to Helsinki. After PS Kemi's 2-1 win over PK 35 Vantaa we took the train on to Rovaniemi which had always been a town of a certain mystique for me as it is the official home of Santa Claus. And as it's in the heart of Lapland, Rovaniemi also houses the outstanding Arktikum Museum where we spent four fascinating hours gleaning all the information we could on the lives and costumes of the reindeer herders and the various other weather-beaten inhabitants of the Arctic Circle. With a choice of restaurants, plus decent running facilities on the paths alongside the Kemijoki River, Rovaniemi had plenty going for it, except perhaps the football. The match, a 2-0 home win by ROPS over VPSD was as disappointing as the Keskuskentta ground they use. Our last stop was Kuopio, home of KUPS who defeated Marieham in a rather better game at an equally prosaic Savon Sanomat Areena. All the more pity then that they no longer play in a pre-war relic at Vainolanniemi, a cape surrounded by a lake which was reputed to be one of the country's most beautiful sporting venues.

The chance of seeing more of my Australia-based son, James availed itself during the October international break which coincided nicely with the ATP tournament in Tokyo. As a tennis coach, James is as eager to tick off the world's top tennis courts as his Dad is to visit the football grounds. Not that I am averse to tennis either. So, Sally and I linked up with the bonus for me of seeing a few more games. Chofu's Ajinomoto Stadium was the stage of FC Tokyo's 2-1 home defeat by Urawa Reds in the J-League Cup and the next night he accompanied me to the 2002 World Cup stadium in Saitama where we saw Japan beat Iraq 2-1 in a World Cup qualifier. But the highlight of the trip came on our visit to Tokyo's Madame Tussauds where David Beckhaaam - as they call him - was among the waxworks, not standing upright but reclining on his back in shorts. A giggling bunch of Japanese girls were among the worshippers and when they thought I had gone on ahead, they took it in turns to sit astride the exhibit's midriff, gently easing themselves up and down. I had sneaked back to see what they were up to. The startled expressions on their faces when they realised that they'd had a captive audience were worth the admission fee alone.

From Tokyo, I flew via Helsinki to Vienna from where I made my way by train to Trnava, which has assumed a rivalry to Bratislava as the home to Slovakia's national football team. Scotland were their opponents this time in a World Cup qualifier which meant that I had the company of Oldham Dave, Chelsea Ian, Scottish Mark, Ross and Wolfgang before and after the game which ended in a dismal 3-0 defeat for the Scots. I was disappointed that Palace's James McArthur could do little in the visitors' midfield to stem the tide of one-way attacks. The Scottish fans and hangers-on were going home the next day. I was surprised that I, alone, had cottoned onto the fact that there was a Czech Liga second tier (FNL) game on offer in Moravia in the mediaeval walled town of Znojmo, only 110 miles distant by train. Not many Czechs were aware of the fixture either judging by the pitiful crowd there for a 2-1 home win. I should have stayed on trains for the journey back to Vienna - instead of taking the boat - as the stretch of the Danube from Bratislava is comparatively soulless. Not so the Austrian second division game I saw in the capital, a sparkling 5-1 win for Liefering in Floridsdorfer's modest ground.

200

Chapter 48.
The woes of relegation

I have always maintained that the despair and pain of relegation is akin to a death in the family, not as bad as losing a parent or a child but, at least, on a par with the passing of a relative or a close friend. Supporting a club like Palace doesn't help. They have forced me to suffer more than my fair share of heartaches over the years but however many times it happens, the depression doesn't easily fade away. Loyalty being a little-known virtue among footballers, relegated clubs invariably get ravaged, forced to sell the majority of their best players before the next campaign. Optimists talk about bouncing back immediately but us cynics know that is easier said than done. We know that several seasons might have to be endured at a lower level or, worse still, there might be a subsequent drop down another tier before the bouncing-back takes on any kind of reality. It's far worse for the supporters than the players because the players can move on, albeit with a blot on their CV, while the supporters are saddled with the club they have supported most of their lives. Unless they are extremely fickle, they stay put. I sometimes feel I have shown more fidelity to the clubs I support than my women.

Arsenal and Everton fans won't, of course, know what I'm on about as they have never experienced the devastation of relegation and that also goes for the vast majority of Liverpool, Man United, Spurs and Chelsea aficionados.

Palace thankfully spared me the fate of relegation in 2017. But within a month I saw two of my other teams fall. Hayes and Yeading had been my favourite non-league side since my days of covering the Conference in the 1990s when the Hayes chairman, Derek Goodall invariably invited me into the boardroom for post-match cups of tea whenever I turned up to report their home games. Terry Brown, their manager, and his assistant, Willie Wordsworth, were also both of tremendous value, approachable and friendly. I developed an ever-increasing affection for the club, burgeoning into fully fledged support and was delighted when they once availed their Church Road ground for me to play on in a Times v Sun game when I was running the Fleet Street League.

Even when the club merged with Yeading and Goodall and his charming wife, Pat disappeared into the sunset, my support never wavered. The free half-time cups of tea had long since disappeared too but thanks to the club's frequent Sunday fixtures as they were ground-sharing with the likes of Woking, Beaconsfield and Maidenhead, I saw them often. Conveniently for me, they were nomads for the eternity it took them to renovate Yeading's ground in order to gain the required safety certificates. So, it was that I acquainted myself with Hayes and Yeading's downward spiral. The loss of Conference - or National League as it is now - status heralded a distressing five-year period of three relegations. The last of them came on Easter Monday when on yet another borrowed ground - at Uxbridge - they went down 2-0 to Kings Langley in a tempestuous game. Relegation was upon us again and with it, all the attendant misery. It felt like another stab in the heart.

Another summer of relentless football-watching on the continent did its best to help me over my melancholy but the priority now was Spain or, more specifically, Real Mallorca's battle to avoid the drop from the Segunda Division. While travelling to and from three successive crucial late-season games - which yielded just four points - I had constantly and perversely reminded myself of the cameo of four years earlier when I had arrived back at the hotel in Soller from watching them relegated from La Liga.

"Was it a good game darling?" Sally had asked after Mallorca's 4-2 home win over Valladolid.

"Yes, it was darling," I had replied through gritted teeth, quietly bemoaning the fact that the other results hadn't gone Mallorca's way. Try explaining all that to a woman who isn't interested or doesn't really want to know. While she spent the rest of the evening without an apparent care in the world, I was contemplating the various methods of committing suicide!

This time Mallorca needed to win their last two games to have a realistic chance of escaping, so I just had to be at the first of those, away to Mirandes even though it meant an 18-hour round trip by train from my base near Alicante, to the distant northern outpost of Miranda de Ebro. An overnight stop was also required which left me with plenty of time to dwell on the repercussions of a desperate 2-2 draw which succeeded in sending both sides down. I had seldom felt so utterly miserable. The players had given their all but now some of them would move on. And others would discover all about the joys of obscurity in Spain's part-time Segunda div B. And so, 48 days after Uxbridge, the knife had been twisted. If the scenery on that return train ride from Basque country was majestic, I didn't notice it. I sulked all the way back.

I didn't bother with the last game at home to Getafe. There seemed no point. I am always amazed that any fans go to witness the last rites. Back in 1973 when I had seen Palace's first 41 games in the old first division to stand on the brink of a 100 percent attendance record for the first time,

I couldn't bring myself to go to the last game at Man City after we had been relegated at Norwich on Easter Tuesday. Although I missed a 3-2 Palace win, I had no regrets. In fact, I already had all the material I needed for a good interview with Mel Blyth, an ace Palace defender when GOAL magazine - for whom I then worked - asked me to do a series under a "What went wrong?" banner. Under Malcolm Allison, Palace went down again the next season, losing at Cardiff on the last day. I had led a sheltered life until then. But now I was a battle-hardened, shell-shocked veteran of relegations.

Chapter 49:
Respite in Poland

The two relegations in 2017 had been interrupted by a trip to Sweden which brought much needed respite. The focal point was the Europa League final and Manchester United's 2-0 win over Ajax which gave them entry under Jose Mourinho to the Champions League. The game took place the night after the Manchester Arena bombing which, some said, was a valid explanation for United's underwhelming performance which others contended was absolute nonsense. Tickets were scarce but on the approaches to the Solna Stadium I managed to acquire one for one and a half times face value. So far as I was concerned the build-up was more entertaining than the big game itself. My overnight trip to Vaxjo for Oster v Helsingborg (1-2) proved fine value as did the boat cabin I stayed in the next night in Stockholm after bumping into Oldham Dave at Syrianska IF v Forward (0-3).

My affection for Poland brought more cheer. They were staging the European Under-21 championship in several grounds off the beaten track such as Kielce, the venue for England's opening goalless draw with Sweden and Gdynia's GOSIR Stadion, the scene of Spain's 5-0 win over Macedonia. I was delighted to see my old Mallorca favourite, Marco Asensio, now with Real Madrid, notch a hat trick. The bonus of Gdynia on the sun-drenched Baltic coast was a surprise birthday present for me, an unexpected third div game the next afternoon in the Narodowy Stadion almost next door to the main one. I saw Baltyk Gdynia overcome Gwardia Koszalini 4-1. With the added spice of another Spain game in Gdynia, a 3-1 victory over Portugal, Sally and I stayed put in the exotically named Hotel Opera in the forest just outside Sopot which is the middle one of the tri-city metropolitan area's three resorts on a 20-mile stretch of coastline. With its 555 yard-long wooden pier, the longest in Europe, and a tasteful pedestrianised zone which includes the famous Crooked House, modelled on fairy tale illuminations, Sopot does its utmost to match the most celebrated tourist hotspot up there which is, of course, Gdansk whose waterfront is an artistic delight.

Years earlier my romance with Alicia had, alas, come to grief before she had had a chance to escort me round her home city of Krakow. No wonder she is proud of the place and thank the Lord the Polish football authorities had seen fit to base their competition round it. There can be few such glorious city centres as Krakow's even if, this time, half of it was fenced off and knee deep in piles of rubble in the process of a new road scheme. We saw two Germany games there, a 3-0 win over Denmark and a 1-0 loss to Italy, either side of an all too short visit to another lovely city, that of Lublin where Slovakia beat Sweden 3-0. The most disappointing stadium by far was the seemingly half repaired Kompleks Sportowy Zawisza in Bydgoszcz where Spain's presence again provided much needed comfort. Their 1-0 defeat of Serbia took them into the last four with a hitherto unblemished record.

Pennie was more pleased than I was at my failure to find a game to announce her arrival on the Sunday but that did at least give us more time to search for a room near the town of Tychy which was to stage England's semi-final with the Germans. And it wasn't any old room that we eventually stumbled upon in a primeval pine forest on the shores of Lake Paprocany, six miles south of Tychy. Originating from the 16th century, the hunting lodge of Promnice had to be up there along with Kuching and Puerto Varas as one of the most magnificent places I have ever rested my head. We were lucky to get a chalet there. The hotel staff were pre-occupied with a wedding party on their spacious lawns, but they indulged us at a competitive rate, so we were happy to oblige them with our custom in their ornate dining room that evening.

With the circuitous paths around the lake inviting heaven-sent running opportunities, the hunting lodge became our base for a few days. From it we could easily reach Tychy's Stadion Miejski where we saw England and Germany's 2-2 draw in the semi-final which led to the Germans inevitably prevailing 4-3 on pens. And, as ever, the early rounds of the Europa League presented another titbit in the shape of Trencin, only 140 miles distant, across the border in Slovakia. The monstrous bulbs on the crest of the floodlights had prepared us for a characteristic East European relic of a ground but ultimately the Stadion na Sihoti was far less memorable than AC Trencin's 5-1 win over the Georgians from Torpedo Kutaisi. We had to hurry back to Krakow for the Euro final the next night. Spain were the dominant force but were unlucky to lose 1-0 to Germany.

There was no stopping us. Pennie and I were bound for Norway the next evening and I, had fortunately found us a direct flight to Bergen as I felt a need to revisit Brann Bergen's stadium which had much improved in the 52 years since I had last been there. There was no sign of the press passes I had ordered in advance so, rather than hang around in the torrential rain, getting soaked, we sped through an open door to find empty seats from which we had a fine view of a goalless draw with Valerenga. Our beds for those two nights were in utter contrast to the luxury of Promnice. We were on a boat in Bergen's harbour that could only be reached by lowering ourselves cautiously onto another boat that was also rocking in the swell. From Bergen the next day we flew to Kristiansund, who were newcomers to the Tippeligaen, which was now known as the Eliteserien. I wanted to get there before they came down again but judging by their contribution to a 3-3 draw against the title contenders of Rosenborg Trondheim, they were going to stay a while. They went from two down to 3-2 up before Nicklas Bendtner, the former Arsenal and Forest striker, saved Trondheim's faces with a last-minute equaliser. With time to spare the next day, we took the bus back to Bergen which was an epic nine-hour journey through fjord country.

Chapter 50:
A relentless rhythm

The summer was still in its infancy and the year was an odd number which meant that the Gold Cup was upon us again in its usual peculiar format. With so many cities up for staging games, Concacaf permits each chosen applicant - 14 this time - one double-header unless they are selected for a semi-final or final. My love of Country music made Nashville an obvious first stop for Pennie and I but you'd have thought that Tennessee was at the very back of beyond judging by the convoluted route required to get us there. From Bergen, we flew to Copenhagen and from there to our overnight stop in a downtrodden hotel just outside New York's JFK Airport. From JFK we went to Charlotte the next day before changing for Nashville. We were exhausted on arrival but there was little chance of lying back to enjoy the comfort of the Rodeway Inn that booking.com had given us. It seemed to double up as a welfare hostel occupied by Nashville's colony of drunks, druggies and hookers. The photograph of the swimming pool in the brochure had appealed to me but it was locked up and there was a turd floating on the algae-ridden surface. We took a look at the other hotels in the complex, but they were similar doss houses.

We stuck it out for one night and complained the next day to booking.com who did, at least, refund me for the other four nights I had booked. The taxi driver who transferred us to a city centre hotel expressed surprise that we hadn't gone there in the first place as we didn't, he said, fit the general category of down and outs who had infested the Rodeway Inn. We were suitably flattered but the cost of the transfer was exorbitant. But it was a huge improvement. It was within walking distance or a hotel courtesy car ride from Nashville's abundance of country bars. Get fed up with one group and there's doubtless a better and noisier one next door. The city rocks to a relentless rhythm. Main Street and all its adjoining streets are the hive of activity and sounds during the tourist season. And then there are museums galore honouring the likes of Johnny Cash, Willie Nelson, Kris Kristofferson, Kenny Rogers, Glen Campbell, Waylon Jennings, Dolly Parton, Lucinda Williams, Emmylou Harris, Linda Ronstadt et al. The Grand Ole Opry was also an essential stop as was the Listening Room which we discovered two years later.

The only bitter taste was left by the odious creep of a landlord in charge of the George Jones bar who poured me a pint when we walked in to see the later stages of one of the Gold Cup games on the establishment's television screen. We had only been there about five minutes and the match was at its 80-minute mark when I was told to sup up. Why he couldn't have warned us that closing time was nigh upon our entry, I don't know. But I do know that I put this point to him ever so politely and asked if we could stay until the end of the game. During the ensuing argument, the cretin behind the bar asked: "Is it because I'm black?" I hadn't even noticed his colour. But seconds later I was frogmarched out by the odious creep while Pennie walked out, acutely embarrassed. We gave the bar a major swerve on our next visit.

Fortunately, the group games the next day at the Nissan Stadium proved a welcome distraction. The USA drew 1-1 with Panama and Martinique beat Nicaragua 2-0. Giving subsequent double-headers in San Diego and Houston a miss, Pennie and I went our separate ways thereafter. She flew home while I went via Atlanta to Tampa for more games in the same group. This time they were USA 3, Martinique 2 and Panama 2, Nicaragua 1. The need to keep costs down meant that I was forsaking more Gold Cup ties in Denver, Frisco and Cleveland. So, I utilised a spare evening with a visit to Tampa Bay Rowdies II v Lakeland Tropics in the USL League Two. Seating was at a premium, so I parked myself among what I presumed were the ground's only few seats. "Are you with one of the teams?" I was asked by a tracksuited lady. "Eh no," I said to which she told me that I was in one of the dug-outs. Somewhat red faced, I still had time before kick-off to find a folding seat in the groundsman's shed from where I had a grandstand view of an entertaining 2-2 draw.

Moving onto San Antonio, I took in Mexico's 2-0 win over Curacao and the 1-1 draw involving El Salvador and Jamaica in the Alamodome Stadium plus the many other attractions offered by this historical Texan city, such as its Alamo Mission, a museum and a world heritage site devoted to recalling the famous siege of 1836 which was made into a movie. The quirky restaurants and bars to be found alongside the San Antonio River were the obvious places to dine out. By now thankfully I had bumped into Dieter, a German groundhopper I knew from old. He was, like me, intent on devouring games for the rest of the Gold Cup. The idea was to share the costs of car hire and petrol, but this was still going to be one expensive ride exacerbated by the drop-off charge of a Dodge, the only car that was available. That was convenient for the rental company, less so for us. We had a long drive ahead through the rest of Texas and the entire width of Arizona. I had been told this part of the

208

world, mostly desert was "nothing special" by an American bar owner I had met in Mallorca, but I was, as ever, intrigued by the endless prairies, wondering which cowboys in Wild West folklore might have ridden over them. Those able horsemen probably made swifter progress than us, restricted, as always by the tedious US speed limits. We were stopped once by a cop on a motorbike, but he let us go after the inevitable lecture.

Our destination now was Phoenix or, more specifically, the University of Phoenix Stadium in the suburb of Glendale. With its towering skyscrapers constructed between a jumble of entwining motorways, Phoenix is the kind of vast metropolis that I'm invariably relieved to leave far behind. I was always far more of a country bumpkin than a city slicker. Somehow, we negotiated the right slip roads in time to survey the last two quarter-finals in which Mexico accounted for Honduras 1-0 and Jamaica overcame Canada 2-1. With little appetite for getting lost in the maze of Phoenix searching for a hotel, or for backtracking to Dallas for the first semi-final (USA v Costa Rica), we drove 80 miles on into the night before finding somewhere to stay.

On and on we drove the next day, towards California in the usually fruitless search for cheap lodgings. We found Oceanside to be an unremarkable though typically costly resort on the eve of the second semi. I had been to Pasadena for the 1994 World Cup, but The Rose Bowl was, I thought, worth another visit which was fully justified and not only by Jamaica's shock 1-0 win over Mexico that came with an 88th minute winner from Kemar Lawrence. Football is full of stadiums that are little more than huge bowls, but this is an iconic one nestling beneath its superb backdrop of the San Gabriel Mountains. It is awesome, second only to Mexico City's Aztec Stadium in its magnificence and magnitude, in my opinion, though I must admit that I never saw the Maracanã before it was scaled down. Pasadena is also worth a visit for its plentiful choice of eateries and, better still, we found a hotel for the night that didn't cost the earth.

The interstate that hugs the Pacific Coast for tantalisingly short stretches before leading to Big Sur got a unanimous vote as the route we should then take northbound for the final but we were both infuriated by the lack of warning signs telling us of a land slip. On the 50-mile diversion I couldn't help thinking once again that America possesses a third world underbelly. Clint Eastwood should have sorted that out, I reminded Dieter as we explored the fashionable streets of Carmel where the great man had once been mayor. Somewhat appositely we found rooms just out of town costing only a fistful of dollars.

The stage for the final was the Levi's Stadium in Santa Clara, just north of San Jose. My failure to get accredited for this tournament continued not to matter too much as tickets were easy and cheap to purchase, even with the hosts in the final and even though Americans don't take too kindly to having their asking prices beaten down. More fool them, I thought. Much to the disappointment of both of us, the USA defeated Jamaica 2-1. Now it was Jamaica's turn to lose in the 88th minute, to a goal from Jordan Morris who, like the USA's earlier scorer, Jozy Altidore, was named in the team of the tournament. As luck would have it, we were both departing from San Francisco the next day with flights back to Europe within an hour of each other. Our marathon voyage had been of 2,342 miles. Dieter had testspiels lined up in Germany. I had the Test match, England v South Africa at the Oval followed by ten days of athletics at the World Championships in the London Arena. By the closing ceremony, I was convinced that it was a stadium far better suited to the likes of Usain Bolt, Mo Farah and co than West Ham's footballers.

Chapter 51:
Sliding door opens for De Boer

The nine countries on the continent I visited before Christmas provided a few highlights, not necessarily on the pitch. Lugano was far more memorable for instance for a glorious boat ride on the shimmering glacial Lake Lugano than the nondescript Lugano v St Gallen game (0-1) I saw the previous evening. Ross County v Rangers (1-3) was preceded by a piping Sunday roast in a nearby hotel which, sadly, had already been trashed by Rangers fans. I clapped myself on the back a fortnight later for all the planning it took for me to go by air from Alicante to Glasgow for Hamilton 1, Celtic 4, which was followed the next day by a stirring goalless draw between Hearts and Aberdeen. That game was at Scotland's rugby union headquarters at Murrayfield, a must for any true groundhopper, because the main stand at Tynecastle, Hearts' home ground was in the process of being rebuilt. There was a late panic for tickets as one of Ivo's Bulgarian contacts in Scotland had failed to come up with complimentaries as promised. The alacrity with which one of Scottish Mark's mates in Aberdeen sprang into action to rescue us with seats for the away end was impressive.

From Edinburgh the next morning I took the train to Burnley where Palace's game, a fourth successive defeat - all goalless - spelt the end of Frank de Boer's short stint as manager. His ideas of man management apparently left much to be desired as did the back pass from Chung-yong Lee that did for him. It is often strange how one simple error by a player can have such huge repercussions. If Chris Wood had not profited from the South Korean's error would the Dutchman have kept his job in which case where would Roy Hodgson have ended up as manager? It was football's equivalent of sliding doors.

Pennie and I stayed the night in Burnley and over dinner eavesdropped on the mother of all rows between a couple after which we swopped notes with another bloke who had also been much entertained by the altercation. Our destination on the Monday evening was Gloucester, or to put it more accurately the new ground at Evesham where they ground shared. As Gloucester's opponents were Hampton and Richmond, I had managed to track down a Hampton fan who could give us a lift back to the smoke after the 1-1 draw which I thought represented the height of clever planning on my part.

Pennie had never been to Prague so of course I had to make sure that she complimented a visit to that wonderful city and a stroll across the famous St Charles Bridge with a game which turned out to be Dukla Prague's 1-1 draw with Slovako. I wondered how these clubs manage to survive with attendances such as the paltry 1,332 who saw that one in Dukla's cavernous Juliska Stadium. Jet 2 enabled us to fly straight back from Prague to Newcastle for Palace's game on the Saturday. The lengths I went in order to save an outward train fare!!! But from thereon in, I was to depend on trains for another complicated journey, this one to Scandinavia in the rush to see two clubs before they got relegated from their respective top flights.

Getting from Newcastle to Helsingor in Denmark via King's Cross, Gatwick and Copenhagen was the easy bit. I stayed the night in Copenhagen after Brondby's 1-0 win but left early the next morning. It took two more changes to reach Jonkoping in central Sweden. From their 2-0 victory over Kalmar, I dashed to the station and a late-night train to my overnight stop in Malmo before a homeward flight the next day.

Sally's early Christmas present was a return flight plus accommodation in Madeira, the catch being that two games were included in the package. Seldom do the island's pair of top division clubs play at home on the same weekend but it's worth scanning the Portuguese fixture lists to find out the rare occasions when that happens, as a double-header can go neatly in hand with a tour of the island, or at least a tour of half of it. Mind you, plotting a path to Nacional's hill-top Estadio dos Barreiros is a feat in itself. I feared the worst on the local bus we took from Funchal city centre as there was hardly anyone else on it, let alone anyone geared up like a football fan going to see them play Gil Vicente. The driver eventually suggested that we get off about three quarters of the way up a steep and meandering slope as he was heading off to remote villages. He told us to carry on walking until we could go no further. It was such hard work that I was glad not to be encumbered by the bags we had dumped at the hotel.

Judging by the mass exodus of vehicles - after the 1-1 draw - from car parks that had, like the stadium, been chiselled out of the mountainside, none of Nacional's regular supporters tended to follow our example of wearing out shoe leather. Thankfully, I managed to talk someone in the press box into giving us a lift back to sea level after the game and, even more thankfully, I discovered the next day that Maritimo's Campo do Adelino Rodrigues is in the heart of Funchal. We saw them beat Braga 1-0.

Fortunately, Palace's game at Leicester the following Saturday was the early kick-off as that enabled me to rush away from our 3-0 win to

Gatwick for a flight to Rome, where I was able to join Chris for the last leg of his three-games-in-three-days extravaganza in Italy. We met up on the train to Naples from where we changed to Benevento who were in the midst of confirming that they really were one-season wonders in Serie A. And neither was the city much in the way of a gastronomic paradise, particularly for the two of us anticipating a lunch of steaming spag bol. The culinary fare proved as big a disappointment as their football team who went down 2-1 to fellow relegation contenders SPAL. The Stadio Ciro Vigorito's floodlights were easily visible from the top of the town, but they were an optical illusion, much further away than they looked. But for a lucky lift from people who stopped to ask us for directions, we would probably have missed the first 20 minutes.

The following Sunday, which was Christmas Eve, I came close not only to missing kick-off but the whole game in Holland thanks to British Rail excelling themselves by cancelling the first Gatwick-bound train out of Clapham Junction. People with planes to catch, hurried out of the station to order cabs. I invited myself to share an Uber taxi with a pretty girl. She had an Uber account, but I didn't, so sensing my desperation, the skunk of a driver ripped me off by demanding £50. I only had £40 in readies which he accepted. My fellow passenger turned out to be a British Airways stewardess serving my flight to Amsterdam. She gave me a knowing smile and greeting when I boarded, much to the curiosity of my fellow passengers. After that it was plain sailing or rather plain railing from Schiphol to Venlo whose team VVV Venlo overcame Heracles 3-1. The obvious need to be home for Christmas Day meant that I was thereafter at the mercy of Dutch trains but with more respect for the timetables than their British counterparts, they did me proud.

Chapter 52:
Maltese melancholy

Time, they say, is a great healer so I was prepared to overlook Frannie's moaning from our previous trip together - to the Euros in France - when, out of the blue early in 2018, she rang to ask if I'd like to join her for a few days in Malta. The fact that it wouldn't have been possible to get from Palace's home game with Burnley to Mallorca's Sunday noon kick-off in Ibiza helped salve my conscience. I had only been to Malta once before to see an international against Spain on a trip more significant for the fact that I got entangled in a timeshare con. It was back in the early 90s when I was on a promenade with Gill. Drops of rain had started to fall when a mother and son in a horse and cart offered us a lift. The pressing need for shelter persuaded us to climb aboard. Big mistake. Within moments they had said they would take us to some refuge which turned out to be the Sunny Coast's timeshare headquarters where I was naïve enough to show interest. The couple who interviewed us, said they would be coming to London the following week when I could sign the various forms. They took us out for dinner and outlined all the benefits of the exchange programme which I was soon to discover were zilch. I couldn't believe how such apparently nice people could be so superficial. To give Gill credit though, she had seen through them and tried her utmost to dissuade me from joining up.

She knew that I was not a great one for spending a week in the same place and I had no great desire to return to Malta, but that exchange programme was tempting as it could provide accommodation for my countless trips abroad on football-watching missions. Or so I thought. Over the years I discovered that the resorts on their list were either nowhere near football hot spots or they were never available when I needed them. I had been a victim of the company's hard-sell policy. Of the several letters of complaint I wrote to the RCI owners, some protested that they never printed my letters in their glossy brochure. Surprise, surprise. RCI only ever printed letters of praise and I suspect that most of them were concocted by staff with nothing better to do. It took about ten years for me to extricate myself from the deal by which time I had wasted thousands of pounds on maintenance of a property that I never stayed in. I won't fall for that scam again. Is it any wonder that timeshare holidays are a declining industry? Too many unsuspecting punters have been ripped off over the years.

So, my memories of Malta were not too positive when Frannie rang but a quick look at Soccerway.com's various possibilities were a persuasive factor. We could do a double header on the Sunday and take a boat trip to Gozo on the Monday. Gozo had looked idyllic on my previous trip but now, much more built up and in midwinter, it somehow looked less of an idyll. Still, I could reflect on the Sunday's two games, not that either of them were cliff-hangers. Fortunately, they had both been in arenas about half a mile from each other. The MFA Centenary Stadium which staged the first div game between Qrendie and Zejtun Corinthians (0-3) was just a few strides from Ta' Qali, the scene of the premier league game involving Floriana and Hibernians (0-1). The only goal, a penalty came from Jorginho who was Brazilian but not the same one, now a naturalised Italian, who has graced Chelsea's midfield. Ta' Qali had been rammed on my previous visit to see Spain but now there were just a few spectators scattered around the redeveloped 17,000 all-seater national stadium. That was as sad as the quality of football. Little wonder then that the real Jorginho was not on show. Much of Malta's supposedly top-class football takes place in those two stadiums. The island is not exactly a hotbed of football.

My next two double headers had much more going for them. I had long since come to the conclusion that there can be comforts if one's team suffers an early exit from the FA Cup. Dreams of Wembley may vanish but the dates of the fourth and fifth rounds are now freed up, ready to be exploited. Palace's third-round loss at Brighton opened up such a weekend late in January, focused around my favourite city, Valencia thanks to the Spanish fixture planners coming to my aid.

I had already been to the Maestella four times, but it is such an imposing venue and due for demolition anyway, that I could not ignore the fact that the galaticos from Real Madrid would be there, possibly for one last time. I had always managed to procure a press pass on previous visits but this time I decided not to risk an application which in true Spanish custom would probably have been rejected too late for me to buy a ticket. So, I got one online at a decent height over the corner flag where I had a perfect view of a player high on my hit list scoring a superb goal. I have never really taken to Marcello or his ludicrous haircut. He can be a thug but, showing the verve of a striker rather than the full back he is, the Brazilian took a return pass from Asensio to restore the two-goal lead that Ronaldo had established with two penalties. Real Madrid eventually won 4-1.

Christine joined me for the second game which was, of course, the raison d'etre of my visit since Mallorca's descent to Segunda div B had not exactly dampened my desire to support them. The host of virgin territories provided added temptation. One of them belonged to Saguntino from the small town of Sagunt, just north of Valencia. The rain teemed down as we made our way to the tumble-down home of a club that had always been among Spain's lower brethren. Pools of water were everywhere and all the seats in the upper rows were taken. To sit anywhere else would mean getting soaked. We both managed to hoist ourselves on top of a ledge at the back of the stand, perching just high enough above the masses to get an acceptable view of Mallorca's 2-1 victory on a puddle-strewn surface. It is doubtful whether an English referee would have let the game finish but, happily, they don't seem to like postponements or abandoned games in Spain. The two clubs would go in different directions at the end of the season.

It was with a haste to see Lyngby before they went down from the Superliga that I arranged my next visit to Denmark, revolving as always around a night's stay in the Star Hotel which is less than a five-minute walk from Copenhagen's main station and within reach of an agreeable choice of Asian restaurants. It was hardly surprising that my application for accreditation had been rejected as the entire Danish sporting press must have wanted to be at the game, a 3-1 home defeat by Brondby, as it had coincided with turmoil at the home club. Lyngby had suffered financial difficulties and irregularities which had led to the owner Hellerup Finans going bankrupt. Local businessmen, known as The Friends of Lyngby had just come to their aid. Lyngby are based in the capital's northern suburbs, therefore easily accessible.

Not so, Hobro which is on Jutland and a near four-hour train ride away. Danish expresses would be ideal if they could only sustain the restaurant cars which seem to have been phased out. There's nothing so wonderful as biting into a delicious smorgasbord while watching the world go by as Michael Portillo, Chris Tarrant, Tony Robinson et al would no doubt readily testify. But get on a long-distance train in Denmark unprepared these days and a passenger is liable to go hungry. Thankfully I found a café in Hobro offering snacks before their game which AGF Aarhus won 1-0. There was a late train to Aalborg from where I had a flight booked the next morning but this time, I was very much an innocent abroad. The hotel I had booked was surrounded by the city's most erotic night spots, all of which remain firmly closed on Monday nights. More's the pity.

Just as Brondby invariably seemed to provide the opposition on my visits to Denmark, I was jinxed with Raith Rovers. I had frequently glanced longingly into their home from the windows of trains slowing down for Kirkcaldy or slowly gaining speed. I have lost count of the times I have tried to arrange to see games there only for flights to get cancelled, trains to run late or television fixture alterations to mess things up. And so it was again on one of the occasions I had persuaded Pennie to link our trips north for Palace with games in Scotland or Wales.

There was nothing to suggest that I would be thwarted again after taking our leave of Huddersfield following Palace's 2-0 win but on arriving at Waverley, we found Edinburgh to be ankle-deep in snow. The postponement of Raith's game with East Fife the next day was inevitable. The onward journey from Yorkshire would have been a complete waste of time and money if Celtic's game at Motherwell went the same way. I had been to Fir Park before but never for a Motherwell home game. The suspense was almost too much as we listened to the weather reports. But by some quirk of prevailing winds and temperatures, the area west of Edinburgh was completely snow-free so off we set with the fates continuing to smile upon us in the form of the genial media man at Motherwell who gave us comps behind the goal. We managed to persuade a willing steward to let us sit on the side to watch the action which included the harsh dismissal of Motherwell's Cedric Kipre before half-time. From then on we were rooting for the Steelmen who held out for a well merited goalless draw.

EasyJet should have given me a season ticket for Spain judging by the number of flights I was taking on their planes for games there. One fest of six games in as many days, illuminated by Spain's 6-1 victory over Argentina in an amistoso in Madrid's new Wanda Metropole Stadium, was followed by an enterprising post Easter sortie I took with Pennie. Things livened up somewhat after a drab first day of two goalless draws involving Elche and Mallorca and then, in the tercera div, Cieza v Churramin as I had noticed that Italy, like Spain, tend to garland their late-season midweeks with full football schedules. Furthermore, flights between the two Mediterranean nations can be remarkably cheap such as the one we found ourselves on, from Alicante to Bologna. The cost of car hire was rather more prohibitive.

Carpi, of Serie B, had been good enough to permit us press passes for their 2-1 home defeat by Perugia in their former velodrome of a stadium but there was no such welcome at Ferrara, the home of SPAL despite my emailed request of a week earlier. My search for supporters with spares fell on stony ground as Italy's paranoia prevents their stewards from admitting anyone whose name is not on the ticket. We joined a line of hopefuls waiting for a late sale, but the queue moved forward at snail's pace, hindered by the fact that every spectator's name had to be printed on their ticket.

I was beginning to despair when the guy at the window said he had one, just one. Pennie was ever gracious and insisted that I should take it.

I was in no mood for chivalry, but I was relieved to get a text from her a few minutes after kick-off to say that she, too, was in. We saw a pulsating goalless draw in a relegation six-pointer against Chievo which was not quite enough to assuage me, such was my anger towards the press secretary for not having the good manners to inform me, at least, that we were not getting press tickets. When I emailed him on my return home to say that I hoped his club would go down from Serie A, it probably wasn't the most sensible thing I have ever done. Forza Crotone, I wrote, but in the end, it was Crotone who went down and SPAL who stayed up.

The countdown to the World Cup in Russia continued with my re-acquaintance with the Groupama Stadium in Lyon, the scene of a one-sided Europa league final between Marseilles and Atletico Madrid who won 3-0. I probably wouldn't have countenanced the fixture, but I had noticed that it could be combined with a visit to the Geneva ATP tennis tournament the next afternoon and some enticing Swiss games over the following few days. The first of them was Wohlen v Schaffhausen.

Christine and I found an obliging hostelry with outside tables for a pre-match feast under the evening sun after which we asked directions to the ground. We got there to find the place deserted. It looked rustic and unworthy of a club in the Challenge League (second division) in any case but there was no indication whatsoever of a match taking place there that Friday night. We found some kids who eventually convinced me that we were in the wrong Wohlen. We were in the picturesque village of Wohlen bei Bern which doesn't merit a mention in most road maps of Europe whereas the match we wanted was taking place in Wohlen Aargau, 65 miles away. Kick-off was within five minutes, so we gave it up as a bad job and headed back to our base in Lausanne. We missed a seven-goal thriller.

Show me a football fan who hasn't made a similar mistake though. I was glad our lapse was not of similar gravity to the Man United fans who found themselves on the wrong plane when they wanted to see their Reds playing a Champions League tie at Deportivo La Coruna. They found to their horror they were not bound for Santiago de Compostela in northern Spain but Santiago, the capital of Chile. Didn't they wonder why their travel agents had booked them such expensive flights?

I had already ticked off Lausanne's Stade Olympique de la Pontaise years earlier but Stade Lausanne-Ouchy, the city's 1 Liga Promotion (3rd div) club's 4pm kick-off on the Saturday afforded us just enough time to hurtle from their 1-1 draw against Koniz to McCarthy's Irish pub which I had researched. They had ensured me they would be showing the Man United v Chelsea Cup Final. The perfect antidote to the pain of United's 1-0 defeat was provided by the barman switching over to the German Cup

218

Final which was in its later stages. I still had a soft spot for Eintracht Frankfurt, so I texted my ex-wife Lissi and son Ben to make sure they were watching back home. We were all ecstatic to see their dramatic 3-1 win over Bayern Munich, secured with two goals from the Croat, Ante Rebic who was to etch himself a place in my affections. It was such a shame he later chose to leave Eintracht for AC Milan rather than Palace. But us beggars are seldom the choosers. We could have done with a striker like him.

Chapter 53:
Russian resistance

The nearer we got to the World Cup, the more I freaked out about going to Russia. I had flights, hotels and match tickets all booked and all the lads would be there, but I was looking at every excuse under the sun not to travel. It was strange. I had been to Russia a few times before, so it was not as if I was unfamiliar with that vast land mass. I'd never experienced major discomfort or mishaps on previous trips apart from the brief theft of my vitamin pills on the Trans-Siberian 16 years earlier. But I could not work up any real enthusiasm.

There must have been more to it than my extreme dislike of the horrendously steep escalators on Moscow's subway system. They seem to descend halfway down to Australia and do nothing to alleviate my fear of heights. They have me clinging on for dear life until the moving staircase gives way to the sanctity of the platforms way down below and all the architectural wonders between them, columns, busts and murals.

Chris didn't believe me when I told him of my apprehension at Wembley on the afternoon, we saw Fulham win the play-off final against Aston Vila. "You'll be there," he said. Thanks to Christine Mathews, the former Chelsea and Brentford press secretary who lived upstairs from me in Wimbledon, I also got to see the other two play-off finals in hospitality before heading off to Spain. All Mallorca's late-season regular fixtures had clashed with Palace, so I hadn't seen them clinch promotion from the dreaded Segunda div B. But I did think it worthwhile boarding a high speed Renfe train from Alicante to see them become champions - for what that was worth - at the expense of little Majadahonda, from the Madrid outskirts. Mallorca's 1-0 win gave them an aggregate 3-1 success in the play-off final. Majadahonda went up too but came straight back down again.

The more I thought about Russia, the greater the dilemma. The flight I had originally booked had long since left and landed. I looked for serious distractions such as a three-day visit to the Balearic's party island which deliberately coincided with the first leg of Ibiza's tercera div play-off against Levante B (0-1). On the first evening in Ibiza, I got prime spot in front of a restaurant's television to see Ronaldo scoring a hat trick in Portugal's 3-3 draw with Spain. Had I made a grave error by not going? I went to Mallorca for the last two days of a ladies' tennis tournament, won by the German, Tatjana Maria. The tennis was in the resort of Santa

Ponsa where I joined a throng of sunburned English tourists under a restaurant awning, watching our 6-1 victory over Panama. Still, I wasn't going to Moscow. But I was weakening.

I flew from Palma direct to Newcastle which gave me easy access to Scarborough where Surrey were contesting a four-day county championship match. I was there in time for the last hour of the first day and saw the rest of the game which Surrey won en route to the title. Each day's play had ended most conveniently in time for the late game in Russia and even more conveniently there was a pub outside the cricket ground with big screens. Every game seemed to be a thriller. I was buckling. Eventually I found a library in Scarborough's town centre with computers. I used one of them to book myself a seat on a flight to Moscow plus a message to the airport hotel I had originally booked, confirming my new arrival date. Of course, the Sheremetevo Novotel refused to honour my new booking which they said they'd never received. Welcome to Moscow. Their charge for a room for the night was grossly inflated so after the usual protracted argument at reception, I used one of the hotel's computers to book myself a room in a small city centre hotel at a far more competitive rate. When I got there, I found it to be next to a park where I could run so I booked more nights for when I would not be staying in the flat rented by my son Ashley and Maria, his lovely blonde Russian girlfriend who had modelling assignments.

I had arrived in Moscow late on the Friday. The round-of-16 ties the next day were all hundreds of miles away so I settled for a Russian third division match which Google told me would be within walking distance or a short taxi ride from a metro stop near Domodedvo Airport. When I got there and asked around, I was met by blank stares and frowns from the cabbies. None of them had a clue where FK Peresvet played. It was an exasperating way of spending a World Cup Saturday. All my misgivings about going in the first place had re-surfaced. But the game must have taken place because the result appeared on Soccerway.com's website the next day, a 2-1 home win over Dolgie Prudy's second team. What had I missed! Anyway, I gave up and found a place in a shopping mall showing France v Argentina which was enhanced by two goals from Kylian Mbappe and Benjamin Pavard's piledriver in a 4-3 France win.

I felt like a gate crasher the next day when I activated the first of my tickets at the Luzhniki Stadium. My first 24 hours in Moscow had gone so badly that the last thing I needed now was to witness a home win, least of all against Spain, but that's what I got, Russia succeeding by 4-2 in the shootout after holding out for 1-1 over 120 minutes. It seems that Spain either win these events or crash out early. There's no grey area. But, at least, I was up and running now with Samara my next stop, via a flight the next morning. I met up with Singapore Steve, who was in his Brazil replica shirt for their 2-0 win over Mexico. Our category 2 seats were in the second row by the corner flag. Have Fifa's imbeciles no idea what constitutes a good view and what is a distinctly lousy view? I told Steve that we should upgrade which, in time-honoured fashion we did, finding a couple of empty seats on the side at a reasonable height.

Back in the capital the following evening, I met up, at last with the others in an extremely well chosen, albeit extremely tight-fitting, Muscovite diner before England's epic game with Colombia in the Otkiritie Stadium which is used by Moscow Spartak. For once, we won on pens, by 4-3 this time, after another 1-1. With ex Palace man, Gareth Southgate now at the helm, I found I was getting behind England again after the dour regimes of Sven-Goran Eriksson, Steve McClaren, Fabio Capello and, dare I say, Roy Hodgson.

As a latecomer to the party, I wanted to fit in as many games as possible to make up for lost time. The quarter-finals were upon us now and I needed to be present on both match days even though that presented massive difficulties. The easy bit was flying to Kazan, a wondrous city decorated by its Kremlin and on this occasion, Kevin de Bruyne's brilliance in Belgium's 2-1 win over Brazil. The hard bit was reaching Samara. I had already been there, of course, but that was from Moscow. Now Leicester Mike, a newly acquired friend - through an introduction from Chelsea Ian - and I both needed to overcome the lack of trains and planes for a return visit if we were to see England oppose Sweden. The only feasible transport was by taxi which presented another problem caused by the guy I was expecting at my hotel the next morning. He reneged on the booking. He texted me 20 minutes before he was due, to say he would not be coming.

Keeping calm in his city centre hotel, Mike used his smart phone to locate and negotiate a price with a more reliable driver who turned up minutes later. Not bad since he had a ten-hour round trip ahead of him. He was a local lad unlike the majority of Russia's ranks of cabbies who hail from such fragmented outposts of the former USSR as Turkmenistan and Kyrgyzstan. Mike must have known something about the driver's predilection for speed judging by the fact that he sat in the back while I was ushered into the front passenger seat for the 225-mile journey through, for the most part, lush countryside. Instead of my usual aerial views of Russia, it was good to see something of the country close at hand as it hurtled by.

The driver was no slouch. It was foot down all the way. I thought he was a risk-taker but for all that he was a fine judge of speed and distance when it came to overtaking with the maximum degree of safety. Several times I saw my life flash by. But he got us to Samara in one piece. We even had enough time to dump our bags in the city centre apartment that Mike had booked with some of his mates who had taken the direct route from Moscow. Our escort spoke no English but with hand gestures I implored him to take it easy on the return leg. Unless he was on a promise the other end, there was no need to hurry, I told him. I hoped he understood. We gave him a generous tip before making our way to the Samara Stadium. Mike's mates were good company. Lawrie was a Luton fan, Keith coached a team near Colchester and Paul was a surprisingly nice chap considering that he was a Brighton fan. We all met up after the game to celebrate England's 2-0 win. And then I made my way to the hotel I had booked which seemed to double up as a brothel judging by the lurid-looking business card I found at reception.

For once I wasn't complaining about the lack of a game on a Sunday or, for that matter Monday. After the suspense of the previous few days, it was good to relax before the semis and so I persuaded the rest of the gang to join me on a boat ride down the Volga River. The first of the semis was in St Petersburg, which fortunately was a direct flight away from Samara. I had been to this magnificent city once before in a bid to reach Zenit's former Kirov Stadium before it was razed. It was for a Champions League tie against Malaga when, unable to find the press box because of linguistic problems, I was forced to sit in the open behind the goal among a score of frozen Spaniards watching the 2-2 draw. It was mid-November. I had wondered how Brazilian players such as Zenit's Hulk had acclimatised to the meteorological conditions of winter, high up in the northern hemisphere. But now St Pete's as we named it, basked in balmier temperatures which France obviously found conducive judging by the manner of their 1-0 win over Belgium thanks to a goal from Samuel Umtiti.

As a train buff, it had been one of my life-long ambitions to travel on and dine aboard the Sapsan which is the St Petersburg to Moscow express so I was dismayed to find that Chris had booked us on the sleeper the next day that trundles along, taking eight hours. Progress was slow but we need not have worried whether we would reach the Luzhniki Stadium in time for England's game against Croatia. The main concern was if England could reach their first final since 1966. After all my years of observing England rather than supporting them, I was now back as a true fan of Southgate's team, feeling the tension as if it was a Palace play-off final. Which was why it came as such a crushing blow when we failed so agonisingly to make it.

Despite Croatia's 2-1 win, I went to the final hoping that Ante Rebic might inspire them to beat France. Chris and I sat just above a girl who seemed to spend the whole 90 minutes texting on her mobile, looking up just occasionally when she heard a roar, to see what was going on We wondered out aloud how tickets for such momentous games could fall so lamentably into the wrong hands. Who had been stupid enough to let her have the ticket when there were thousands outside who would have given their right arm to be inside. And it was not as if it was a bad final. For a long time it was a gripping one enhanced for France by Mbappe's devastating acceleration. It was good to see a final with a few goals even though at least one of them, Mario Mandzukic's - at the right end for Croatia - was handed to him on a plate by Hugo Loris. That meant, at the least, a respectable 4-2 scoreline in adversity for the Croats.

For once I had achieved nothing like a clean sweep of all 11 venues, but did it really matter? I had seen eight games on five grounds, leaving the likes of Kaliningrad and Nizhny Novgorod to be done another day. I had thoroughly enjoyed myself. So why all the brooding beforehand? I couldn't explain it.

Lots of fans might have wanted a World Cup final to provide the climax to their summer but, needless to say, I was not among their number. The following lunchtime I met Pennie at Stockholm's Arlanda Airport where, most conveniently, both our flights were landing within 35 minutes of each other. A few games, and especially, some new grounds in the Allsvenskan, would be the liqueurs on my menu over the next ten days. With time to spare before the first of them, we headed for the resort of Hudiksvall which not only has a glorious sandy beach but an annual music festival clashing nicely with our visit and appealing to all tastes, except perhaps, lovers of classical symphonies. The town rocked. Old ladies wanting to get to bed early might have grumbled at the noise but for three nights we relished the variety of sounds bashed out from that stage. We spent most of the days chilling out at a café overlooking the beach, which was full of dog walkers including, on one afternoon, rather surprisingly an English trio with a mongrel. One of the boys was wearing a Brighton shirt so we got talking. The father was such a jovial soul that we forgave him his choice of favourite club.

People had come from far and wide to attend the music festival which perhaps explained the multitude of vintage American cars such as Chryslers and Chevrolets chugging their way around the streets. Hudiksvall proved the perfect halfway stop on our journey to Östersund which is a drab town hardly befitting of a rejuvenated team judging by their display in a 4-1 win over Trelleborg. It was Östersund's first home outing since Graham Potter's exit for Swansea and, on the evidence of the reaction to tanoy announcements, the club's fanbase seemed more grateful for the contribution the Englishman had made to their

224

emergence - that led to Europa League qualification - than any bitterness at his departure for richer financial pickings. Neither did the players appear too downcast. They seemed determined to maintain the progress.

From Östersund we faced a long drive back down the coast to Uppsala's half renovated Studenternas Stadium for Sirius' 3-2 win over IFK Goteborg the next day. And then, continuing south, it was the turn of Hammarby to welcome us in their new Tele2Arena that the club shares with Djurgarden. And if the response to the goals in the 4-1 win over Dalkurd was anything to go by, the home crowd have matched their decibel levels since moving from one Stockholm suburb to another. They seem keen to retain their reputation as the noisiest fans in Sweden. Not to mention the most boisterous. Dalkurd, formed by Kurdish immigrants, were, by contrast, doubtless the quietest. They were the least well supported of the nation's top flight clubs before dropping into the Superettan.

Chapter 54:
Runway to the Rock

My reluctance to go to Russia until the tournament was well under way threatened my target of 200 games a year. It was a stupid ambition, I know, but addictions are also fairly stupid and virtually impossible to prevent, albeit without the aid of psychiatric treatment and Chris was charging too much for that. Once at a party my daughter, Jessica had asked him: "Can you have a word with my Dad. Football is ruining his life."

"On the contrary," replied Chris. "I think football has enhanced your Dad's life." I tended to agree with him, never more so than on one of the few occasions the fixtures had squeezed so perfectly into my schedule that they could have been arranged by my good self. It was almost three months after I had returned from Sweden. And I was in Spain again for Mallorca's return to the Segunda div. I had already seen them a few times, most notably in Lugo (1-1) not the easiest of venues to reach as it is in the far north west of the mainland.

Reaching Granada for their next away game was a far simpler task as I only had to step on a bus at Alicante - which was near my base - for a five-hour ride. With its Alhambra and various other attractions, Granada is a tourists' haven and not, therefore, the best city to be on one's own. I was in no mood for solitude after Mallorca had lost 1-0 to a late goal but that's what I got. Still, I would have agreeable company over the next couple of days.

Granada had been the start of a hectic four-games-in-four-days fest. With a combination of another bus and trains, I got to my next stop, Sevilla which was due to stage Spain's Nations League qualifier against England in the Estadio Benito Villamarin, belonging to Betis. People had been quick to criticise the Nations League as it was deemed surplus to requirements in an already overcrowded fixture list but the ensuing progress of Southgate's men at the expense of Spain and Croatia was to quieten the critics. I met up with Leicester Mike and Lawrie for a pre-match bite before witnessing the almost unprecedented sight of England romping into a three-goal lead through two goals from Raheem Sterling and one from Marcus Rashford before hanging on for a 3-2 win.

The next stop was Gibraltar who were now playing international matches at home instead of borrowing Loule from the Spaniards which was never much of an harmonious arrangement given the way they feel

226

about each other. Martin (dos metros), my Aldershot train driver mate and his pal, Michael Rainbird had both, like me, travelled down from Seville for the game which was to be a Euro qualifier against Liechtenstein and I met up with them for a pre match drink in the La Linea hotel where we were all residing. I have never known an approach to a football ground like it. The Victoria Stadium stands just the other side of The Rock's airport so, from Spain, we had to walk across the runway to get there. Flights in and out of Gibraltar are few and far between, thankfully, and it's not as if pedestrians are allowed anywhere near the landing strip if a plane is due. But it was a bizarre means, all the same, of accessing a stadium.

As Gibraltar's 2-1 win was their first ever in international competition, we witnessed scenes of wild joy before helping Martin collate all the programmes that had been left on seats by fans who didn't seem at all grateful to the organisers for dishing out free ones. Not so Martin who is one of Britain's top traders in football memorabilia. Foreigners don't collect programmes the way us Brits do so there were some easy pickings for him and profits to be made at the national programme fair in Russell Square. He also deals in tickets and badges. Many a time have I come across him outside a ground after a game, holding up a piece of cardboard with the words of "I collect tickets" scratched on it. Lots of Germans have followed his example but Martin reckons that he started the trend at the 2002 World Cup when he got a local lass to help him with his mission. She wrote a rather wordy request in Japanese which Martin trimmed down to the essential translation for 'please can I have your ticket if you don't want it.' Or words to that affect.

Sometimes he is so grateful that he doles out a badge in exchange. Many of the tickets he gathers go on Ebay for sizeable sums. I am constantly amazed at the number of people who pay big money for tickets for games they have never been to unless, of course, those tickets are for ancient and significant games such as World Cup finals. There is a burgeoning market out there for such items.

By the time we departed the stadium weighed down by progs, most of Gib's finest restaurants - if there are any - had long since closed so I treated the three of us to a pizza each. We crossed the runway back into La Linea where we did, at least, find a funky bar.

The two of them were heading back home the next day but I had discovered another gem. I had always been intrigued by Ceuta and Melilla, the two Spanish enclaves on Morocco's coastline. Both of them are the homes of Spanish tercera div clubs and now, glory be, one of them - Melilla - were staging a Copa del Rey tie. Their opponents were hardly illustrious, just another tercera div club, Ontinyent, from the Murcia group, but this was a chance not to be missed. I could have virtually swum across the straits of Gibraltar to reach Ceuta but to get to Melilla, I had to take a coach to Malaga Airport from where it was a 50-minute flight. With kick-off beckoning, I had to dash from my hotel to the ground but with my homeward journey via Malaga to Gatwick not beginning until late the following afternoon I had time to explore this mysterious citadel. Mellila's 2-0 win earned them a tie against Real Madrid in the next round which did, of course, signal the end of their run in the copa.

I had only been back three days when I was off to Russia again, this time with far more eagerness than before. In a bid to boost tourism, the Russian authorities had told football fans attending the World Cup that their visas - which were match tickets - would not expire until December 31. It was an invitation I seized upon after scouring the fixtures to examine the possibilities. Visits to the World Cup venues that had proved beyond my scope would have been preferable but nothing availed itself except perhaps a game at Ekaterinburg but that would have meant an expensive return flight from Moscow at the weekend. The alternative was far cheaper. And nearer.

I was grateful for Lokomotiv Moscow's participation in the Champions League and the fortune which had paired them with Porto on the most convenient date for me. Not only that but the two clubs under 19 teams were meeting before the big one. I had gone to Moscow ill prepared. Most of the World Cup had taken place in conditions suitable for t-shirts and shorts. I hadn't realised temperatures would plunge so drastically by October. I had shivered at the under 19 match which was a 2-1 home win. Luckily there was a major shopping complex in the half mile between the Sapsan Arena and Lokomotiv's RZD Arena, so I forked out the equivalent of around £100 on a heavy padded and hooded coat which I thought was a bargain seeing as I'd forced the salesman down from his original asking price of about £180. And, at least, I was warm for the second game which Porto won 3-1.

This time I had to make the most of my own company. It's something to which the single-minded football watcher has to become accustomed if he is to accumulate the games in foreign climes. Not everyone's schedule fits in with his own. It can be a lonely pastime. There's only so many hours a person can devote to sight-seeing on his tod, even in a city with so many sights to see as Moscow. I was ensconced at the same hotel I had stayed in three months earlier with its advantages of the park across the road for running, easy access to the metro and an ornate café which served up tasty omelettes and coffee for my breakfasts.

228

I also discovered that the chaps pressing the bell of the establishment next door were entering a dodgy nightclub. For all that, I was glad to have the excuse to be on the move again.

The excuse came in the shape of Tula or, to put it more precisely, Arsenal Tula, the club based two hours train ride south of Moscow. The red tape that goes into purchasing a ticket for this simple journey seemed to take hours. I was glad I had checked out the station and its booking hall, full of endless queues, with a day to spare. Like Kazan, Tula turned out to be another Russian city with a kremlin which meant that it was on the tourist beat with plenty going for it. I walked everywhere, including up a fairly steep hill to the basic but perfectly acceptable Arsenal Stadium where, for the equivalent of £5 for a seat on the side, I saw an entertaining 2-2 draw with Orenburg who had travelled 750 miles for the fixture. Mind you, I had probably travelled further. I got the train back to Moscow and stayed in a modest hotel near the airport - as I was loathe to give the Novotel any custom - and flew back the next morning. I was in time for Palace's lunchtime kick-off against Arsenal, another 2-2 draw. I thought I must have been the only person on the planet to see two completely different Arsenal clubs within 24 hours. A peculiar claim to fame.

Chapter 55:
Ode to Patrick

Within days of my return, another combination of football and culture was generated around Palace's Carabao Cup tie (1-0) at Middlesbrough, of all unlikely places. The Settle to Carlisle railway had gained a prominent place on my bucket list so here was a golden opportunity to sample the dales and moors of that 63-mile return journey. In fact, it was a few miles less for Pennie and I as Martin who knows everything there is to know about train travel, had given us the sound advice to disembark at the penultimate stop of Appleby so as to take an exploratory stroll round that quaint town which is famous for its horse fair, frequented by gypsies. We did as we were told and got back to Leeds in time for our journey to Gateshead's Sage Theatre via Newcastle.

The attraction this time for us Country music nuts was Kasey Musgraves, the American singer who was on tour. She proved well worth our diversion as did Bridget, the daughter of my erstwhile oldest and dearest friend, Patrick. When Bridget - who worked at Sage - met us for a post-concert drink, it was the first time I'd had a chance to reminisce with her in depth about her late father who had been my travelling companion on the first few road trips I'd done for Palace away games in the late 60s. And to England games abroad.

She was compiling a memoir about his early life which had taken him to Paris for a while, working as a waiter, and she grilled me relentlessly before we got the late train back to our Leeds base. I had heard the sad news about Patrick's death in a phone call from Pat, his wife, during the half-time interval of the Ludogorets v AC Milan game eight months earlier. It had quite ruined the second half for me and put a dampener on the rest of the trip.

Patrick who had retired from driving a cab to live out his late years in Gravesend, would doubtless have admired my stamina which enabled me to take two more overseas trips before Christmas. The first one came during the November international break when Mallorca's Saturday fixture at Zaragoza (2-2) followed Andorra's Nations League tie with Georgia (1-1). I had seen Andorra in their former Estadi Comunal home on the occasion of their first ever victory in international football over Macedonia (1-0, att 116) but never before, of course, in their new sparkling new city centre Estadi Nacional. Not that I was over impressed. It's one of the tragedies of progress that crumbling old relics of stadiums

230

give way to the modernised versions, all built around roughly the same model, which are soulless and completely lacking in character with the result that they fade quickly from the memory. As Christine and I had flown into Barcelona and taken one route up the hill to Andorra, we were able to see more of the undulating Aragon countryside by descending along a different route towards Zaragoza and our Sunday tercera div game at Tamarite (3-0 v Sabinanigo).

Christine, who had taken to the hotel bars for the first two games, sat through this one gritting her teeth as Tamarite de Litera is a small town, more dead than alive on a Sunday afternoon. There was nowhere else for her to go.

I hadn't been back a week before I was heading off again, this time to Germany, so as to complete the Bundesliga stads. Lufthansa did their utmost to upset all my best laid plans however by delaying my Frankfurt-bound plane by two hours out of Heathrow. Airlines wouldn't do this if they realised the stress and heartburn they cause punters heading for a match. But luckily everything thereafter worked like clockwork as it does so frequently in Germany. My train connections were spot on as was the match--special bus at Sinsheim Bahnhof taking stragglers to Hoffenheim's Champions League group game against Shaktor Donetsk. The added worry was the bag I was carrying that I had been assured I could not take into the Pre-Zero Stadium. Not to worry. The bag drop was opposite my entrance. There was a girl there arguing with the fellow behind the window. She didn't have enough cash to access her match ticket and he wouldn't give her any. Her bloke was already inside the ground. She seemed genuine so I gave her the 15 euros she needed. She promised to leave it for me at the bag drop after the game. I got in for kick-off. My faith in humanity was restored not only by the spectacle, a thrilling 3-2 win for the Ukranians but on finding, after the game, that she had left the 15e for me to collect.

Hoffenheim is little more than a village. As the brainchild of Dietmar Hopp, the software entrepreneur and billionaire, the football club is, like Red Bull Leipzig, reviled throughout the rest of Germany for being a money bags operation, a bit like Chelsea. The place is distinctly one-horse, not exactly the size of urban community you would expect to be accommodating a top club, so it was not exactly festooned with cabs when I wandered back after the game in search of my bed for the night. I eventually stumbled into a bar where they understood me well enough to order a cab that took me six miles further away from the heart of commerce and industry to the small hotel where I had booked a room. The cab company returned me to civilisation the next morning from where I continued my journey in a southerly direction.

231

Munich was my destination now. I re-acquainted myself with the city's Englischer Garden and discovered the Bratwurstherzl restaurant which specialises in sausages of every hue, proportion and taste. But the main purpose of my visit was the suburb of Unterhaching whose stadium was only two metro stops from where I was staying with Nadiya, my blast from the past. Like their Liga 3 opponents, Kaiserslautern who had been Bundesliga champions as recently as 1998, the hosts had fallen on hard times. They had enjoyed two seasons in the top flight at the turn of the century. I wondered at the sharp declines of the two clubs. But then I thought of Sunderland, Portsmouth and Bolton to name but a few. Such transformations in fortunes don't just happen in Germany. Unterhaching won 5-0. No wonder the Berger twins, Jurgen and Bastien had long since given up on Kaiserslautern. I flew back to Gatwick the next morning in plenty of time for Palace's 2-0 win over Burnley.

When Nadiya had lived in Berlin, the joke had always been: "Nick's relationship with Nadiya would be over as soon as he had done all the grounds around Berlin." There was an element of truth in that as we went several years without contact. But now she was Munich-based. And harder work than ever even though I couldn't resist seeing her again on the occasion of Munich 1860 against Bayern 11 in a Liga 3 derby (1-1) by when our affair was well past its sell-by date.

Chapter 56:
Getting in with a squeeze

I had heard about Patrick's death while at a game and regrettably there was a similar scenario when I combined Britain's Federation Cup tennis event at Bath with a Western League football match at Plymouth Parkway. The match against Cadbury Heath (5-0) was well under way when I got a call from a girl to say that her father Clive White had died. And I hadn't even known that Clive was on his death bed. He had become a great friend during my 12 years on The Times. Not only was he a superb writer, so good that he should have been the paper's football correspondent, but he was also the most affable of blokes. No one ever had a bad word to say about Clive. We had met up occasionally since our departures from Wapping - both on the same black Friday in November 1992 - and now I could only feel sorry that it hadn't been more often. The rain that teemed down in Plymouth that evening did nothing to improve my mood.

Clive had spent most of his later years as a tennis correspondent, most notably at the Sunday Telegraph with whom he had a spectacular falling-out. He wasn't of football hopper mentality so he would have found it hard to comprehend my enthusiasm for such trips as the one I had already booked for the following weekend to Denmark where coincidence decided that I would be watching Brondby yet again. Their hosts were Nordsjaelland from Farum, a small town just outside Copenhagen's city's boundaries. I'd had a tetchy correspondence with the home club's press officer leading up to the game and, ultimately he chose not to give me accreditation. When I got to the exquisitely named Right to Dream Stadium, the unguarded media entrance proved too much of a temptation, so I went in. I was surveying the scene when a chap who might well have been the aforementioned press officer, asked me what I was doing. "Just looking," said I before making a hasty bolt for the stand where, out of visibility of the press box, I found an empty seat permitting me an unobstructed view of a splendid 3-3 draw. I celebrated my good fortune over dinner in the Thai restaurant almost next door to my favourite Star Hotel.

By now a veteran of Danish railways, I knew enough to do a circuit of the food stalls in Copenhagen station the next morning, knowing that I would go hungry if I wasn't properly equipped for the forthcoming six-hour journey on trains minus buffet cars. The country's trains lack

233

nothing in comfort except for the one basic necessity required by the long-distance traveller. Not to worry though. Chris had spotted the game that had also caught my eye, newly promoted Vendsyssel v Midtjylland and he seldom goes anywhere without his Michelin Guide. The far northern outpost of Hjorring seems to have little else going for it, certainly not a decent team judging by the manner of Vendsyssel's 1-0 defeat, but the restaurant he had earmarked for us after the game, cooked one of the juiciest steaks it has ever been my pleasure to devour. We walked back the couple of hundred yards to the station, a distance I had undertaken by cab earlier in the evening so as to make kick-off, thanks to the trains not honouring my faith in their punctuality. We found that we were both staying the night in Aalborg, albeit in different hotels before flying back to Stansted the next morning.

I was back in Denmark five weeks later. Oldham Dave and I had long since cursed our failure to get to Silkeborg's former Mascot Park home but now I had noticed that this town in central Jutland was acting as one of the group hosts for the Uefa Under-17 championship. I flew to Copenhagen from Las Palmas where I had seen Mallorca maintain their promotion push from the Segunda div with a 2-1 win. I should have known better than to risk the last possible train to Silkeborg because, by the time, I found the only open entrance to the new JYSK Stadium and gained free admission, I had missed Croatia's first two goals in their 3-2 win over the hosts. Most of the crowd, such as it was, had vanished by the time England took the field for the second instalment of the double-header, a 5-2 victory over Switzerland.

The UEFA under 17 event was, of course, the start of an international week which in normal circumstances would have represented a trip for me to see Mallorca so, overcoming my guilt at forsaking their home fixture with Zaragoza, I embarked on a hectic week by flying to Budapest instead. Hungary's Euro qualifier with Croatia in the new Ferencvaros (Groupama) Stadium had stood out and an outstanding game it was too. Rebic scored early for the Croats, but Hungary recovered for a shock 2-1 win over the World Cup runners-up.

This trip had warranted meticulous preparation. From Budapest I caught a late-night train to Vienna where Judy, a sexy Singaporean lady, was awaiting me at the end of the platform. It was straight out of a Graham Greene novel. I had met Judy when I noticed her sitting in the seat behind me at a Brentford v Sheffield Wednesday match the previous August. I could scarcely concentrate on the first half, so I used the half-time interval to make her acquaintance before any other chancer did so. She was a football nut, in London on an auditing mission. But now she was in Vienna sight-seeing. From the Austrian capital we took a direct flight the next day to Podgorica for England's game against Montenegro. The England travel club had only been granted 500 tickets which meant that a relatively new member like myself was way down the list of no-hopers. I met up with Leicester Mike and Lawrie who had no spares between them, so I tried the local bars. In the lounge of a five-star hotel I came across two English fans in the process of getting drunk. One of them said he wouldn't be using his ticket. He wanted 75 euros, three times face value, but it still seemed a bargain, so I forked out, feeling extra glad that I had done so later in the light of England's 5-1 win. With only one ticket between us and the match in the humble Stadion Pod Goricom long since sold out, there was nothing else for it but to tell Judy that we were both going through the turnstile together which was some feat considering the extent to which I had to hold in my stomach so as to squeeze in behind her. We found two empty seats easily enough.

I couldn't help but wonder if the slob who had sold me the ticket, had any regrets. I am often mystified as to why some fans will travel huge distances to support their team only to spend the duration of the game getting plastered. It doesn't matter if there are no televisions in the bars where they are soaking up their ales. Luke, the West Brom fan we had met in Argentina, liked to boast of going to away games in places such as Blackpool where he would drink the afternoon away - and probably the night too - in preference to entering Bloomfield Road. His drinking sessions would invariably cost far more than the price of admission. Danny was another one. He would go halfway round the globe and end up in a bar full of drifters while the game was on.

The kindly staff at our pleasant hotel on Podgorica's outskirts helped us hire a car which was essential for the next leg of the journey which was into Bosnia. The primitive border crossing, high up the snowclad hills on unkempt roads was straight out of an Alfred Hitchcock black and white, spy-gate movie. From there, it was hazardous enough for our Polo, let alone the drivers of coaches and trucks also inching their way down through the drizzle. We finally made it to Sarajevo in time for a pre-match snack in a café outside the very same Stadion Grbavica where I had seen Terry Neill's Arsenal side face Zeljeznicar in a pre-season friendly 43 years earlier (1-1). The occasion this time was Bosnia v Moldova in a Uefa Under 21 qualifier which the hosts won 4-0.

With snow falling and a 45-mile journey ahead of us, we hurried away on the whistle in the belief that we would have to source tickets for the evening game, the Euro qualifier involving Bosnia and Greece in Zenica. Ultimately there was no need as, following a fruitless quest, we located the press entrance. The chaos there was just what we needed. Television crews and photographers were all jostling their way down a narrow passage. Telling Judy to look like she owned the place, she followed me as we were shoved past security. And then we climbed up into the crowded press gallery where we took advantage of the two remaining empty seats. We made ourselves look busy. I was relieved that we had made the effort as the game was a dramatic 2-2 draw. Greece fought back well from going two goals down inside 16 minutes.

My one regret was that we saw little of Zenica which looked an attractive city in the dark - straddling the Bosna River - as we had decided to break our journey back by staying the night in Sarajevo. On the drive back to Podgorica the next day, we stopped off at the historic Ostrog Monastery which had been carved out of a cliff face 2,700 feet above the Zeta Valley. It was known as Sv Vasilije's Miracle after a bishop responsible for its creation in the 17th century. It took a precarious drive to get there and for anyone on foot such as a monk with second thoughts about devoting his life to the Almighty, it would have been a long and sweaty descent in his robes.

Chapter 57:
Storks have the best view

Southampton Steve or Saint Steve as he was now known had long since extolled the virtues of Deventer as a town of ancient artistic merit and charm in Holland, so it was an obvious base for my next trip to Holland the following weekend. Celia who had familiarised herself with the world of football in the four months since I'd met her on a train, was my companion. This time, press passes were at the ready at the pick-up point at Zwolle where we saw a 3-0 home win over Emmen which took me to within one ground of completing the Dutch (Eredivisie) League. Only Fortuna Sittard was left to do now. Celia and I took the train to Deventer where we accessed the tiny craft taking folk across the River Ijssel to find our lodgings were in the attic of a boutique bed and breakfast owned by a garrulous chap who was an avid hunter judging by the number of trophies of animals competing for space with the various antiques on his shelves and walls. There was no denying the comfort of the place or the quality of his breakfast, but we couldn't share his enthusiasm for the heads and horns peering down on us as we ate. I'd like to think that we made it clear we weren't in favour of killing proud and innocent beasts for the mere sake of it. I am an animal lover and as the widow of a vet, Celia also responds to living creatures around her instead of reminders of their demise. We explored Deventer's cobbled streets and The Brink, its main square during our two-night stay which was rounded off by a lively second (Eerste) div game in which the town's club, Go Ahead Eagles lost 3-2 to Telstar.

The stadium there, indeed, most stadiums everywhere are put in the shade by the grandeur of the next stadium I was to visit, the imposing edifice of Tottenham Hotspur's new home which is a complete juxtaposition, akin to a mirage rising from a desert of ethnic fast-food joints and inner-city developments on the High Road from Seven Sisters. Palace were, I am sure, honoured to be the first visitors but we seemed to freeze on the occasion of our 2-0 defeat. I was just thankful that our fans did not soil the event with any rendition of "This is a shit hole, I want to go home." Somewhat incredulously, I had heard that tiresome ditty three months earlier at Craven Cottage, sung by Oldham's congregation, if you please, during their surprising FA Cup win. The cheek of football fans. Or indeed, the perverse humour.

Feeling like a jetsetter, I was off again at the weekend, rejuvenated by the Luka Milivojevic penalty that gave Palace a late 1-0 win at Newcastle. In a perfect world I would have flown direct from Geordie country to Poland but there were no such flights, so I had to return to London for a plane to Katowice on the Sunday morning. I had feared it would be a complicated journey from there to Zabrze so I couldn't believe it when I stepped out of the airport to find a coach leaving within five minutes. Which was just as well. When I got to the Ernest Pohl stadium - named after a former Gornik player - it was heaving. I'd received no reply to my request for a press pass so I went to a ticket booth and bought the highest priced ticket believing that would get me in quicker. Every entrance was rammed but I managed to circumvent the snarl-up outside my block to sneak under a bar and in, missing only the first five minutes of an enthralling match that Legia Warsaw won by the odd goal in three.

Zabrze is on the edge of Poland's polluted industrial heartland so it doesn't abound with good restaurants or, indeed any restaurants at all that I could find during my subsequent search. I had a couple of hours to kill before a late-night bus to my overnight stop in Krakow, but I eventually gave up and settled for an unsatisfactory meat pie and chips at a stall. That meagre offering was in stark contrast to the menu in the buffet car of my train the next day. Unlike Denmark, the embellishment of long-distance rail travel in Poland is to linger over a meal as the world races by. Never had a simple ham omelette and French fries with all the sundry garnishes tasted so good. By the time I had changed trains to reach Plock I was hungry again but the restaurant I found near the station took such an eternity to serve up my steak that I left before it arrived. I did not want to miss another kick-off. I need not have worried. The frenzy of Zabrze was a world away. The steward at the modest Kazimierz Gorski Stadium named after a former national team manager - who had no connections with Plock so far as I could gather - gave my press card a cursory look. He directed me towards hospitality where I ordered the same pork dish that everyone seemed to be consuming. Kick-off was beckoning so I took the plate in with me and ate the pork off my lap. I was in the directors' box, but no one seemed to give me a second glance. Their mellow mood was doubtless helped by Wisla Plock's 2-0 win over Slask Wroclaw.

Sweden was next on the agenda as I wanted to get to Falkenberg before their possible relegation from the Allsvenkan. It was the day of the Champions League final so people, even in Sweden, were showing off their allegiances. Judy and I were overjoyed to be served our pre match beers in a marquee near the ground by a sexy barmaid busting out of a Spurs replica shirt. Judging by the permanent smile adorning her

238

winsome face, she was basking in the attention. After that, Falkenberg's goalless draw with Kalmar was quite an anti-climax although the point helped the hosts stay up.

The barmaid must have been disappointed by the evening's outcome. But she was not the only one. Judging by the wild cheers and the groans of misery which were the reactions to the goals in Liverpool's 2-0 win, there were few neutrals in the packed bar we found near the mouth of the River Atran that winds its way through the town. Just about everyone seemed desperate for one team or the other to win. And here we were on the west coast of Sweden. The establishment did a roaring trade. From that Scandanavian outpost, it was good to witness the appreciation for two of our top clubs. On that evidence the Swedes obviously hold our Premier League in high esteem. Would it have been a similar scenario if the final had involved two Spanish, Italian or German clubs? I doubt it.

Our live match the next day, a short train ride up the coast was a big improvement on the first instalment. Varberg's challenge for promotion from the second div gained momentum with an exciting 2-1 success over GAIS from Gothenburg who had fallen on such hard times that they were in the midst of a relegation struggle. Varberg had been reduced to nine men by the end, but they held on, much to the delight of the majority of the crowd in their tiny 4,500 capacity Paskbergsvallen ground, the second smallest in the Superettan.

Three days later, my carelessness almost cost me a trip to the first ever Nations League finals. As someone whose interest in cricket had been revived, I was on the early stages of wanting to visit all the top-class grounds. I had driven past Surrey's secondary home of Guildford hundreds of times, but I had never actually seen a game there. So, the first day of the four-day county championship match against Somerset had long since been pencilled in. It was the day before my departure for Portugal. Pennie and I left after an entertaining day's play but, to my horror, I found I was lacking my jacket when I got back to London. It contained not only my wallet but my passport. Cursing my stupidity and the possible onset of dementia for leaving it hanging over my seat at Guildford, I rang my photographer mate, Mark who had contacts galore among the Surrey hierarchy. He obliged by giving me the number of the chief steward from where I was directed to lost property. The chap there said he would look for it but I had suffered a sleepless night by the time he rang in the morning to say he had found my jacket with everything intact. I vowed never to be so absent-minded again as I set forth for Porto via a flight to Lisbon as I had reckoned that route would be cheaper.

The balmy evening of the tournament's opening game, Portugal's 3-1 win over Switzerland, gave way to a torrential downpour up the road in

Guimaraes the next day. The bedraggled rabble of England fans drinking from plastic glasses outside the plentiful bars of the picturesque Largo da Oliveira - named after an olive tree that had been planted in the square - made for an incongruous sight. A group of us took refuge for a long lunch in one of the town's finest restaurants. I got talking to Peter and Sue, a couple from Hampstead. He seemed too middle-aged and too well spoken to be the type to be wearing a Fulham replica shirt. He could have been a bank manager. Such aficionados must spend long hours praying that their customers don't spot them in their England garb. Or even Fulham kit. But there he was with his wife, about to join England's disreputable army of fans shouting on Southgate's men who nevertheless slipped to a disappointing 3-1 extra-time defeat against Holland.

Over lunch Chris had also outlined his crazy idea of filling the Saturday which had threatened to be a football-free day. The Portuguese domestic season had finished but not the Spanish campaign. Even so, Mallorca's game over the border at Extremadura was a nothing match so far as I was concerned. Mallorca had already secured their place in the Segunda div play-offs and, if ever a contest was expendable this was it. If there was a saving grace, it was that Extremadura would complete a clean sweep of segunda div venues for me. It was a persuasive factor so, without too much ado, Chris talked me into it though I had to talk him out of doing the whole 610-mile round trip in a day. That would have been madness. With a hotel in Porto booked for the duration, he wanted - as usual - to save money. I was not having that especially as I knew that my hotel would be more flexible.

We tracked down an agreeable car hire company and set off early for the 8.30pm kick-off. I was glad he had coerced me into the trip as the busy Portuguese motorways soon gave way to minor roads passing alongside olive groves, forests, sweeping valleys and the tiny endearing towns of Iberian border country, one of which, Porto Alegre, had an elegant hotel where we booked ourselves rooms for the night. Carrying on, we explored what little there was on offer in Almendralejo before a goalless draw which was memorable, if only for the storks rising to stretch their limbs from their nest on a flagpole behind one of the goals. The birds had a grandstand view of Mallorca's hard-earned point to which only a handful of regulars contributed. The rest were being saved for the play-offs.

I hadn't realised that Chris was intent on doing both games on the Sunday, England's third-place match in Guimaraes as well as the final in Porto. Somewhat reluctantly I went along with it although I didn't have a ticket for the first one. Third-place games can be misleading. They can be surprisingly hot tickets as I was to find, almost to my cost. Eventually

I got one for face value. The last thing we needed was for Switzerland to take us to extra-time but, of course, sod's law was not on our side We would have to leave on the whistle for Porto. I went out after 90 dreary and goalless minutes to move to a section closer to where we had parked the car. At least that was my intention but having left the Estadio D Alfonso Henriques, I wasn't allowed back in by the mass of stewards and policia at the exits even though all the gates had been opened for the benefit of the early leavers. It was pathetic, heavy-handed nonsense. Talk about erring on the side of caution. It was just an excuse for numbskulls in uniforms to exercise their strength and bullying tactics. I told one of them that I had left a bag inside but, of course, when one of the cretins escorted me inside, there was no bag.

I was in danger of losing my head completely and getting arrested when I called Chris and told him we would be leaving pronto. The game was so dire that he duly came out. All we really missed was the shoot-out, won 6-5 by England. We dashed to Porto's Estadio do Dragao for what was a far better contest. Portugal beat Holland 1-0 with a goal from Goncalo Guedes to become the first Nations League champions.

Taking the train north the next day, I had to kill a few hours in Santiago de Compostela before flying onto Alicante. It's the last stop on the weary road for thousands of pilgrims on the religious Camino de Santiago. The narrow streets of the city centre offer a welcome respite to those hikers wanting to jettison their heavy rucksacks. Most of them flock into better restaurants for plates of tapas than the one I chose. I left most of it on the plate.

My next mistake was not to book a return flight from Alicante to La Coruna for ten days later as soon I saw it offered for 73e. By the time I looked again the fare had shot up to 255e so I settled for watching the first leg of Mallorca's play-off final, a 2-0 defeat against Deportivo in a bar. By then I had seen both legs of the semi-final against Albacete, a nervy 2-1 triumph on aggregate but I was still more or less resigned to disappointment at the second leg of the final. Son Moix was rocking though and few seemed to share my sense of pessimism. The crowd roared Mallorca to a 3-0 triumph that took them back into La Liga after an absence of six years. They became the first club to go straight up to the top flight from segunda div b in successive seasons.

241

Chapter 58:
Foiled by Damo

The late kick-off meant that there was no time to celebrate Mallorca's elevation. Furthermore, all the hotels in my favourite resort of C'an Pastilla were booked solid, so I had to settle for a second night in the less savoury surroundings of Arenal before jetting off to Los Angeles via Barcelona where I met up with Pennie. We were off again to the Gold Cup or, more specifically to some of the Gold Cup's venues that we had not already done, plus the odd game in the MLS, plus a return visit to Nashville.

Our schedule allowed a modicum of breathing space before the games came at us thick and fast. We had just enough time to acquaint ourselves with our Airbnb and take a stroll along Venice Beach that is infested with every dreg of California's drug-ridden society. Some of them evidently don't just use the local library for taking out books. We found a sign in the toilets there asking people "not to wash their clothes in the basins." With no garments that needed washing at this early stage of our adventure, we utilised Ubers and the metro to find our way to the Bank of California Stadium for that evening's double header which would be the third round of group games.

There had been the usual pre-tournament fiasco with accreditation. Concacaf invite journalists to apply but then they do their utmost to make it impossible for them to get in. Or, at least anyone unfamiliar with the intricate mechanisms of their website was not getting in fast. Chris and I both fell into that category with the result that we both went to the tournament lacking accreditation. With so many Salvadorian exiles in town, tickets to purchase were also at a premium and I had to pay way over the odds for a pair from a scalper with no interest in the game.

It was another reason to despise Americans and one more reason was soon to present itself on entry or, on attempted entry. The supervisor at the gate, an archetypal jobsworth, refused to let Pennie go in with the cosmetics bag that had been tucked into her handbag. "Take it back to your car," he said but of course we hadn't come by car. "Take it back to your hotel then," he shouted at her. Our hotel was on the far side of town and kick-off was beckoning. I told him where to go to which he replied that we were now banned from entering. We disappeared into the middle distance and she emptied the contents of her cosmetics bag onto the grass. Fortunately, I had come armed with my rain jacket which had

242

several pockets. We stuffed some of her bottles of perfumes, insect repellent and asthma inhaler into those pockets and her few pockets. We changed our appearance, doffing hats and sunglasses, and hurried towards another entrance where there were no problems getting in. What a palaver over nothing. Once inside, she transferred all the items that were inside my jacket pockets back into her cosmetics bag.

The Salvador supporters had taken over the stadium. Their team still had a chance of qualifying unlike their opponents, Honduras who nevertheless played as if their lives depended on it and won 4-0 with the result that both countries went out. The first game had been a 1-1 draw between Jamaica and Curacao which succeeded in taking both teams into the knock-out stages. After the second game, we filed towards the same exit where the buffoon who had originally stopped us, might still be stationed. I was all for saying something abusive and for Pennie to wave her handbag in his face but somewhat fortunately perhaps, he was long gone.

Kansas City was staging the next day's group games, but Chris and I had been there, so we settled for an MLS fixture at San Jose whose unprepossessing stadium was a new one as far as we were both concerned. We were in airbnbs close to the ground, so we took an Uber there, arriving in enough time to buy tickets at the ticket booth and sample the tasty burgers in the diner on the complex across the road. Watching the game, we were constantly distracted by the movement behind one goal. Spectators, forever hurrying back and forth between the bars carrying flagons of beer, were doing little to dispel the notion that American sports fans are incapable of concentrating on an event for longer than fractions of a second.

San Jose Earthquakes defeated Houston Dynamo 2-0. As Houston was, coincidentally, to be our next port of call, I'd had the supposedly bright idea of writing to the Dynamos asking if we could hitch a lift back to Texas with them, but I was politely informed that their charter plane would be flying onwards to Boston for their next MLS obligation against New England Revolution. Silly me for overlooking that possibility. But the tides of fortune had not completely deserted us. Pennie had got talking to a lady on our scheduled Spirit Airlines flight to Houston who said that her husband - on arrival duty - would give us a lift into town. He turned out to be a Vietnam vet. They were a charming couple. There were some nice people in America after all. Not everyone was objectionable. The girls at reception endorsed that opinion when they directed us to a restaurant which specialised in guests cooking sumptuous slivers of steak over a flame. But parts of America still had a third-world feel about them. To get there, we had to sidestep numerous piles of earth, the residue of roads that were in the process of allegedly being dug up and resurfaced though we never saw the bulldozers at work.

We were in Houston for the first two Gold Cup quarter-finals at the NRG Stadium which was filled almost to the brim by Mexican immigrants, most of whom Donald Trump had presumably tried to keep on the other side of his precious barricade. The swarms of Latinos in their dark green replica shirts tolerated the first match in which Haiti gained a shock 3-2 win over Canada and got behind their team in the second game against Costa Rica. It was sheer bedlam. Helped by a goal from Raul Jimenez, the Wolves striker, Mexico took the lead only to be pegged back by an equaliser from the penalty spot for Los Ticos by the elegant Bryan Ruiz, once of Fulham. The countries were still level at 1-1 after extra time but Mexico prevailed 6-5 in the shoot-out.

In normal circumstances I wouldn't have considered the semi-final in Nashville's Nissan Stadium as I had been there so recently but as the hub of country music, Nashville has so much more to offer than the socca there. We spent two days exploring the CMA Museum that had escaped our attention two years earlier and returned to the bars that were on our beat the first time only to find that Nashville was echoing much more now to the sounds of rock from the multitude of groups vying for attention. That was sad but the Listening Room did at least provide a respite in the form of more recognisable Country music to the accompaniment of the clinking of knives and forks from folk dining from the tables laid out in the auditorium.

The food on offer the next night contained rather less nutritional value, nachos and chips in the main stand of the Nissan Stadium during the electric storm that caused an interruption of 90 minutes during the USA v Jamaica semi-final. We were glad to see Scottish Mark who had joined our trio from Brazil where he had been watching the Copa America. When it was deemed safe for the players to reappear, the game resumed and the hosts confirmed that they were the superior side, winning 3-1 to secure a place in the final against Mexico. By the time of Mexico's 1-0 win in Chicago, we were in Ireland but not without a costly hitch.

I had found a cheap flight from New York to Dublin with Norwegian, little knowing that the so-called New York airport, Stewart is, in fact, about 60 miles north of Manhattan. On arrival at La Guardia from Nashville, we were astonished to discover that no one had heard of Stewart. It was akin to arriving at Gatwick to find that no one knew the whereabouts of Stansted. It just goes to show how parochial the average Yank is. We had six hours to find Stewart and get there so we eventually

244

boarded a coach from La Guardia bound for the Port Authority Bus Terminal, only to find that the once-a-day Shortline service to Stewart had departed hours earlier.

There was nothing else for it but to hire a taxi. I did a circuit of the cabbies in the vicinity to find who might be the cheapest, but they all wanted well in excess of $200 for the job. Pennie eventually found one on Uber who would do the trip for $175 so he was summoned. I'd had a good impression of Norwegian until then, much less so after that expensive caper. They should, at least warn their passengers of the pitfalls ahead of them in locating this far distant airfield at the back of beyond.

There was a simple, two-pronged reason for going home via Ireland. The League of Ireland season was well advanced and Waterford's home game against St Pats had caught my eye because I hadn't been there and they now had Damien Delaney among their ranks. Or so we believed. Delaney had been a firm favourite at Palace for all his eccentricity and occasional lapses. It's strange how some players can achieve cult hero status from fans for obscure reasons. Alan Pardew was another. He gave so many distinctly prosaic performances in Palace's midfield, forever defying Steve Coppell's judgement on keeping him in the team, that he became perversely known as Super Alan Pardew.

A gangling left-footed central defender, Damo's popularity had stemmed not just from the stunning goal he scored against Liverpool to begin our rally from 3-0 down to 3-3 in one of the ten most exciting Premier League matches, according to Match of the Day pundits. His trademark pass was from the centre circle out to Wilf Zaha on the right wing. More often than not, they flew into touch.

We took the bus from Dublin airport to the south, checked into our hotel near the River Suir, ate our pre match meal at the Bodega Restaurant - which Chris had recommended - and headed for the game. Imagine our dismay then on pitching up at Waterford's Regional Sports Centre ground - that is as ordinary as it sounds - to be informed that Delaney had retired the previous day. We were told that he would not even be at the game as a spectator. The news of Delaney's decision to hang up his boots had not even been relayed to Pennie by her great pal Liz who followed his every move on Facebook and treasured numerous copies of his autograph plus a collection of Palace shirts, all with his name imprinted on the back. Maybe Liz's temporary ignorance was hardly surprising given that she was in hospital having a brain operation. Pennie's masterplan had been for Delaney to sign a 'best wishes' card that she had brought along to hasten her friend's recuperation. With no Damo to focus on, the game was a disappointment, a 2-1 away win. There was a

245

blank fixture list over the weekend, so we spent the Saturday afternoon on a boat ride up the River Suir before flying back from Cork on the Saturday evening.

That was the start of a barren ten days for me without a game. Consolation came in the form of a reunion in Spain with my son James, his wife and kids. I would have to make do with watching Wimbledon and world cup cricket in the bars of Torrevieja. I found one bar with several screens, meaning that I could watch the men's final, Djokovic v Federer and the world cup final simultaneously.

But, with the Premier League season five weeks away and the Spanish campaign on an even more distant horizon, I was still like a junkie craving his next fix. I was overjoyed therefore to get a text from Ivo telling me that one of his scout mates had been told to check on players in a friendly between Bournemouth and Wimbledon at the La Manga training centre only 50 miles away. Never was a friendly or an amistoso, as the Spanish call it, so keenly anticipated. We spent the afternoon taking in the sights of Cartagena enroute to La Manga where we found the open stand of the football complex packed with expats. Word had obviously got around. Some of them were even in replica shirts. The grandchildren who had been brought up on a diet of tennis and more tennis, were not impressed. It only took ten minutes before Zanzi - who was sitting next to me - was asking "how long does this last?" James took them all out at half-time, leaving me in peace to enjoy the rest of Bournemouth's 3-2 win.

Chapter 59
A relic from the past

A week later, I flew back from Spain to Newcastle where thanks to astute planning, Celia was waiting to greet me. She was a well-chosen accomplice albeit hardly a football lover. The early rounds of the Betfred Cup or the Scottish League Cup as it's more commonly known, have come to many an addict's rescue and I was no exception. The fixtures had fanned out, almost to my complete satisfaction. I had yet to do about a third of the stadiums in the Scottish leagues and now here was a heaven-sent opportunity to get more of them under my belt so to speak. We could go up the west coast and return down the east coast.

From Newcastle we hurried to Stranraer to locate our Airbnb on the edge of Loch Ryan before Stranraer's 2-1 home defeat by Livingston. Stair Park possesses a certain rustic charm unlike our next stop, Excelsior Stadium, the utterly charmless, modern symmetrical, all-seater home of Airdrie whose tie with Queen's Park went all the way to a lengthy penalty shoot-out, won 12-11 by the hosts. It had been 2-2 after 120 minutes.

We had driven north through the lowlands, stopping off for refreshments in the town of Lanark where I showed my ignorance by asking an old boy if there were still any remnants around of the long since defunct Third Lanark club. "Och nay, not around here," he said. "Third Lanark played in Glasgow and as far as I know, there's nothing left of the club." He was wrong there, however, as I was subsequently reliably informed that close to Hampden Park, a few steps of moss-covered terracing still exist as well as the pitch which is still played on. I'll have to go there some time.

With no game on the Thursday, we spent the balmy evening dining on the terrace and admiring the glorious views across the Cairngorn National Park from the magnificent Laggan Hotel which we had fortuitously stumbled upon while looking for somewhere to eat. With little sense of optimism, I had gone up to reception to ask how much they charged for a room if, indeed they had a spare one as we'd seen a coach party milling about. The cost was prohibitive so I enquired as to whether she could recommend any restaurants nearby. "I tell you what," said the gorgeous brunette who doubled up as maitresse d, "for £125, you can have a room and dinner for the two of you." I almost snapped her hand off. She was obviously not expecting any more stragglers. It was on a par with the most outstanding places I have ever stayed. The girl was so enchanting that I wondered what she was doing with her bloke, covered in tattoos, with whom I settled up the next morning. That was her loss.

Friday would have been another matchless day but for television's unsurprising interest in Elgin's tie with Hibernian which had obvious shock appeal. The game had been moved forward and I, or rather, we took advantage. Accommodation in Elgin was scarce, so we stayed six miles up the road in Lossiemouth, home of an RAF base whose Typhoon Combat Squadron jets thundered into land from the Moray Firth as we sped underneath. The balmy night of 24 hours earlier had given way to a downpour which might have handicapped Hibs' chances of avoiding an upset. But they looked every bit the premier div team. Their 2-0 success was little more than a formality.

Cove Rangers, newcomers to the Scottish second div from the Highland League, had been pencilled in for the Saturday but their tie with Raith was now meaningless as neither side could advance. It would have been a wasted afternoon so far as I was concerned. So, we gave that game on Aberdeen's outskirts a mighty swerve and drove a further 55 miles down the coast road to Arbroath whose tie with Alloa had far more going for it. Both clubs could still qualify for the knock-out stages though ultimately neither did so despite Alloa's 3-2 win in the most entertaining game we had seen yet. Gayfield Park must be much developed since it gained a place in the record books as the scene of Arbroath's 36-0 win over Bon Accord in an 1885 cup tie - the biggest victory ever in global senior football - but with its terracing on three sides, it's a still a worthy relic from the past. It overlooks the North Sea whose waves batter the ground's perimeter when there's a storm brewing. I was glad we had chosen a sunny afternoon in July for our visit rather than a freezing Tuesday night in November.

The only game on the Sunday was at Dundee so there was nothing else for it but to take in Dens Park. It was 20 years since my one previous visit, a seven-goal thriller with Hibs. There are far worse grounds to go a second time but if ever a stadium was a fire risk, it must be this one with its ageing wooden stands. It reeks of history. We'd got complimentary tickets through Ivo's friendship with his fellow Bulgarian, Nikolay Todorov who came on as a sub for Inverness, too late to prevent the visitors from sinking to a 1-0 defeat.

As the dutiful driver, Celia deserved some reward, so I was more than happy to combine the game at Dens Park with a visit to the Queen Mother's former home at Glamis Castle which she had wanted to see. More culture followed when we drove through the gates of Floors Castle near Kelso. It has been the home, over the years, of the dukes and earls of Roxburghe. I speculated that Andy Roxburgh had possibly lost an e

248

from his name through the mists of time, but it was probably just as well that I lacked the courage to ask our guide if the former Scotland manager was a family descendant. The next stop on our to-do list was Traquair House, dating back to 1107, making it apparently the oldest inhabited house in Scotland though it looked extremely well preserved.

The group games in the Betfred Cup had now petered out but as we were in no hurry to return across the border, I was relieved to find that the Lowland League's midweek schedule could occupy us. The Vale of Leithen was one such prospect. They play at Victoria Park in Innerleithen which we were told by our hotel staff could be reached by walking down their garden and opening the gate at the end. I wish it was always that simple. But we had been misinformed. Because of the lack of floodlights, the game had begun at 7.15, half an hour earlier than we had been led to believe. So, we missed the first two goals in Gala of Fairydean Rovers' 5-1 success. That was frustrating so I vowed not to make the same mistake the next night which represented an enormous improvement. Not only could we take a seat at Dalbeattie Stars, in their Islecroft Stadium's impressive main stand but there were also floodlights, more than a quorum for a crowd and a closer contest which East Kilbride won 2-0. The visitors, who were well supported despite the 175-mile return journey from near Glasgow, had been the club ousted by Cove in the promotion play-offs which led to poor Berwick Rangers relinquishing their place in the Scottish second div.

I still had nostalgic and romantic memories of sitting with Louise Taylor, from The Times, among the sheep droppings on one of Berwick's grass slopes to watch them defeat Cowdenbeath 2-0 some 30 years earlier. But I digress.

The Lowland League fixtures had fitted in well with our last stop. From our four-poster bed in Dumfries, we left the next morning for Holmfirth, the quirky Yorkshire town, which had somehow managed to book the celebrated Country singer, Lucinda Williams for a date in their unorthodox century-old Picturedrome Theatre. It was a sell-out. We were lucky to obtain tickets, never mind seats.

The Premier League season was almost upon us. Palace got off to such an inauspicious start by drawing 0-0 at home with Everton and losing 1-0 at Sheffield United that I could maybe have been forgiven for giving our game at Old Trafford a miss. I was glad I hadn't. As I was in the middle of a holiday in Mallorca with my kids who had rented a villa, I chose to fly to and from the UK for the game. From our 2-1 victory, I dashed back to my favourite Manchester Bar in C'an Pastilla to find that celebrity status had instantly been thrust upon me by the bar owner Darren Hankes, who is not a great United lover. His claim to fame was

249

that he had, in his football-playing prime, appeared for half a friendly game for his beloved Man City. "Do you know what this man has done?" Darren asked anyone who cared to listen. "He's flown back to see Palace beat United and he's here now watching it again on Match of the Day."

"Top man," said one of the regulars, inviting me to take a glass from a tray load of liqueurs he was transporting to a table. I was brought back to earth by Mallorca's 1-0 home defeat by Real Sociedad the next evening.

For once my next trip to Denmark did not coincide with a Brondby away game. And neither did it mean a visit to the home of toy bricks. I had flown into Billund - which happens to be Legoland's headquarters - from Stansted following Palace's abject 4-0 surrender to Spurs. Randers were the visitors to Esjberg and they were easy 3-0 winners after which I faced the usual complicated trek round southern Scandanavia by rail in order to reach Eskilstuna the next evening. They were doomed for the drop from the Allsvenskan and I wanted to get there before their fate became mathematically certain. The point they took from an enterprising 2-2 draw with Elfsborg did not ultimately save them and judging by the pitiful 1,923 crowd, few cared. It didn't even look that many. I flew back from Stockholm the next day as Eskilstuna is only 70 miles from Sweden's capital.

All this time, I was travelling to and from Mallorca's games on the island and the mainland but after witnessing them three times on their return to La Liga I had yet to see them score. I was so desperate to see them get a goal, never mind a win, that I used up one otherwise blank Sunday by booking a day return flight to Bilbao plus a hired car in order to see their game at Vitoria-Gasteiz. But it was the same old story, a 2-0 defeat against Alaves. I felt duty-bound to watch them. It was crazy.

The international break would bring relief in the form of a visit to Croatia who were fast becoming my most watched national team although I felt no sense of allegiance towards them. But they obviously had a sensitive press department judging by their acquiescence when I requested a ticket. The only difficulty was getting hold of that blessed ticket for the return Euro qualifier against Hungary. Few people in Split seemed to speak English so I was quite literally stumbling around in the dark on the confines of the Stadion Poljud, the home of Hajduk, when I located the sports centre, whose gymnasium transpired to be what I was looking for. They were using it as a press office. The man there duly handed me a pass for the game which the Croats won 3-0 to avenge their defeat in Budapest.

I was with Nadiya on our swansong of a trip. We had taken the motorway from Dubrovnik to reach Split but with time on our hands, we

250

dawdled down the far more scenic coastal road on our return drive and I took a dip in the Adriatic though it was mid-October. For some inexplicable reason, I had always fancied a game in Dubrovnik in the belief that the ground there might provide an additional jewel to the walled city itself. I was not far wrong. The Gradski Stadion Lapad is a gem, partly walled, terraced, a low stand in the open and overlooked by trees, a hedge row and an attractive variety of pastel covered buildings. The third div game we saw, GOSK Dubrovnik against Neretva Metkovic wasn't bad either. It was 1-1 until the dying seconds when the home goalkeeper suddenly took it upon himself to race up for a corner. We thought he had taken leave of his senses. It was the kind of thing a keeper might be instructed to do with his team behind in a cup replay or in a relegation scrap when they needed another goal. But not in a mid-season league game with less at stake. Anyway, he volleyed in a terrific winner and went suitably berserk, jumping into the arms of his manager on the bench.

I was still mulling over the incredible finish on my flight back to Luton that night, an apt stop for me as it was from there that Celia and I took a flight to Talinn the next morning. My one visit to the Baltic states, to Latvia had been for a basketball international in Riga. Their football grounds had to be explored. Estonia's game with Germany was like a beacon the way it stood out, so long as it was not a repeat of Germany's 8-0 slaughter four months earlier. We were caught out by the two-hour time difference but on this occasion, we arrived at the ground far too early than too late. We could have done with a more hospitable kiosk than the one we encountered in the main stand. When the match got under way, we found we were a few seats along from Helge, a German friend of much hopping history. We were just above the dugouts. Helge and his pal were probably the worse for a few beers. Along with most German fans he didn't take kindly to Red Bull Leipzig or their players, so he let Timo Werner know what he thought of him when the substitute returned from a warm-up. "Werner, you're a motherfucker," Helge yelled. The insult was heard by the security man standing a few yards from Joachim Low. The security man bounded up the few steps to Helge and told him that he would be thrown out if he didn't behave. Helge was as quiet as a mouse after that, hardly daring to stand up and cheer the first two goals from Ilkay Gundogan in his team's 3-0 win. He wasn't overjoyed to see Werner net the third.

With a day to spare before our next game, Celia and I braved the torrential rain to board a hop-on hop-off bus, finding the only sheltered part of the top deck from where we could see what we could of Talinn through the steamed-up, rain-splattered windows. Thankfully the

251

weather dried up over the next 24 hours and we were able to savour the 70-mile coach ride through forests to Parnu, a medieval city, full of timber villas, which is not only the country's top resort but the home of the basic Rannastaadion where we saw Estonia's Under 21s defeated 5-0 by their Russian counterparts. On our way from our hotel to the match, we had passed a bistro where we warmed up afterwards. I was stuffed by the time I'd finished the soup. It would have been sufficient for a main course. Talinn's old town is a centre to savour. With time on our hands before our flight home the next day, we took the tram in the opposite direction to the airport before heading the right way. It was two euros extremely well spent.

Chapter 60:
Refs wave play on

Scandinavia beckoned yet again the following weekend as, like Eskilstuna in Sweden, Ranheim in Norway would be graced by my presence before they went down. Their home game against Odd Grenland was an ideal one on a Sunday when nothing else appealed. Ranheim is just outside Trondheim so, forgetting my grievance towards Norwegian, I booked up with them again. They fly to Trondheim from Gatwick. I had looked up Ranheim on the map and wasn't complacent about getting there from the airport without spending a fortune. But it was like finding Zabzre from Katowice Airport, no sweat at all, as the buses to the city centre stop off there or, at least, on the main road above the town. I spotted the floodlights as I descended down the steep slope and there was even time for a snack before kick-off. The EXTRA Arena is tastefully designed with its open stand opposite the covered main one, an example of fine town-planning as it merged neatly with the apartment blocks behind it. Stadium staff were friendly and the hosts romped to a 4-1 win with two goals from Michael Karlsen, one of them a staggering 45-yard volley. They played with such gusto that I wondered what they were doing at the wrong end of the Eliteserien. But, sadly, they obviously didn't recapture that form or indeed win another match with the consequence that they were relegated after a two-year stay.

It's strange how some clubs can etch a place into one's affections so much easier than others. It's like the chemistry between lovers. Unlike Eskilstuna who left me cold, I'd got the hots for Ranheim, so much so that I checked their results until their fate was decided. In usual circumstances I'd have linked their game - which had enabled me to complete the Norwegian top flight - with another one but this time a double header was beyond me so the next day I acted the part of a tourist in Trondheim before flying home.

Most of the lads were heading to England's game in Kosovo at the next international break but fearing that the supporting act would be the usual booze-up, I made my excuses as I had found a ready alternative in the form, once again, of Croatia. Maybe I should have donned a red and white chequered replica shirt by now as this was the sixth time I would see Zlatko Dalic's side in 17 months. Yes, they play fluent, attacking football but I'd been swayed more by the descriptions I'd heard of HNK Rijeka's Kantrida Stadium, wedged at the foot of a cliff. Everyone who had been there had raved about it as if it was one of the world's wonders. In that respect I was to be sadly disillusioned as the Euro qualifier with Slovakia was destined instead for the new tediously modern Stadion Rujevica on a hill overlooking the city. I sympathised with the majority of the spectators who were sitting in the open as the rain lashed down but, at least, they had a 3-1 home win to provide scant comfort. And yet I couldn't fathom why Croatia would want to play such a game in a nondescript 8,000 capacity stadium when they possessed far grander alternatives in Split and Zagreb.

We'd probably had more fun during the afternoon when the spate of third div fixtures threw up the chance of an obvious time-filler. Christine and I, who were based in the opulent resort of Opatija, a dozen miles from Rijeka, opted for the game at Senj because it was an excuse for a drive down the Adriatic coast. The game couldn't compete for curiosity value with the one I'd seen in Dubrovnik five weeks previously but, for all that, it was a welcome bonus. Nehaj took on Grobnican on a quagmire of a pitch which the visitors swiftly adjusted to, winning 4-0. It would never have started in the UK, but we were both suitably grateful to the referee for waving play on.

Some fanatics express rather less gratitude towards Uefa for the suspense they generate before announcing their venues for their Euro Under 21 qualifiers. The vast majority who ignore such meagre titbits, may scoff at such a notion but for us desperados needing to expand our knowledge of obscure pitches, they can be an invaluable addition to the calendar. Happily, this was the case on the eve of our departure from Zagreb whose fascinating city centre we had seen from the top of another hop on, hop off bus. I wondered why Croatia couldn't stage a game of any representative level in the capital, but this time Velika Gorica had been chosen for Croatia's Under 21 group tie against the Czech Republic who won 2-1. A few miles from Zagreb Airport, its Gradski Stadion is the home of the town's club whose less solvent fans must watch in the open from seats mounted on a low grass bank opposite the one and only stand. It's not one of the world's great stadiums and would scarcely pass muster for a club in our Ryman League. We could hardly complain though as it was free entry.

The decision by Sky TV to delay Palace's game with Brighton for a Monday night screening came as an early Christmas present. Mallorca's visit to Celta Vigo on the Sunday could be accommodated as the focal point for a bonanza weekend of four games in Spain and Portugal, aided by flights to and from Porto which were the most expedient. Benefitting from the same hotel, car hire company and café for breakfast that had contributed to my contentment at the Nations League six months earlier, we made an early start for the 200-mile drive north for Racing Ferrol's Segunda div 2 game with Langreo. We missed the start of the hosts' 3-0 win after a prolonged argument with stewards who called for the girl in charge of the press to sanction our entrance to the Estadio Municipal de A Malata which is a tad better than the average municipal stad.

Our stop for the night was in Redondela, a few miles east of Vigo and its suburb of Coruxo, the home of another segunda div b club. As the weather deteriorated the next morning, we followed directions to what we assumed was Coruxo's Campo do Vao until a sports centre loomed into sight on a distant hilltop where there was a kids game in progress on an all-weather surface. They were exceptionally skilful, but it was not what we were looking for although another all-weather surface would have come in handy at Coruxo's ramshackle home which we located just in time for the 11am kick-off. Confirmation of the conditions that constantly bedevil this westerly outpost of Europe came with the puddles on the pitch which made us wonder if we would have suffered a postponement had the opposition been any other than Las Palmas B. They wouldn't have wanted their trip from the Canary Islands to have been in vain, so the game went ahead, much to the joy of the locals who won 4-1.

As clubs in La Liga tend to follow a policy of not telling applicants for press passes if they have got lucky, we went along to the Balaidos stadium more in hope than expectation. We were making little headway at the window until an Englishman from Celta's media department came to our rescue, leading us high up the stand to seats beside the press box where we witnessed a dramatic relegation six-pointer. Mallorca were down to ten men by the time they secured their first away point of the season from a 2-2 draw with an 83rd minute equaliser from Ante Budimir who thereby found himself added to my list of favourite Croats. Mallorca were still in the bottom three, but it was with an overwhelming sense of relief that I took the wheel for the 75-mile drive to the third game of our hectic day in the Portuguese city of Barcelos, home of Gil Vicente whose opponents from less than 30 miles away were Guimaraes. It was a rousing derby and the visiting supporters, crammed behind one goal, added an extra atmospheric flavour to proceedings. From 2-0 down, they roared their side to a 2-2 draw with the first goal coming from Marcus Edwards who was on loan from Spurs. We traipsed round Barcelos after the game and found what we sincerely believed to be the best restaurant in town before beginning our homeward journey.

With most countries on the continent taking a festive breather, I made use of the free Sunday after Christmas to complete the 92, albeit not for the first time. Clubs have come and gone, promoted or relegated from and to the Conference - as it was known - or the National League. Some, too, have folded but here I was again, one short of the full set. It was at the same time of year and for the same reason that I'd taken the train north two years earlier, to Chesterfield for what I reckoned - correctly - would be a last-gasp opportunity to see them at their Proact Stadium before they were deprived of their League status. That left only Rotherham to do and their 3pm kick-off against Peterborough had long since earned a place in my diary as I always prefer such occasions to be in daylight. Not only that but it was a promotion six-pointer. On the evidence of their 4-0 win, the Yorkshire side looked the better bet to go up. There was something surreal about the New York Stadium and its surroundings that merely added to the satisfaction.

The second and third Sundays of the New Year were also hugely enjoyable. Chris and I spent the first one Shuttle-bound for Belgium where the village of Sint-Eloois-Winkel accommodates a club in the first amateur division, effectively the third tier. They gave their best in a 2-0 defeat by Lierse Kempenzonen but the pre-match meal, a divine steak as good as any we'd had in Belgium, was probably worth more merit marks than the game. The restaurant was down a country lane which we wouldn't have hit upon but for some helpful signs for which we were eternally grateful. No comparable feast availed itself a week later but, at least, and at long last after many years of trying, I was able to get to a game at Farense in the Portuguese segunda liga. I had risked a British Airways flight that only got Sally and I into Faro 65 minutes before kick-off but thankfully BA did me proud. We even had time for a coffee before taking a seat in the sun on the large open terrace for the goalless draw with Sporting Covilha and, better still, I found a bar later in the afternoon showing Liverpool's home game with Man United.

Subconsciously I must have sensed that lockdown and with it, enforced quarantine, was fast approaching judging by my haste in accumulating the games on overseas trips. But I could have done with less red-eye Sunday morning flights such as the one I took to Amsterdam for the purpose of completing the Eredivisie in Holland with Fortuna Sittard's 2-1 victory over Herenveen. I flew to Barcelona the following Saturday evening from Manchester after a misguided attempt to cheer myself up after Palace's 3-1 lunchtime defeat at Everton. From Goodison Park, I had dashed by cab to Bootle for their 3-0 home loss to Rylands in the North West Counties League. But if there is a more soulless ground anywhere than Bootle's Berry Street Garage Stadium, I haven't set foot in it. It's as bleak as it sounds. I should have known better than to seek solace in Barcelona where Mallorca had a must-win game, or at least, a must-not-lose game against Espanyol on the Sunday which of course, they lost by a solitary, scrappy goal. It's always scrappy, isn't it, when it goes against your team? There was plenty of time after the noon kick-off to fit in a segunda div B match. Cornella's game with Taragona, a 1-1 draw got the vote as I judged it to be nearer and therefore a cheaper taxi ride to El Prat Airport than Barcelona B's new home, the Estadi Johan Cruyff.

My son, Ben had behaved admirably by arranging his wedding in Islamabad to the beautiful Rafia around Palace fixtures but hard as I tried after the ceremony, I could find no sign of goalposts let alone any indication of football taking place on my week-long visit to Pakistan. And yet, Soccerway's website assured me there had been top flight games there 12 months earlier. No one I spoke to came up with a rational explanation for this sad lapse. There was nothing else for it but to plunge headlong into games on my return with Celia on my arm. And so, we flew to Zurich from where we caught a train to St Gallen whose new Kybunpark I had yet to visit. I, or rather, we had chosen well as the top-of-the-table clash against Berne Young Boys was a fluctuating and mesmerising 3-3 draw. Is there ever a bad 3-3? The last two goals came in added time, including a 99th minute equaliser for the Young Boys from the penalty spot by Guillaume Hoarau.

That game was as exciting as the fare on offer the next evening, a five-hour train ride away, was awful. Or, at least Eintracht Frankfurt were awful in their 2-1 defeat by Union Berlin. Their ultras boycotted the match in protest at the Bundesliga taking television's slice to stage matches on Monday nights. Not helped by an empty terrace behind one goal, Eintracht appeared to have gone backwards since I'd seen them beat Arsenal 2-1 in a Europa League tie three months earlier at the Emirates. But, at least the wurst mit brot was as tasty as ever. I'd not been to the Waldstadion since my early days with Lissi, so I was no longer familiar with the environment. Markus Linke who had our tickets, had told us to get the metro but, of course, the tram had been more convenient from our city centre hotel. I was naïve enough to think it wouldn't make much difference, but I had reckoned without the forest which surrounds the stadium. Big mistake. We had to tramp more than a mile down a bridle path in the dark to find him. It could have been a mugger's delight on any other night.

And talking of being mugged, that's what Mallorca must have felt when I subsequently saw them lose 1-0 at home to Getafe after dominating the game. Two weeks later lockdown was upon us. The entire first-class programme was called off, leaving only a scattering of non-league games such as those in the Wessex League. As I had been due to see Palace at Bournemouth, I headed off in the same direction for AFC

Stoneham v Solent University, a lively 2-2 draw. I sat next to a wizened hopper who was also a part time Palace diehard. He was with his mate. They were completing the Wessex League. I could have got nearer the same target with a visit to a Solent University home game on the Monday night. But it was off. Like everything else.

Part Two

Up For The Cups

Chapter 1:
Who needs a goalkeeper?

I often pity football-loving kids growing up these days because they never witnessed an FA Cup final when it meant something of a far greater significance than it does today. The previews would dominate the back pages of the papers for several days beforehand instead of the day beforehand. Television would take a much keener interest and people would talk about it for weeks leading up to the big event. And yet, you could get into a discussion in a pub the night before the big game these days and some people professing to be football know-alls, might struggle to name the finalists.

I suppose that it was no coincidence that my interest in the great competition began in 1957 at a time when Manchester United had come to the fore under Matt Busby since United were at that time my favourite club. I remember my irritation when my father who was an Aston Villa fan for various spurious reasons, managed to get one ticket for the final but not two. It was a few weeks after he took me to my first game, England v Scotland. But this time he went to Wembley alone, leaving me to watch on television. I went with my mother to meet him at the station on his return from Villa's 2-1 triumph a little while before he sat down to dinner to suggest that United should have done without a goalkeeper after Ray Wood had been stretchered off with a fractured cheekbone following his dreadful collision with Peter McParland. My Dad often liked to make outrageous comments just to get an argument going and this was, I thought - even at the tender age of nine - an outrageous comment. He thought that United's ten men should have persevered with Jackie Blanchflower in midfield instead of him donning Wood's jersey until Wood returned in goal, much the worse for wear, seven minutes from time. It was, of course, the era before substitutes were permitted. I got to thinking to what extent Busby might have been pilloried had he followed my Dad's advice and United been slaughtered.

By the time United's revamped post Munich team made it to the following year's final against Bolton, we were, frustratingly for me, in Mallorca. With no consideration for my wish to stay behind for the final, my parents followed their habit of taking us kids on a family holiday at the same time of year. We returned from Palma to find that Ray Wood's successor, Harry Gregg was dominating the sports pages, even though it was several days after the event. He had been bundled into the net by Nat

261

Lofthouse and with the help of dramatic photographs as evidence, the top football writers were continuing to debate the legality of Bolton's second goal in their 2-0 win. Today, the game would have been done and dusted by the Monday morning's editions. There was similar exasperation in 1959 when it was only when I got home from Mallorca on the Sunday that I caught up with the drama of Nottingham Forest's ten men holding on for a 2-1 win over Luton after their first-goal scorer, Roy Dwight had broken his leg. In those days, fortunately, BBC replayed the final the next day.

I had no trouble watching Wolves beat Blackburn in 1960 but Spurs v Leicester in 1961 was a troublesome affair. I was needed to play cricket at Westminster School on that very same Saturday afternoon when Bill Nicholson's team were bidding to become the first club in the 20th century to complete the double. The cricket at Vincent Square wasn't an inter schools game, just a pick-up match of no consequence but I still thought I would have problems getting out of it.

My parents were members of a group called the Georgian Group who like to go round the country visiting National Trust homes of the aristocracy. So, I came up with the bright idea of forging a letter from my Dad to my housemaster asking him "to relieve Nicholas from playing cricket as Phoebe and I would like him to join us on a visit to a delicious house in the west country." Delicious was one my Dad's favourite words. He would frequently use it to describe a meal or a dress but never, so I learned later, to enthuse over a house. Delightful maybe but not delicious. My housemaster Jumbo Wilson, a canny Scot, obviously smelled a rat although I thought I'd done a good job in emulating my Dad's artistic hand-writing. But Mr Wilson said nothing. He excused me from cricket, so I dashed back to Godstone from morning classes, arriving by taxi from Oxted just as the final got under way. I watched Spurs beat Leicester 2-0 and thought no more about it. But about six weeks later, after my parents had returned from a parents teachers evening, my Dad handed me the letter I had written and asked me about it. There was nothing else for it but to confess. I'd have got away with it but for my misuse of the word 'delicious.' But I was spared a beating from Mr Wilson on that occasion because the three of them had agreed that I had, at least, shown initiative in order to watch the cup final.

Spurs v Burnley the following year presented no such problems but in 1963 I was old enough to go to Wembley on my own and agonising about not having a ticket for the Man United v Leicester final. I was suffering the ordeal of a CCF night exercise in the Ashdown Forest on the Thursday, hating every minute of it, when a teammate from the school's first XI, Michael Petit, asked me as calmly as you like, if I wanted to go with him to Wembley on Saturday. He had a spare ticket. He knew I was a United fan, albeit a United fan in the process of discovering Crystal Palace. Michael didn't have to ask me a second time. Suddenly the night exercise didn't seem so awful after all and my khaki uniform didn't itch quite so badly. With ease now, I could abide the nonsensical tramps through the heather on the Surrey/Sussex border. It was a brilliant final so far as I was concerned with United winning 3-1 thanks to two goals from David Herd and one from Denis Law. I got back to Victoria Station to pick up the classified Evening Standard to read that their excellent football writer, Bernard Joy had poked fun at Gordon Banks for making a crucial mistake by saying that "Banks had performed like an England goalkeeper in his attempt to save Herd's second goal." How those words must have come back to haunt Joy in the years to come.

Another Westminster pal, Mark van de Weyer, with whom I used to go to Upton Park when I was not playing and Palace were not at home, got me a ticket for West Ham's final v Preston the following year. By now I had well and truly got the bug. By hook or by crook I would get to cup finals, but my confidence took a hit in 1965 when the demand for tickets for Liverpool versus Leeds was far greater than the pocket money I had saved. Touts were doing brisk business. I was not getting in. It was long before the days when a person could wander into a pub in mid-afternoon and see the game on their television. What's more, I was miles from home. So, I plucked up courage and started knocking on doors around the confines of Wembley, asking residents if there was any chance I could enter their parlour and see the game. Needs must. These days, I still wonder at my audacity. But I was wearing a red scarf and imitating what I thought was an acceptable Scouse accent. A genuine Scouser would doubtless have laughed me out of Merseyside. I gave people a sob story about coming down from Liverpool and not getting into the game. Eventually some gullible bloke took pity and let me in to watch the game.

Over the next 40 years I didn't miss a single final. Talk about using one's contacts. Or even exhausting them. Ralph Finn who had employed my budding journalistic skills to contribute to his books on England's World Cup win and the first all London final, Chelsea v Spurs in 1967, helped me with tickets over the next few years. And then it was through a devious combination of buying tickets from touts, acquiring press passes, utilising the scam Chris was operating with the London Football Association or exploiting the various loopholes, that I somehow always got in. One such loophole presented itself in 1973. My great pal Rob Freeman - who sadly died during the pandemic though not from the virus - had a ticket as did his mate. I was with another friend who like me, didn't have a ticket. So, there were four of us wanting to see Sunderland

263

oppose Leeds. We presented the two tickets at the turnstiles, each one of them separated by a fiver. £5 was worth a lot more those days than it is now. Calmly accepting the bribe, the turnstile operator didn't blink an eyelid as he clicked us all in. In 1974, I acquired two tickets thanks to working on GOAL magazine which was on its last legs before folding. I took Lissi who was banging on about not taking enough sandwiches the moment Kevin Keegan raced through for Liverpool's first goal in their 3-0 win over Newcastle. Just as the controversial 1927 final between Cardiff and Arsenal became known as "the ball over the line final," 1974 was forever fondly recalled in our household as the "liver sausage final."

I couldn't believe how easy it was to purchase tickets for Fulham v West Ham the following year even though it was a sentimental reunion with Bobby Moore facing his old club. Remarkably Fulham still had tickets for sale the day before the game, so I went along to Craven Cottage and bought two. Simple as that. I thought there'd be no problem in 1976 thanks to making a friend of Mel Blyth when he was at Palace. He promised me a ticket for Southampton v Man United but with a profit to be made, Mel decided that my ticket should go elsewhere. But thanks to my membership of the London branch of the United supporters club, I got one at the last minute for United's 1-0 defeat.

Chapter 2:
Revie to the rescue

Desperation was close at hand when United returned to Wembley in 1977 for their final against Liverpool. The touts were making a killing. I hadn't been able to source a ticket and wasn't prepared to part with a fortune, so I explored the area behind the stadium occupied by scores of vans belonging to television crews. Security was surprisingly scarce so, sensibly attired in jacket and strides, I kept on going. And going and going until I suddenly found myself in a lift with Don Revie plus a couple of other well-heeled bods and the uniformed lift operator. "Aye, aye," said Revie who didn't know me from Adam. Somewhat sheepishly, I said, 'hello Don,' and exited the lift when everyone else got out. I didn't want to risk the embarrassment of being thrown out of the press gallery in front of journalists I knew so I made my way to behind one of the goals where I had an excellent view of Lou Macari's deflected winner for United. As Revie had indirectly assisted my entry, I couldn't help but think fondly of him when, years later, I assembled his obituary for The Times. But I omitted mention of his "aye, aye" to me in the lift as it was not, I reckoned, one of the highlights of his career as a manager with Leeds and England.

By the late Seventies, I was sports editor of the Hampstead and Highgate Express. With Arsenal in the next three finals against Ipswich, Man United and West Ham, I had no problems getting press passes. Would that it was always this easy. As I had spent the first six years of my life in a hamlet in Suffolk, I'd always had a soft spot for Ipswich, so I ventured into their dressing room after their 1-0 win to hear Brian Talbot regaling anyone who cared to listen with talk of how the victorious midfield of him, John Wark and Roger Osborne were "the three musketeers." Of course, the one final I really wanted Arsenal to lose was the next one but Alan Sunderland's late winner did for United who had fought back from two goals down in what became known as the "five-minute final." The rest of it was absolute tedium. Gordon McQueen and Sammy McIlroy came down to the press conference. I asked them if they'd ever felt so bad. McQueen said it was "the worst experience he had ever known as a footballer."

If I wasn't getting passes for the press box once I joined The Times in 1980 as a sports sub editor, I was getting regular tickets through Chris. He had once played for a club called Pointers who had folded which was

265

fortunately not a morsel of information gleaned by the London Football Association. The Football Association's ludicrous ticket distribution scheme for FA Cup finals means that, at the expense of supporters of the two competing clubs, local football authorities such as the London FA are given allocations of tickets to dispose of, usually through a raffle. More often than not, Chris came up trumps with two tickets even though Pointers no longer existed. If he was not taking his wife or brother Ned - a United fan - I was usually offered the spare one.

I didn't need anyone's help in 1988 which was a bit like 1975 in that Wimbledon, like Fulham, still had tickets for their final against Liverpool for sale the day before the game so long as the purchaser could prove he'd been to previous games at Plough Lane which was no problem for me. The year after the Dons' shock win, Louise Taylor and I took a short cut across the Wembley pitch to the press bar following Liverpool's post Hillsborough 3-2 win over Everton. That was a thrill. And neither did Man United's frequent excursions to the final come amiss. Lissi was in charge of sport at the German School in Richmond whose team - fortified by the up and coming Robert Huth - had once, extremely fortuitously hosted a game against opposition from a Manchester school whose coach happened to be David Bushell, Man United's development officer. Lissi 's decision to give David and the other master beds for the night in Wimbledon was a master stroke. Over dinner I discovered that David was a good bloke, good enough indeed to furnish me with tickets for United's big games for years to come. In 1999 he got us seats right next to the steps leading up to the Royal Box. I took Ben, then an impressionable 14-year-old who was able to touch the United players and the Cup as they descended, following their 2-0 win over Newcastle.

Of course, the one final I didn't want United to win was in 1990 when Palace were the team they faced. I have never known suspense like it as we clung onto our 3-2 lead during extra time. With his two goals, our super sub, Ian Wright was playing like a man possessed. I could feel my heart beating. The excitement was intense. We were seven minutes from glory when Mark Hughes burst through to equalise. Oh, the agony. I sensed the worst for the replay. We had lost our chance, I was sure, and I was right, but I had no idea we would besmirch the occasion the way we did, not only with our wasp-like kit but by the way we played, trying to rough up United. I was sitting in the same row as Steve Kember who came past me at half-time. "Doing a job aren't they," he said. But what a job. I couldn't see why Steve Coppell had allowed all our good football of the first game to become a foul-ridden contribution to the replay. "We're proud of you," our fans sang as the players went up to receive their runners-up medals after Lee Martin's solitary goal had won it for United. I started to join in but I couldn't. The words stuck in my throat.

One way or another I was getting into finals. From 1992, I was freelancing for The Daily Telegraph, Independent and Guardian. Unbelievably some of those papers usually had a spare press pass although I wasn't usually told until the day before the game. In 2006 I was wondering how I might get into the Liverpool v West Ham final in Cardiff when the Telegraph asked me to report on a league two play-off semi-final between Wycombe Wanderers and Cheltenham later the same day. It seemed an expedient time to end my run. I got to Adams Park early and watched the 3-3 thriller from Cardiff in the Wycombe press room. I had done 40 successive cup finals plus a few replays. But I own up. I had, in fact, missed the 1983 replay as I had booked a family holiday in Greece with Lissi and Jessica to coincide with Athens staging the European Cup final between Hamburg and Juventus. I had arranged the holiday, reasoning that the cup final was unlikely to go to a replay three years running following Spurs' draws with Man City and QPR. The last thing I wanted was another replay so as Gordon Smith swung back his foot, I was willing him to score for Brighton even though it was against United. But Smith shot feebly and Gary Bailey saved. It was the "Smith must score" final. I watched the replay, won 4-0 by United, in a taverna on the island of Poros. In my haste to get there, I tipped Jessica out of her buggy and she screamed the place down. Luckily, she has forgotten the incident.

Even in that taverna which was rammed and noisy, I could hear the jubilant United fans chanting 'oh Stevie Foster, what a difference you have made, what a difference you have made.' That was in sarcastic recognition of Foster's return to the Brighton side from suspension. Brighton had threatened legal action in a vain attempt to have Foster in their side for the original 2-2 draw.

Chapter 3:
A low blow in Maastricht

It wasn't just the FA Cup that gained my attention over the years but lots of other cups too, beginning in 1974 when my fondness for Eintracht Frankfurt through my marriage to Lissi, led us to Dusseldorf for Eintracht's German Cup final against Hamburger SV. August 17th was an unusual date for a final but that was because the game had been pushed back because West Germany were staging the World Cup. I was suitably grateful for Lissi's mum and brother, Heiner for getting us tickets but not for where they'd got them. We were second row up on the side, peering through the holes in the fence that surrounds the Rheinstadion. It wasn't the best sight of a football match that I'd ever had. In a later era I wouldn't have tolerated such a so-called vantage point. I'd have ascended the stairs and found an empty seat but here I was trying to impress my mother-in-law, cursing her quietly for not having had the good sense to ask for seats higher up the stand. It was a boiling hot afternoon and I was glad when the game was over and Eintracht were holding aloft the trophy after their 3-1 win in extra time. Bernd Hölzenbein, one of the German heroes of a few weeks earlier, got their second goal.

Eintracht's return to the final 12 months, or rather ten months later was an altogether more positive experience even though Lissi and I were forced to drive through the night to Hannover from London and doss down by the autobahn for a few hours kip. Not only did we have far better seats this time but the final against Duisburg was probably the best club game I have ever seen. It was a magnificent end to end contest in which both Hölzenbein and Eintracht's captain, Jurgen Grabowski, another West German World Cup winner, excelled although it was Charly Korbel, their excellent centre half who notched the only goal. Ten years later the Germans moved their final to Berlin's Olympia Stadion as a permanent neutral venue unless, of course, Hertha Berlin ever get there.

The chance of meeting up in Paris with Patrick and my old school mentor John Goodbody - who got me a press ticket - took me to the climax of the Coupe de France in 1979. Auxerre were then a little-known club from the second tier, albeit coached by the celebrated Guy Roux and they took Nantes all the way over 90 minutes only to be swamped 4-1 in extra time by the Ligue 1 side. Easy access to press passes in the Parc des Princes led me to four further finals there. I saw Marseilles lose 2-0 to Bordeaux in 1987 and overcome Monaco 4-3 in a thriller. Monaco's manager was a certain Arsene Wenger and Glenn Hoddle was in their midfield. After our glorious family holiday in Corsica in 1984, I had adopted Bastia as my favourite French club which was a good enough reason for me to witness their 2-1 victory over St Etienne in 1981. The outcome for them was not so satisfying in 2002, a 1-0 defeat by Lorient in the final. Thereafter Bastia slid towards obscurity.

The Italian cup final in 1983 was the culmination of a holiday of hectic travel that bordered on the insane. Diana, the mother of our four-year old son, James, had often accused me of having a one-track mind and not always for the obvious reason. She was pleased enough to hear that I had rented an apartment in the south of France belonging to Ron Noades, the Palace chairman, and his ex-beauty queen wife, Novello. Di was less ecstatic to learn that we would divert from our 700-mile drive from Calais to Cassis, just east of Marseilles, by going to a game at Nimes which happened to be the first leg - against Tours - of a barrage, the French equivalent of a play-off. While she played the martyr by looking after James in the car, I played the part of the selfish father by going in and stepping onto the base of a floodlight pylon for a strained view, above a 14,000 capacity crowd, of the hosts' 3-1 win. Di would never have understood if I'd told her that I had to get to the Stade Jean Bouin before Nimes moved out years later. So, I didn't bother to try.

The French season was over now but my personal season was far from over if I was to insert the metaphorical needle for my next fix. At least now though, I could travel, knowing that Di and James were safely ensconced, poolside for most of the time, at Ron's gaff. I didn't want to leave them alone for too long however which partly explained my departure, far too late, for Switzerland's friendly with Brazil in Basle. James hadn't helped by throwing my car key into the deep end of the pool from where I had to fish it out. I was supposed to be covering the game for The Times. By the time I was approaching Geneva, I knew I had no chance of making it to St Jakob Park for kick-off. There was only one thing for it. I followed the signs for Geneva Airport in the vague, slim hope that there might be a flight leaving for Basle that could get me to the match on time. Eureka. There was one and they had a seat for me at a reasonable cost. With an English referee, Alfred Grey, there was even a home angle for my report of the game which Brazil won 2-1 with a late winner from Careca. I found a hotel room in Basle and got the train back to Geneva to pick up my car the next day. There must be better ways though of spending one's birthday than on a solo 300-mile drive.

According to L'Equipe, the French sports daily, there was just one more game within my geographical scope and that was the Italian Cup final between Juventus and Hellas Verona. Juve were two goals down from the first leg so the second leg in the crumbling Stadio Communale had a lot going for it. The 200-mile drive to Turin was a doddle compared with the tension of my longer journey five days earlier. Nor could I believe how easy it was to buy a ticket outside. They'd have charged more if they'd known what was coming. Inspired by Michel Platini who added to Paolo Rossi's early goal with a late equaliser -on aggregate - Juve forced extra time during which Platini got the decisive goal. Bedlam followed. The Frenchman was worshipped. How sad it was then that he lacked the moral fortitude to avoid the temptations of all Uefa's corruption years later. By the time, I had returned to Cassis to pick up the threads of my vacation, I was exhausted and feeling like a holiday. But there was still the arduous drive home to contemplate.

No connoisseur of cup finals can ignore the Taca de Portugal 's climax although it is invariably staged on the least convenient of days, the one following the FA Cup final. So, I was in two minds and in a state of torment, enduring the later stages of Chelsea's game with Portsmouth in 2010. Much as I longed for Pompey to cancel out Didier Drogba's goal for Chelsea, the last thing I needed was extra time which would have almost certainly cost me my flight to Lisbon. Chelsea obliged by holding on, so thanking Blues' fanatic Robert Stein profusely for the ticket he had sold me, I left Wembley on the whistle, bound for Heathrow where a frantic Sally was awaiting me. We were to make use of her friends' apartment on the Algarve after the game in Portugal.

Like Portsmouth at Wembley, Chaves were major underdogs in the Portuguese final as they were from the Liga Vitalis, effectively the second tier, and up against the mighty Porto. The annual venue for the final is not one of the most renowned stadiums belonging to Benfica, Sporting or Porto but it's the Estadio Nacional Oeiras, up a hill and in the picturesque setting of a forest among the western suburbs of Lisbon. It was the stage of the first ever game in the European Cup between Sporting and Partizan Belgrade in 1955 and where the Lisbon Lions of Celtic famously defeated Inter Milan to win the competition 12 years later. Now it looked like being the scene of the kind of one-sided contest feared by all neutrals, when the Colombians, Fredy Guarin and Radamel Falcao shot Porto into a two-goal lead. That would have been increased had the Brazilian, Hulk accepted one of many chances. Happily he didn't and Chaves made it respectable, on the wrong end of a mere 2-1 defeat, when Paolo Clemente scored for them near the end.

The happiest cup final of them all for me was in 2003 when Real Mallorca won the Copa del Rey for the first time with a comprehensive 3-0 defeat of Recreativo Huelva who had hitherto never got this far in the competition. Spain tend to move their finals around, doing their seeming utmost to find a sizeable venue somewhere between the participating clubs. So, Elche got the vote this time or rather the Estadio Martinez Valero which had been a World Cup venue in 1982 and was only a bus ride away from Alicante Airport. I had managed to acquire press passes for both Sally and I. It was one of my most euphoric sporting days. The Uruguayan, Walter Pandiani gave Mallorca an early lead with a penalty after which Samuel Eto'o took over with a starring role and two goals for Gregorio Manzano's side, making up for the club's two defeats in previous finals. We found a restaurant in the vicinity for our post-match paella during which I was struck by the exemplary behaviour of the Mallorca supporters who flocked in. Whereas their English counterparts would have been leaping around and chanting and shouting the place down, the islanders sat down to eat quietly, all of them smiling broadly.

As the Belgian correspondent for World Soccer magazine as well as a train buff who enjoyed rides on Eurostar, I went to a few Belgian cup finals but two stood out. Remarkably, KV Mechelen's 2-1 win over Gent in 2019 was the first time a club from outside the top flight had captured the trophy but that was largely because the victors had been accused of match fixing the year before and were therefore demoted despite winning promotion. They were also denied participation in the following year's knockout competition and entry to the Europa League. As for Gent, they could perhaps have expected more from Alexander Sorloth, their Norwegian striker on loan from Palace. He would go on to Trabzonspor in Turkey and become their top scorer before moving to Leipzig. I had always maintained that Palace never gave him a proper chance, especially when you consider all the chances they gave Christian Benteke to come good. Pennie and I digested all this over a sumptuous post-match meal in one of the dozen or so restaurants outside the Roi Baudouin stadium where we raised a toast to Danny Goyvaerts, the KV Mechelen press secretary who had got us tickets in the press box.

I had got to know Danny, an affable bohemian who wears his hair in a ponytail through my ill-chosen friendship with Maryan Mahieu who I had met on my first visit to a Belgian final. I was filing a short report for the Telegraph on Germinal Ekeren's 4-2 triumph over Anderlecht in 1997 when Brian Oliver, the paper's sports news editor asked me if Ekeren had ever won the trophy previously. I asked the person next to me who happened to be Maryan. "It was the first time for them," he said after which we got talking with the result that we became firm friends. He got me tickets for the 1998 World Cup and I bought him a meal on my frequent trips to Brussels for Anderlecht's champions league ties in exchange for the nuggets of information he gave me for my World Soccer column. Separated from his Nigerian wife, he sometimes put me up for the night if we could find enough space in his flat for a mattress. That was no simple task. Although on the right side of middle age, Maryan lived like an ageing recluse in that he had piles upon piles of old newspapers which made a mockery of my collection back home. They looked trifling in comparison. His head-high stacks of old papers were, he explained, for the benefit of his work as a statistician with one of the Belgian TV companies. That would have been fine had he chucked them away when he'd finished with them. Easier said than done. Maryan would go out to buy at least three newspapers every morning, Belgian, Dutch and English, plus all the football magazines, plus three chocolate eclairs which were his staple diet for breakfast. Not surprisingly he was on the plump side.

We got on well over the years until he asked me for a loan of 2,000 euros just before the 2006 World Cup in Germany. He wanted the money for a down payment for the rent of a new apartment he was moving into. He promised me he'd repay me within a fortnight. I had no reason to doubt him. A fortnight came and went and I made the huge mistake - in hindsight - of getting him a free ticket for the World Cup final in Berlin. A month, six months, a year all went by without me seeing a sniff of the money I had lent him. Our friendship began to deteriorate amid a flurry of angry exchanges via email. He kept on promising me the euros, but none was forthcoming. I looked elsewhere for my Belgian info as I had begun to doubt the veracity of the information he gave me for my column.

I went to one of Anderlecht champions league ties at home to Lyon with the intention, not so much of seeing the game which was virtually meaningless with Anderlecht 5-1 down after the first leg, but of getting my money. Judging by the look of alarm on his face when the hacks came down for refreshments at half-time, I was the last person he wanted to bump into. I grabbed his arm in front of the assembled throng and dragged him into the street. "Where's my fucking money?" I asked him. "It's at home," he said, to which I replied: "ok let's go home now and get it." With Anderlecht a further three goals adrift and therefore 8-1 behind on aggregate, I thought I could afford to miss the second half. "What time is your train tomorrow?" he asked. I told him and he replied that he would be in the Eurostar ticket hall the next day to hand over 500 euros towards the debt. We went in for the rest of the game. He was there in the booking office all right the following afternoon, but he only gave me 400e, placating me with the promise that the eventual balance would come with interest.

All my friends and fellow journos got to hear of the saga as it dragged on and on. They told me they'd seen him at remote footballing outposts

272

which wouldn't have cost peanuts in travel. In 2008 on the occasion of the Champions League final in Moscow, I was astonished to be told by Jurgen - who was sitting next to me - that Maryan was in the row behind us, desperately trying to conceal himself. I knew that no one would have paid his expenses to Moscow so at half-time, I turned round to confront him, incensed by the fact that he could find the money to travel to Russia for Man United v Chelsea, but not to repay me. "I suppose you are going to the Euros in Austria and Switzerland as well?" I said. "Why would I want to go to that?" he said. Which was a joke as he was spotted there in a press box using someone else's press pass with the result that he was thrown out. News of that was music to my ears but I still hadn't received any more money. It got to the stage that he refused to take my phone calls or acknowledge my texts. And yet I was sure he was still lashing out on petrol for the fortnightly 150-mile round trip to support his team, Lens in northern France. Not to mention treks to their away games. I went to one Lens away game in Vannes in Brittany in the hope of finding him. He must have got wind of my presence and gave the press box a swerve.

By 2011, I was livid. Danny told me that he was now covering women's football as no one would give him accreditation for men's games. I scanned the fixtures and spotted a Belgium v South Korea women's friendly in Maastricht that he'd probably be covering. There are worse places to go than Maastricht on a wild goose chase. So, I took Nadiya as my accomplice. We deliberately got in late. I spotted him standing up behind the television cameras. I wasn't too proud of my next manoeuvre but at half-time I crept up behind him and hit him hard in the solar plexus. There was enough padding there so I probably didn't hurt him too much. And yet I hadn't been in the ring with John Conteh many years earlier for nothing. Mind you, Maryan's fat gut was a far easier target than the Observer footballer who had provoked me years earlier in a Fleet Street League cup tie. "You need to improve that left hook of yours," said one of his team-mates in the bar afterwards. "It looked like you were hanging out the washing."

"Where's my fucking money?" I asked Maryan after my low blow. "Didn't you know, I paid it into your account yesterday," he said. I didn't believe him. But I escorted Nadiya back to Brussels Airport the next day and carried on driving towards the ferry. I was interrupted by a phone call from the head honcho of the Belgian sporting press association. "Maryan Mahieu tells me that you hit him yesterday," he said. "Yes, I did," I replied. "He has been owing me money for five years." It appeared that Maryan had only told the guy half the story. "It's ok," he said, "we have taken away Maryan's accreditation and he only covers women's football these days."

273

I got home to find that Maryan had indeed paid the balance minus 200e. I went along to the women's champions league final at Fulham expecting to find him in the press box and watching Lyon v Turbine Potsdam (2-0). He was there. I told him about the missing 200e. It arrived a few weeks later but our friendship was well and truly over. I never received the interest payment that he had promised. I didn't have the heart or strength to pursue him for that.

Chapter 4:
A bunch of five

I often wonder how many people can truthfully match my claim to have gone to all Man United's five European Cup or Champions League finals. Although my affection towards the Old Trafford club has waned over the years, I still have enough of a soft spot to want to see them to do well - especially in Europe - now that the deadly dull reigns of Louis Van Gaal and José Mourinho have been consigned to the past. Nowadays I scoff at the club's long-range fans who travel up from Croydon or the west country or Billingshurst to lend their support instead of backing their local club. I even revel in the chants of "we support the local team," or "see you on the motorway." But in 1968 I was a long-distance red, far more committed than I am now. I got a ticket for the 4-1 win over Benfica through my membership of the London branch of the United supporters association. If ever there was a bright move on my part, it was to join up. The only aspect of that joyous evening at Wembley to which I didn't take kindly was that United played in blue. Somehow George Best, Bobby Charlton and Nobby Stiles didn't look right when they were not clad in red. I felt sorry for Denis Law who missed out as he was in hospital recovering from knee surgery.

The London branch of the United supporters club had probably long since been disbanded by 1999. Maybe it was still an ongoing concern, but I was no longer a member which meant that I was in desperate need of a ticket as the countdown to the final against Bayern Munich ticked on. Fortunately, my falling-out with Maryan was still seven years down the line. We were still on good terms and he came to my aid in my hour of need. On the Monday evening he rang me to say that he had a spare ticket. Did I want it? Is the pope a Catholic? Of course, I wanted it. The only problem would be getting to Barcelona by the Wednesday evening as all flights from the UK's airports to Catalonia were booked solid. I could have driven but I was banned. Trains would have cost a fortune.

I looked at all the possibilities which were not as easy to resolve then as they are now with such helpful websites as Skyscanner.com. Eventually I found a flight to Valencia and one back from Alicante. I told Maryan I was coming. He booked me into the same hotel as him. My flight and train from Valencia were on time. We met up before the game. He was in the press box. I was high up the Nou Camp's slopes from where I had an unobstructed view of the action. United looked out of it, a goal

275

down and not playing well. A few minutes before the added-time goals from Teddy Sherringham and Ole Gunnar Solksjaer that won it for them, a group of United fans in front of me, grabbed their bags and left. To this day, I wonder how they felt afterwards and over the intervening years, knowing what drama and euphoria they had voluntarily walked away from. Unless they had a very good reason such as a flight home what could have possessed them to have left then? How have they lived with themselves since? They have probably lied to their mates over the years, pretending that they stayed until the end. They should have known that it is never over until the fat lady sings.

For any normal run of the mill game between Man United and Chelsea - if there ever was such an event - I'd probably have few problems getting a ticket seeing as I've got contacts at both clubs. But the 2008 champions league final in Moscow was no run of the mill game. Although I wasn't eager to be among the Chelsea contingent, I tried my blue-tinted friends all the same, but to no avail. I was hopeful that Dave Bushell might help but United's development man wanted to give his comps to his wife and daughter. For someone on the United staff, I thought he'd get more than two extra ones. Bearing in mind the massive exodus from the UK, I reasoned that I'd have no chance of getting a seat on a flight to Moscow if I got the late offer of a ticket. So, I went to Cologne to spend a few days with Eva.

The ballot had let me down, but Uefa seemed to be dithering as to whether I could have a late press pass or not. Eventually I got an email from them saying I could have one. The venue had probably come to my rescue as Moscow is not the easiest city in which to find cheap accommodation and nor is it the simplest place to fly to at short notice. From Germany, it was more accessible. I found a flight out of Dusseldorf and the print-out of the email from Uefa would serve as my visa on arrival. Accomodation came in the form of a twin-bedded room I was sharing in a Holiday Inn with Angus Loughran, he of Statto fame in the Fantasy Football League comedy programme. He is a big United fan. The game was tight and engrossing all the way to its denouement. As John Terry would never find a place among my list of favourite footballers, I was delighted to see him miss the crucial penalty in the shoot-out, won 6-5 by United. I had a post-match drink with Oldham Dave who had got a ticket in the ballot. And then I went to bed. Angus woke me at 4am having been at United's celebration party. He told me that I could have come too but that wouldn't have been my scene at all. Talk about hangers-on...

My luck continued to hold in 2009 when I forsook the Burnley v Sheffield United play-off final to go with Judy for a short holiday to

Venice, knowing that I would be within easy reach of Rome should anyone contact me at the last minute with the offer of a ticket for United's final against Barcelona. Maryan was persona non grata by then and I had tried the usual avenues of applying for a press pass and entering the Uefa ticket ballot, both without success. I didn't fancy taking the train to Rome on the extreme off-chance of finding a friendly tout with a fistful of tickets. Poor Judy was having to tolerate my disconsolate mood on the Monday evening as we sat down to a plate of pasta when my phone pinged into action. It was Wolfgang texting me from Austria to say that his German pal, Uwe who had got lucky in the ballot, had been let down by the mate taking the spare one. Did I want it? Thankfully for Judy, that was the recipe for my swift change of mood. I took the train south and introduced myself to Uwe whose seats were for high up in the lower section on the side of the Stadio Olympico from where we saw Messi at his best against United who most certainly were not.

Barcelona's 2-0 win was followed by another two-goal success, this one by 3-1 when the clubs resumed acquaintance in the final two years later. Even though the game was at Wembley I was without a ticket until the morning of the final. I was annoyed that Chris, who had succeeded in the ballot was giving the spare one neither to his brother, a United fan, nor to me but his girlfriend who was and never will be the world's biggest football fan. She had said she wanted to go. Big bloody deal. I bet she wouldn't want to watch Tooting and Mitcham on a wet Tuesday night.

As I had just been paid up by Maryan which, to be honest, was never an outcome I anticipated, I went along to the fan fest with 1,000 euros in my pocket. Hyde Park was swarming. The first two Spaniards I encountered looked vaguely suspicious. "Do you have a spare ticket?" I asked them. "Si senor, you can have it for 1,200 euros." Concealing ourselves from the cops who were stalking the area, we did the deal. I beat them down to 1,000e and later admonished myself for not offering 750e which they would probably have accepted. Not to worry. I was in, so long as the ticket was not a forgery. It seemed to have a water mark. It was the most I have ever paid to get into a football match but, in reality, I was forking out with euros that I never expected to have in my possession. Barcelona were so good that evening that I considered it money well spent.

My first memories of the old European Cup had been in 1960 when Real Madrid completed their fifth successive triumph since the competition's inception. Ferenc Puskas and Alfredo Di Stefano starred in the breathtaking 7-3 win over Eintracht Frankfurt which was the first one to be screened live by the BBC though a power failure cost the corporation's viewers four minutes of the first half during which, luckily

277

for them, none of the goals were scored. But those were four frustrating minutes for us budding fanatics. My father's wish for family harmony had the undesired effect of further frustration in the form of a sullen dinner in 1961 when he insisted that we should eat first and then watch the second half of Benfica's 3-2 win over Barcelona. I sulked my way through the meal, little knowing then to what extent I would become hooked. Between 1975 and 1985 I went to ten of the 11 finals.

The last of those was in Brussels.

If I was not getting press passes in those days, there were still few problems getting in. Chris and I bought tickets for a song outside the ground, then known as Heysel, and went for a meal in a marquee just beyond the turnstiles. We heard sirens during the course of our pre-match dinner but thought nothing of them. It was the kind of sound you'd get before the majority of big matches. We wandered back to our seats to be greeted by scenes of devastation to our far right. Various items of clothing and bags were strewn over a wide section of terracing. We asked people next to us what had happened and they described the riot perpetrated by Liverpool hooligans that had led to 39 deaths. We wondered about the fate of our friend Paul Fry who had a ticket for that area but he had apparently escaped the mayhem and made his way to the press box where he gave a close hand account to all and sundry. The Mail on Sunday kept him in Brussels for a few days after the disaster. They wanted the full story.

I have never known such a sombre atmosphere as we awaited the delayed kick-off to the game which Juventus won with a penalty that would have been hotly disputed on any other night. On this one, it hardly mattered. Chris and I were stopped at the border by gendarmes wanting to know if we had any jewels in the boot. There had been a robbery in Brussels also caused by Liverpool fans. I dropped Chris off at Dover and carried on driving through the night, to the gite near Rouen where I had been staying with Di and James. When I got there, well into the early hours, she was waiting up for me. She had heard reports of the calamity on the radio, but her mastery of French was not good enough for her to grasp the magnitude of what had happened. I filled in the gaps.

278

Chapter 5
Laugh time in Lisbon

The next time I saw Liverpool in a final, it was an altogether more joyous occasion even if the annual process of persuading Uefa to part with press passes came, as always, tinged with tension. It was a hit or miss affair although it undoubtedly helped if there was an English club in the final. But once they had allocated their tickets to the national dailies, UEFA still liked to keep the rest of us hacks in suspense, sometimes until the very last minute. I eventually got one for Istanbul in 2005 and met up with Jurgen in Turkey. He had already been to the out-of-town moonscape - on which the Ataturk Stadium is housed - to collect his ticket so he knew the way. I was forever impressed but, of course, he was doing a ticket deal with some fellow Germans enroute. It wouldn't have been Jurgen if he hadn't. But he drove on with all the confidence of a local postman on his daily round. He got us there in good time.

At half-time with Liverpool 3-0 down to AC Milan, all the talk in the press tearoom was of record-winning scores. We were all wondering if Milan could eclipse the four-goal margin of which they were joint holders following their 4-0 defeat of Steaua Bucharest in 1989. Steve Gerrard's subsequent header looked no more than a consolation for Liverpool at the time but, of course, we reckoned without the heroic recovery culminating in their success in the shoot-out. A few of us met up for a quiet drink afterwards feeling like we were shunning an invitation to someone else's party. None of us were Liverpool fans, however, although that didn't stop me from flying to Thessalonica from Eva's hometown of Cologne when the two clubs met again in 2007.

My plan was to take a bus down to Athens but in the arrivals hall I got talking to four Scousers who had chosen the same point of entry to Greece. They would have room for me in the van they were hiring for the 630-mile round trip. They were engaging company, so much so that I thought we would become lifelong soul mates but, as so often, in these instances, distance gets in the way of such bright ideas. I was staggered to hear that they were not intending to stay overnight in Athens but were heading straight back through the night to northern Greece for their flights home the next day. I was welcome to tag along even though several hours of restlessness and snatched moments of kip in the back of the van were not what I had bargained for. Take it or leave it. I took it but might not have done so had I known that Graham, the driver, was not keeping an eye on the petrol gauge with the result that we stuttered to a halt on the long road back after running out of fuel. The mood, not great, following Liverpool's 2-1 defeat, soured drastically after that. One of the lads summoned help on his mobile and while Graham was out of hearing range on the roadside awaiting the recovery vehicle, I heard another one say: "Why the fuck did he allow that to happen? He is just not the sharpest tool in the box."

As an Arsenal sympathiser, I bemoaned the defeat of their ten men by Barcelona in 2006 - following Jens Lehmann's red card in the Stad de France - but I couldn't bring myself to applaud an English triumph in 2012 although my Chelsea pal, Robert Stein had got me a cat one ticket among his club's faithful in Munich's Allianz Arena for the game against the host club. When I think back to some of the first few games my father took me to which were at Stamford Bridge in the days of Jimmy Greaves, Barry Bridges, Frank Blunstone, the Sillett brothers and Peter Bonetti, I often question my feelings towards the club and why they have gone from fondness to plain antipathy. My Chelsea mates probably outnumber my Palace friendships, but I can never bring myself to go to the Bridge these days supporting anyone other than the opposition. Quietly of course.

Over the years, the eras and antics of Ken Bates, Dennis Wise, Roman Abramovich and Terry have done nothing to enhance the club's image. And nor have the supporters. "They'll all fat, bald geezers with tatts and mobile phones growing out of their ears," said Yann Tear once with great profundity. And so, I had to pretend to Robert that I was pleased to see his side win. But he must have suspected how I really felt when I left on the whistle after Didier Drogba had knocked in the decisive penalty. I told him I had to make an early start the next morning. I'd better hope that neither Robert nor Chelsea Ian nor Mark, the photographer, read this or I'll never get another ticket for The Bridge.

There were no problems finding a ticket for the all-German final at Wembley in 2013 but that was in sharp contrast to Lisbon 12 months later. Pennie and I had travelled across Spain by car and sleeper train from Salamanca into Portugal for the game between the two Madrid clubs. With every sports journalist in Spain wanting a press pass, there was no chance of Uefa coming up with the goods this time. But Scottish Mark had got lucky in the UEFA ballot, naming his father as the person he wanted to have the spare one. Which would have all been well and good but for UEFA's ridiculous stipulation that only the people named on the original ballot form can go in. Mark's Dad had no intention of travelling from Edinburgh to Lisbon for the game so there was nothing else for it but for me to go up to the UEFA help desk with Mark an hour before kick-off, pretending that I was his father. Which would have been fine had I resembled in the slightest the photograph of the man on the driving license that we proffered as proof of identity. I had emptied my wallet of any cards with my name on it. We substituted them with Mark's Dad's credit card, driving license and library card which turned out to be a master stroke.

Mark had watched over me for 20 minutes beforehand while I practised his father's signature and tried to remember how to spell his surname which was Trzebiatowski. There must be easier names to sign and remember to spell than that one. The family had originated from Poland and the story we gave the UEFA people was that we had left Poland when I was a baby and therefore too young to learn Polish. UEFA wanted my passport, but we had prepared for this one. I had left it in the hotel in Estoril for fear of pickpockets among the crowd, I told them. It was too far to go now. "But you look nothing like the man in the photograph," said the UEFA man. "He has very short hair. You have much longer hair."

"It was taken long ago," I said. "Is it a crime to grow your hair?" Mark almost cracked up. We should have waited until there was a queue at the help desk but with only us to attend to, UEFA's jobsworths gathered in strength as the rigmarole unfolded. There was a lot of coming and going during which I whispered to Mark that maybe we should come clean. He ignored me. We carried on with this fiasco until suddenly they relented and dished out two tickets, one for me with the name of Mark's father on it. We kept straight faces as we turned away, but we almost cocked up. I left the credit card and driving license on the ledge. Mark almost yelled out, "Nick you've left your cards," but he corrected himself in time to say Dad. They were surprisingly good seats right next to the press box where, of course, I reckoned I should have been all along. We enjoyed Real Madrid's 4-1 extra time victory over Atletico all the more after the escapade we had endured. Alas, I couldn't get a ticket for Pennie who watched it in our hotel bar.

Chapter 6:
Hooping along

Any more dramas like Lisbon and they could have been heart-attack inducing. That was a health warning if ever there was one. I am not sure that I could go through that again. But there are few games more difficult to get into than Champions League finals. With no wish to join those who told me that they had travelled to Kiev and Madrid for Liverpool's finals and not got in, I stayed put. Fortunately, the finals of other competitions such as the Uefa Cup represented less of a challenge. I saw the decisive second leg of Spurs v Wolves in 1972 and both legs of Spurs v Anderlecht in 1984. My devotion for Eintracht Frankfurt led me to both legs of their victorious - on away goals - all German final against Borussia Moenchengladbach in 1980. Porto v Celtic in 2003 was a must for anyone wanting to step foot in Seville's other ground, the Estadio de la Cartuja, scene of the 1999 world athletic championships. Porto's 3-2 win came in a wonderful game. This one bucked the trend with the inevitable invasion of ticketless Jocks in Spain all wanting to see their hoops. It wasn't until 15 minutes before kick-off that Maryan and I were granted press passes after hanging around the Uefa media portacabin with long looks on our faces. When I got home, I heard a lovely story, possibly apocryphal, of a Celtic fan hitching a lift home from the depths of nowhere in Spain. "I'm going to Edinburgh. Is that any good to you?" said a driver, flinging open the passenger door. "Och nae, that's nae good to me," said the fan slamming the door shut. "I'm going to Glasgow."

At least, the Celtic fans did not trash Seville which sadly was the outcome in Manchester after Rangers had lost the 2008 final to Zenit St Petersburg. There was an air of hostility in Manchester before the game which the Russians won 2-0. That began for me a sequence of nine visits to 12 finals. Ironically the three I missed all involved London clubs, Chelsea twice, understandably, Fulham once, inexplicably. More often than not I came up trumps in the Uefa ballot. It was a good excuse to trawl round some of the continent's slightly less salubrious hot spots, such as Istanbul's Sukru Saracoglu Stadium - home of Fenerbahce - Dublin, Turin, Basle, Stockholm and Lyon.

The 2012 final in Bucharest's Arena Nationala was the focal point of quite an adventure. Seemingly every Englishman and German who had got tickets through the ballot for Atletico Madrid's 3-0 win over Athletic Bilbao in a disappointingly one-sided final had also spotted the

282

possibility of a hors d'oeuvre to the main feast. That came in the form of a re-arranged Romanian League game taking place a few hours earlier in the Stadionul Regie. The miserly crowd of 200, mostly foreigners, was there to see already relegated Sportul Studentesc lose 2-0 to Otelul. Watching already relegated teams has never been one my favourite pastimes but sadly they were to be a regular feature of that trip. The train ride that Sally and I took into Hungary the next day was majestic and the town of Paks proved a good bet for our overnight base but Paksi's opponents on the Friday night were the already doomed, albeit once great Vasas who lost 2-1. They were going down with Zalaegerszegi who, as luck would have it, were the visitors to Siofok, our next stop, on the shores of Lake Balaton, 24 hours later. The hosts won 2-0. I couldn't help but wonder at the apathy of football in Hungary. There was a quorum of 1,381 at Paksi but the attendance at Siofok was a pathetic 300. Could this really be the birthplace of Ferenc Puskas, Jozsef Bozsik and Nandor Hidegkuti among other magnificent Magyars?

Knowing what lay in wait, I consoled myself with the thought that games involving a relegated club in front of a low crowd on pastures new had to be marginally better than no game at all. We had hired a car which we dropped off at Gyor before taking the train to Vienna where Wolfgang was awaiting us. As an influential member of the Rapid Wien supporters club, he had used his clout to get us seats on their coach going to yet another down and out club, Kapfenberger SV on the Sunday. This was a novel experience. I had seldom been on supporters club coaches in England let alone Austria. Rapid duly won 2-0 to finish runners-up, six points behind Salzburg. The Rapid fans were in good spirits on their homeward journey as we listened to reports of the drama back in the Premier League of Man City's Argueroooo moment against QPR.

Wolfgang who was in a reciprocal mood for all the times I had put him up, paid for our hotel and then, the next day, drove us for an hour out of Vienna before putting us on a boat chugging up the Danube. He knew me well enough by now to realise that my perfect trips were a combination of football, train rides and boat trips in delightful female company. Sally and I stayed on the vessel until it pulled in at Passau which must be the most enchanting border town on the world map. The next day we took the train to Munich from where we flew home.

My delight at Warsaw winning the vote to host the second of Sevilla's three successive triumphs, in 2015, turned to dismay when my son Ben texted me to say that he had missed his flight out from Stansted, leaving me with a spare 80 euros ticket. He never was the best timekeeper. Punctuality was not his middle name. On most other occasions, there would have been no problem getting rid of the ticket but on this occasion, there were too many people holding aloft spare ones, either side of the bridge spanning the Vitula River, leading to the stadium. They couldn't give them away. More's the pity then for those who stayed away as Seville's 3-2 win over Dnipro was an outstanding contest.

Chapter 7:
From the depths to Palace's zenith

Supporters of some clubs must have a blasé outlook when it comes to competing in Europe. For the likes of the so called "big six" it's virtually taken for granted. For season after season, these clubs will be facing continental opposition, if not in the Champions League then almost certainly in the Europa League. For the likes of Palace, we can only dream although we did actually qualify for the old Uefa Cup in 1991 as the third-placed team in the old first division only to have Liverpool scupper our hopes because of the ban on English clubs after their fans' culpability in the Heysel disaster. We have, therefore, fed on scraps such as the Anglo Italian Cup and the Intertoto Cup both of which took me on wild and wonderful adventures. The Anglo Italian Cup had been formed in 1970 to generate funds for players' wages for the extended close-season caused by Italia 90. The first final had ended prematurely in violence with Swindon leading Napoli 3-0 so the English club took the trophy. A year later Palace found themselves in a group with West Brom, Cagliari and Inter Milan.

Palace beat Cagliari 1-0 at home, but it was immediately after the 1-1 draw with Inter at Selhurst Park that six of us, including Marilyn a Liverpool fan we had befriended at the World Cup in Mexico, set off in a dilapidated van for the return games in Italy. It was long before the Channel tunnel and the Shuttle, so we drove straight down to Dover and caught a boat to Calais from where we sped through the night. Speed was the essence as the game in Cagliari was on the Tuesday. The others, not all of them Palace fans, were on the trip for the craic and the beach, so along with Chris Wright, a rebellious Palace man, I took the overnight ferry from Civitavecchia to Sardinia. We saw Palace lose 2-0 to a Gianni Riva-inspired home side, socialised with the players at their hotel after the game and then headed straight back to the mainland the next morning. There was little time to admire the scenery as Milan was our next stop on the Friday. By overcoming Inter 2-1 thanks to two goals by Bobby Tambling, Palace became only the second British club - after Birmingham in the 1961 Inter Cities Fairs Cup - to win in San Siro. Inter might have had bigger fish to fry but Tarcisio Burgnich, Sandro Mazzola and Giacinto Facchetti were among the ranks of the reigning Serie A champions who were on the back of a 23-game unbeaten run, so it was no mean feat by Bert Head's boys. Nevertheless, David McClelland, the

285

Croydon Advertiser reporter, got slightly carried away. He wrote: "Palace revealed a stature that marked their breakthrough into European soccer."

While the vanload headed home, they dropped me off at Alassio, the beautiful Italian Riviera resort where Edward Elgar incidentally wrote his concert overture 'In the South' in the winter of 1903/04. More significantly so far as I was concerned, it was where Gillian, my girlfriend of the time, was staying at her parents' holiday home. I was delighted to see her again, but she was a bit miffed that my football travels were incomplete. Luckily her Dad was a football man and brusquely dismissed her objections to give me the moral support I needed to satisfy my burgeoning knowledge of Italian stadia, not least Bologna's artistic Stadio Renato Dall 'Ara which was hosting the final eight days later. I became a Blackpool supporter for the day which was a boiling one in the furnace of a hot sun and near capacity crowd. Without the protection of a hat or sun cream, my face was a bright red by the end of extra time during which Micky Burns had scored to give Blackpool a deserved 2-1 win. I must have looked like a typical Brit abroad. Gillian gave me a wide swerve on my return to Alassio.

By the time Palace competed again in the tournament two years later we were heading for the drop and I could not summon up the enthusiasm to go to our games in Bari and Florence (Fiorentina) from which we gained sufficient points to reach the semi-finals. Under Head's successor, Malcolm Allison, we were down by the time we faced Newcastle in the first leg at Selhurst and the air was heavy with the stench of relegation. We drew 0-0 and lost the second leg 5-1 at St James Park.

The Anglo Italian Cup was short lived as was the Intertoto Cup, a competition Palace 'graced' for all of two games against Samsunspor after being relegated again in 1998. It was bizarre that a club so down on its luck could nonetheless be admitted to a European competition from which it could qualify for the Uefa Cup. Clubs gained entry not so much on merit but merely because they had applied. Wimbledon and Tottenham had been banned three years previously for fielding under strength sides which was understandable given that they had only just started pre-season training. That was also the case with Palace whose defender Dean Austin remarked after his debut: "Fitness-wise, we were a long way from where they were."

Long before Palace lost the first leg 2-0 at Selhurst Park, I was surprised at the lack of enthusiasm from supporters wanting to see the second leg in Turkey. Maybe people have better things to do and places to go in the height of summer. The club eventually put me in touch with a few exiled fans from the Midlands who were planning to go and thanks to them I was soon on board a flight to Ankara and a minibus they had hired for the six-hour ride to Samsun, a container port on the banks of the Black Sea. Somehow, we survived the reckless driving of both our man and seemingly every other vehicle on the long road north east, to reach Samsun a few hours before the Saturday evening kick-off.

The rest of the lads were on an insane schedule. They were heading straight back to Ankara after the game but with eight reports to file by the next evening, I had already warned our ringleader that if I was to be included on the trip, I needed to return 24 hours after the main party. I booked myself into a cheap hotel. Terry Venables, who was then the Palace manager, was surprisingly affable considering that Palace had just lost 2-0 and 4-0 on aggregate. When he saw me, he asked: "What are you doing here?" I might have asked him the same question. He seemed astonished that any journalist would make the effort to travel so far for such a game but gave me all the quotes I wanted for my various and varied pieces. I had taken on so much work because no sports editor had deemed the match worthy of a large expenses claim from one of his paper's reporters. With the English cricket team engaged in a nail-biting Fourth Test against South Africa at Trent Bridge, an Intertoto Cup tie at the back of beyond was considered almost surplus to the requirements of their readers.

While the Turkish hacks were attending their manager's press conference, I borrowed one of their phones to dictate my first piece to the Observer and was up early the next morning to get to grips with the rest of my sizeable task which was no simple chore seeing as this was well before the age of laptops and mobile phones had only just come into vogue. I was close to panic mode but struck up a rapport with a friendly hotel receptionist who allowed me to use their landline for my transfer charge calls. Some of them took an eternity to get through so I hit upon the ruse of asking one paper's copytaker to phone the next paper to get them to phone me back and so on.

With a personal deadline forced on me by the bus timetables and my need to get on the road back to Ankara, I skipped lunch so as to give myself more time to compose my reports and ring them through. Progress, laboured at first, steadily speeded up with the result that I breathed a huge sigh of relief when I finished two hours before the bus departure. I ambled onto the promenade and chanced upon a small boat rocking on the waves. It was a floating restaurant. I had a simple dish of fish, chips and salad washed down by a glass of white wine, but no meal had ever tasted so good or cost so little. Palace were not making it to the Uefa Cup but my professional sense of pride at a job reasonably well done was so overwhelming that it felt like we had just won the thing. The

287

beginning of the interminable 255-mile bus journey in daylight brought added enjoyment. I found a hotel near the Ankara bus station from where it was easy to reach the airport the next day.

The desperate wish to see Palace win at Wembley for the first time had taken me to their Zenith Data Systems cup final against Everton in 1991, the year after we had lost the FA Cup final to Man United. For a secondary competition with no passport to Europe awaiting the winners, both sides played as if their lives depended on it. It was a brutal affair. I would love to ask Ian Wright, Mark Bright or Andy Gray some time what Martin Keown had ever done to offend them. But the Toffees' central defender ended up with a broken nose as his team ran out of steam in extra time during which Wright scored twice to give Palace a 4-1 win. "We beat the Scousers 4-1," sang the Palace fans on our subsequent trip to Anfield where we lost 3-0.

Play-off finals have formed an important part of Palace's history. From the joy of beating Blackburn over two legs in 1989, we went to the despair of 1996 when Leicester pipped us late in extra time with Steve Claridge's winner off his knee. And then it was the sheer ecstasy of defeating Sheffield United, West Ham and Watford in our next three finals. As I stood on my seat to salute the lads on their lap of honour after David Hopkin's last gasp winner against the Blades, Jessica asked me if it was the happiest moment of my life. "Yes, I think it is," I said. "What about when we were born?" she asked. "Well apart from that," said I. She always was one for choosing the wrong moments to ask pertinent questions. Chris came to Cardiff to lend his support for the West Ham game, won by Neil Shipperley's close-range winner in 2004. He held six fingers aloft after the game. "What's all that about?" I asked him later. "That's how many points we (Spurs) are going to take off you next season." In fact, we took four points off them. I bumped into Shipperley some years later and asked him why Ian Dowie had refused to give him a single league start the following season when we went straight back down. He was at a loss to explain. We followed up the defeat of Watford in 2013, secured by Kevin Phillips' penalty, by beating them again in the 2016 FA Cup semi-final.

A few other play-off finals stuck in the mind. Swindon were so masterful in their 1990 1-0 triumph over Sunderland that I told their manager Ossie Ardiles that it was the best display I'd ever seen from a championship side. He was fairly unresponsive, fearing perhaps the repercussions that was Swindon's subsequent demotion for financial irregularities. Sunderland took their place in the top flight. The 4-2 wins by Ipswich and Swansea in 2000 and 2011 over Barnsley and Reading respectively made me feel almost as glad all over as a Palace victory because of my soft spots for the victors. Likewise, Fulham's 1-0 win over Villa in 2018 and to a lesser extent, Villa's 2-1 win over Derby in 2019.

Chapter 8:
Deep pockets

As the Telegraph's non-league man, I had long since formed an affection for the clubs outside the established 92 and their various managers and officials. But from 2002 I was to discover that they were not all decent people. The Telegraph told me that I was entitled to invite a guest on expenses to the Football Writers' Association dinner. I considered myself a reasonably good judge of character so I asked Steve Evans, the manager of Boston who had just become Nationwide Conference champions, much to the fury of second-placed Dagenham and Redbridge who thought they had been cheated out of promotion to the fourth division. I had got to know Evans when our paths crossed at Stevenage's Monday night games when he was spying on future opponents. He seemed at worse a likeable rogue so when he asked if he could bring his assistant, Neil Thompson to the dinner, I had no hesitation in saying "that's fine Steve, so long as you pay for him as I'm only allowed to bring one guest on exes."

"Of course, Nick, I'll be happy to pay for him and give you the money," answered Steve who duly came to the Lancaster Gate ballroom accompanied by his assistant. When they rose to leave with the speeches under way, I made a gesture with my fingers asking Steve about the contribution to cover Thompson. "I'll send you a cheque," he replied. To this day, I have never received the money and I have long since given up texting or phoning the fat slob. It was only £55 but there was a principle at stake. The sum was peanuts to a football manager worth thousands, if not millions. They say there's nowt so tight as a Scot with deep pockets and that was certainly true of this overweight Glaswegian in baggy trousers who had somehow managed to score a few goals in his prime as a player with lower league clubs north of the border.

He had been prosecuted for tax evasion and had been in trouble with the FA over players' contract irregularities. He was fined £8,000 after pleading guilty to conspiring to cheat the public revenue and now here he was, cheating not only me but the Daggers. Boston suspended him after which he resigned but astonishingly they took him back, only to lose their place in the Football League under his management. He pledged his allegiance to the club only to join Crawley 19 days later. A few years later on a non-league visit to Crawley Down FC, I got talking to a woman standing on the touchline. She told me that she had previously worked for Crawley but had left because she detested Evans so much. We were kindred spirits. She found that I was a willing listener.

Although he was ostensibly a Villa man, my father's greater love was the amateur game which was why he had extolled the virtues of the great Pegasus team he had watched capture the Amateur Cup twice in the early 1950s. He didn't take kindly to the changing nature of the sport which led to players at non-league level expecting payments of some kind or other or 'expenses' for their efforts. My dad was very much old school and gave up supporting the Amateur Cup once it became the FA Trophy which it was my duty to cover in my role as the Telegraph's non-league correspondent. The first final I reported on was an eye opener, such was the brilliance of the spectacle, Macclesfield's 3-1 win over Northwich Victoria in 1996. The victorious manager was Sammy McIlroy who had in his team such luminaries as Tony Hemmings, a tricky left winger who scored a dazzling third goal. The game deserved a far bigger crowd than the 8,672 who attended Wembley.

With his rosy cheeks and cheerful bonhomie, Geoff Chapple was a friendly soul who obviously liked the feel of Wembley judging by his record there of three wins in four years with Woking and two successive triumphs with Kingstonian. "Look out the Telegraph are here," he said whenever he saw me at a game. But his teams seldom challenged for league titles. That was the province of Steve Cotterill who was a fiercely ambitious manager on behalf of Cheltenham whose bitter rivalry with Kettering got me into trouble. Kettering, under the management of the former Ipswich and Norwich player, Peter Morris, were going for the Conference title with the advantage of facing many depleted teams. Most of their opponents finished with nine or ten men during a remarkable spell of about a dozen games. After Morecambe had had two players dismissed in a 6-0 defeat, I rang their manager, Jim Harvey with whom I got on well. Harvey told me that the Kettering players were "diving and rolling all over the place and conning the referee." The kind of quotes any journo would die for. The trouble was that the Telegraph had restricted my word count to 200 with the result that I didn't want to bite into those juicy quotes by ringing Kettering for what would probably have been a curt "no comment." It was unprofessional of me, I know, but probably even more unprofessional of the Telegraph not to ask me to do just that when my report came in.

The Telegraph sports editor Keith Perry got in the next morning to find a fax threatening legal action from the Kettering chairman Peter Mallinger and I was rung up by the paper's barrister telling me to substantiate Harvey's claims with quotes from other managers and even Kettering players who had been told to deliberately fall over. That was

291

ludicrous. No player would ever admit to such foul play. But John Baldwin, the manager of Hednesford whose players had been expelled in both games against Kettering, came to my rescue, so I thought, by saying that Kettering were "a bunch of fucking cheats." If that wasn't good enough to win a libel case, what would be? I was therefore surprised and annoyed to pick up the Telegraph one morning to read that the paper had apologised to Kettering with an out of court settlement of £5,000. Thereafter I was told to always get the other side of the story even if it was "no comment." Cheltenham went onto capture the title with Cotterill admitting to me after a conclusive 3-0 defeat of Kettering at Whaddon Road that he couldn't find it within himself to pen his usual 'welcome to the opposing manager' column in the club's programme. "I fucking hate them," he said. As I wasn't so keen on Kettering myself, I was delighted to see Chapple's Kingstonian beat them 3-2 in a stirring Trophy final at Wembley.

Keith Perry turned out to be a staunch fan of Stevenage or, more specifically a fan of Paul Fairclough, the club's manager with whom he socialised. As Stevenage were in the habit of playing their midweek matches on Monday evenings, I saw a lot of them and their various challenges for the Conference title. But by the time of their unsuccessful Trophy final against Yeovil in 2002, a 2-0 defeat at Villa Park, Fairclough was on borrowed time. His second sacking by the club's chairman Phil Wallace, did like the first one, lead to me being summoned by Perry to do a feature on the ex-manager. I went to Fairclough's home on the outskirts of St Albans and got the story which must have favoured him too much for the liking of Wallace who was a nasty piece of work. I found that out for myself on the occasion of an England v USA non-league international that Stevenage staged. I was making my way out of their Broadhall Way ground when Greg Fee, one of the FA officials invited me for a drink. I went up to the boardroom and had a beer with Fee, a likeable former Sheffield Wednesday defender, until he decided it was time to leave. I was stuffing my face with canapés when Wallace came up and asked what I was doing. I told him of Fee's invitation to which Wallace replied: "You do realise, don't you, that at no other time would you be welcome in my boardroom." Lower leagues would be a better place without the likes of him.

I had often quietly wondered why the Telegraph and other papers would have a regular non-league column yet give little or no space to leagues one and two. They must have heard me for it was not long before the non-league columns were being phased out. But my interest in the non-league game was still keen, fuelled to a large extent by my friendship with Robert Holmes, the president of Halifax who I had met early on my

292

travels round the Conference. He had spent part of his youth in Halifax with the result that he had got to love the town and its football club who eventually gave him an honorary position even though he ran an estate agents' office far away in Wimbledon. Holmes has a debonair appearance and an academic background of public school and university. He is in his element whether it is greeting the posh totties of SW19 or sitting down among the broad Yorkshire accents of the Halifax directors. I met them over pre match dinners at Aldershot, Orient and Cambridge United and, on one sunny afternoon in 2016, gloriously at Wembley. I had long since retired from reporting on non-league matters but Halifax's advance to the Trophy final could not be ignored so I was delighted to join Robert's table for a pre-match meal in hospitality. Halifax beat Grimsby 1-0 after which I was delighted to meet up again with Jim Harvey who was not to retain his job as their manager for more than another two days. Football works in mystifying ways.

Chapter 9:
And finally

I had booked return flights to Doha some nine months before the 2022 World Cup began. But as the tournament approached, my enthusiasm for it waned to the point that I was close to deciding it could go ahead without me. The Middle East is a long way bottom of my list of the world's favourite places to visit and I had already been to Qatar for the Asian Championships in 2011 when I saw nothing to alter my view.

As the countdown gathered momentum, all the guys were putting in enormous amounts of work booking tickets and accommodation. They were spending longer hours in front of their computers than I could contemplate. I couldn't see how they managed to devote so much time to the exercise and still get to games in the UK. After months of soul searching and with no match tickets or accommodation secured, I finally decided not to go. Three days before the opening ceremony, I rang the Royal Jordanian airline and asked them to reimburse me for my return flights. I would watch the World Cup on television and comfort myself by going to as many matches as I could in the UK.

But as the World Cup games unfolded on TV, I began to harbour regrets that I was not there and not careering between one stadium and another with the likes of Chris, Oldham Dave, Scottish Mark, Leicester Mike, Chelsea Ian and John Bethell. Some of them were doing three or four games a day, exploiting Doha's futuristic transport system and compatible cab fares to race between matches. They were making light of occasional ticketing hitches outside grounds by spending vast sums of money to see the action. But it was well worth it, they reckoned. Mark was texting or phoning me twice a week to keep me informed, adding the carrots of information as to how accessible it all was. Along with Chris, who had taken my room, and Jurgen, they were evidently ensconced in a plush, albeit expensive apartment costing each of them about £150 a night.

On the final week, by which time I was close to breaking point, Mark rang to ask if I would be prepared to come out via Paris. Jurgen was apparently supplying match tickets to a French charter company. Did I want to pay 1,700 euros for a package that included a category three ticket or 3,700e for an all-in deal including a cat one ticket? As I did not want to be stuck, standing in all probability, low down behind a corner flag, I opted for the costlier option. At first it looked like I might make it for both semi-finals plus the final but then as time elapsed, only one semi-final became possible and then not even that. On the Thursday before the final, Mark had still not been able to confirm when I should make tracks for Paris. But on the Friday morning, he rang and said, 'Get yourself to Paris pronto as your flight is leaving tomorrow morning.' I checked flights out of the UK but as train strikes were creating a hazard in reaching Gatwick, I opted for Eurostar. The cost of a return was nearly £300 because of my last-minute purchase. A room in a hotel near Orly Airport added another £100 to my outlay.

The flight was due to leave at 6am (aaaagggghhhh) but no sooner had I booked an alarm call for 4am and cab -- as it was too early for the hotel's shuttle service -- than Mark was ringing me again to say the departure time had changed to 9am, which enabled me to save some much needed euros by taking the shuttle after all. I never did discover why this French charter company was using an Italian airline's plane but whatever the anomalies, the flight finally took off at 11am.

Jens, a young German who was acting as Jurgen's henchman, had befriended me at the airport because he had apparently been made responsible for ensuring that this inexperienced English traveller -- who had hardly been abroad before -- was familiar with airport procedure. I was mystified as to why the plane was required to go via Catania in Sicily, where we were treated to superb views of Mount Etna. No one got on or off except a change of flight crews. Our two-hour wait on the tarmac finally put paid to my faint hopes of adding the third-place final to my hectic schedule.

Arriving in Doha, Jens and I replenished in a Turkish restaurant before sharing a smart twin-bedded apartment, which was part of the deal. We took a cab the next morning to the abode shared by the others. Jurgen barely had time to welcome us as he was hunched over a mighty computer screen, completing the last of his 2022 World Cup ticket deals, which was all part of his dubious profession. On his desk were a plethora of mobile phones. He handed me one of them to take to the stadium as my ticket was on it.

I had always assumed that the advent of tickets-on-mobile-phones would signal the end of ticket-touting but obviously not for a tout as enterprising as Jurgen, who circumvents such trivial obstacles by merely buying up a counter full of phones. He has made such a fortune it's no great loss if someone makes off with the odd phone to compensate for being overcharged for a ticket. With only hours to go before kick-off and more profits to be pocketed, Jurgen was unable to join the rest of us for a sumptuous pre-match meal in a Qatari restaurant half a mile from the

Lusail Stadium which I soon entered feeling like a gate crasher at a party.

I was dismayed to find that my cat one ticket was for Row YY on the seventh level which could only be reached by a tortuous climb. There were no lifts. The players resemble insects from those breathless heights. Those of us who have sat right at the top of the fifth level at Wembley or have managed to ascend, gasping, to the peak of the visitors' gallery at Newcastle, or have sat among the gods at the 02 feel like asking for our money back when we have discovered the mistake of forking out for such seats. It was why I was so exasperated at being lumbered with such a ticket.

If this was Jurgen's revenge for my alleged misdemeanours in our past contretemps, he had done a good job. But I was having none of it. There were two unoccupied seats in row D, so I sat in one of them until, after about 20 minutes of the game and Argentina getting on top, two local women, who were obviously the rightful ticket holders, told me to move on. As I switched to a vacant seat, I had clocked in row F, I kept an eye on the women. They took a couple of selfies, saw glimpses of the action through glazed eyes, looked bored and then left. A similar scenario was repeated by the local chap who usurped me from my new seat at half-time. With money to burn but with no real love of the game, the Qataris buy up the best seats so that they can tell anyone who cares to listen: 'I was there.' And so, they invariably were for a while but not in most cases for the whole game which in this case was 120 minutes, plus added-on minutes at the end of each half, plus a penalty shootout. Far too long for the average Qatari.

I feared I would have to witness the rest of the game from an inferior seat when a steward who had obviously seen what was going on, approached. But instead of checking my ticket and ordering me back to YY, he grabbed my hand and led me to a spare seat in row B. I was in seventh heaven, with a perfect view thereafter of an engrossing game, embellished by the brilliance of Messi and Mbappe.

It had been a one-sided contest for 80 minutes but since 2-0 is the dodgiest score to lead by, I could not feel over-confident of Messi capturing the winner's medal that was his by divine right. Mbappe's subsequent hat-trick for France challenged that view but for once Messi could not be denied. Argentina's triumph (by 4-2 on penalties after 3-3) was one of the great finals but I was so incensed to read the Guardian reporter claiming the next day that it was the best ever that I wrote in to insist that West Germany's 2-1 win over Holland in 1974 was the outstanding final. Not that they printed my letter.

The journey back home had all the usual mishaps associated with charter flights. I went to Hamad Airport and was then told to go to Doha International Airport -- where we had arrived -- only to find that I shouldn't be there. So back I went to Hamad, admonishing the poor chap at the information desk who had misdirected me in the first place. But he was so full of apologies that I asked him to excuse my rage.

I wondered how all the French passengers on my flight managed to avoid such confusion. It all made for a sleepless night veering between airports and the furthest flung departure gate. My flight back for Paris, originally scheduled for 3am and then 6, finally pulled out at 8. Etna was puffing away slightly as we detoured again via Catania. My huge sense of satisfaction at getting to my 14th World Cup -- albeit only the final this time -- was enhanced by the helpful Eurostar lady in Paris who permitted me to take, at no extra cost, an earlier train to St Pancras than the one for which I was originally booked.

So why the reluctance to visit the World Cup when the next one can't come quickly enough?

Acknowledgements

Any book like this is a collaboration between those that remember well and those that write well so my thanks to the following:

Mark Burton, Bob Pryce, Pennie Turrell, Siobhan Payne, Jonathan Payne, Janette Weedall, Celia Howard, Jason Jones, Paul McDermott, Sally, Martin Scott, Hy Money, Robert Stein, Richard Rawles, Sophia Longdon, John Ashcroft, Ian Willsmer and, lastly but not least, Mr Google for confirming score lines and facts from a distant and murky past.